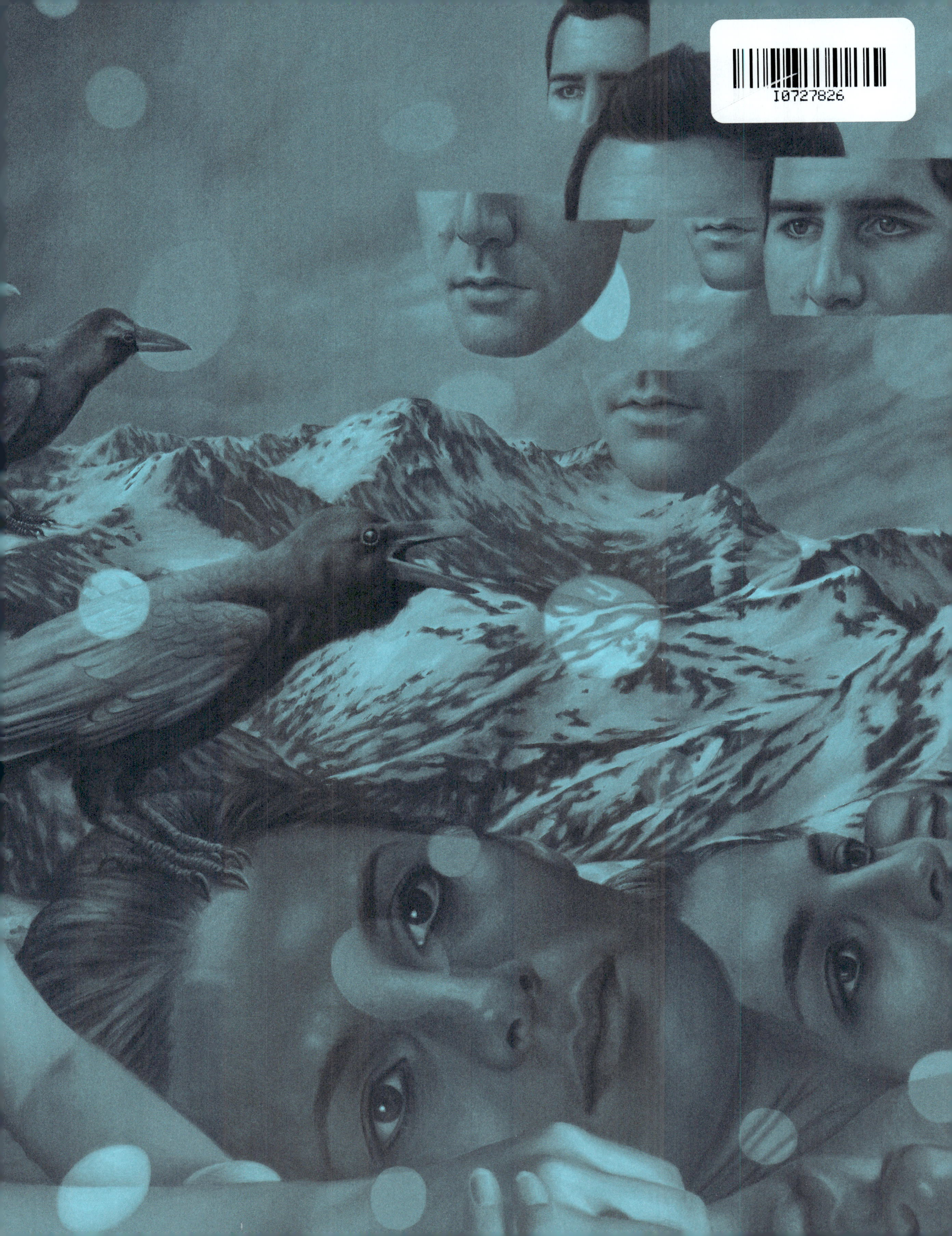
I0727826

Prison Of The Mind

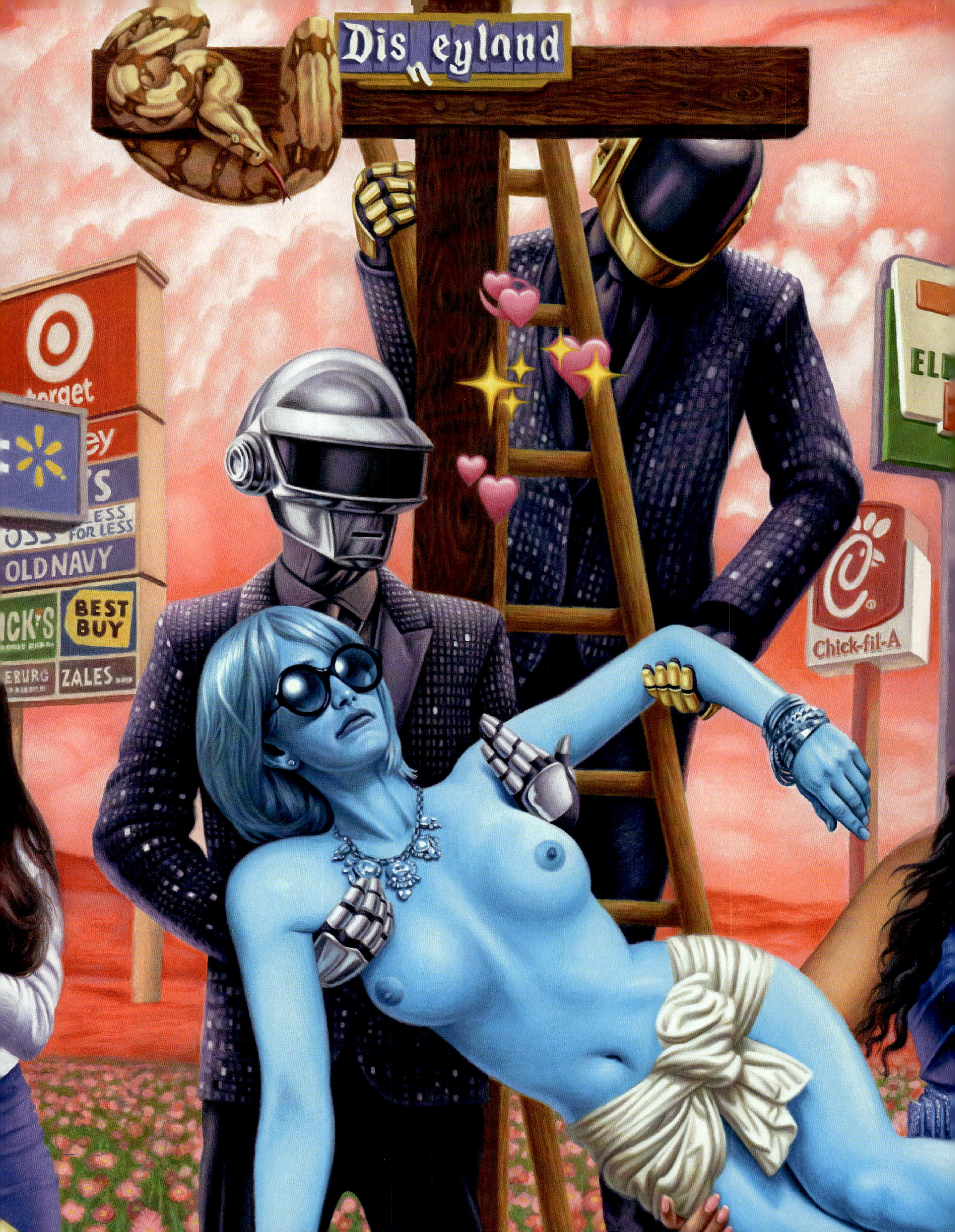
Disneyland
Target
OLD NAVY
BEST BUY
ZALES
EBURG
ELD
Chick-fil-A

Prison Of The Mind

Paintings By Alex Gross, 2014-2024

GINGKO PRESS

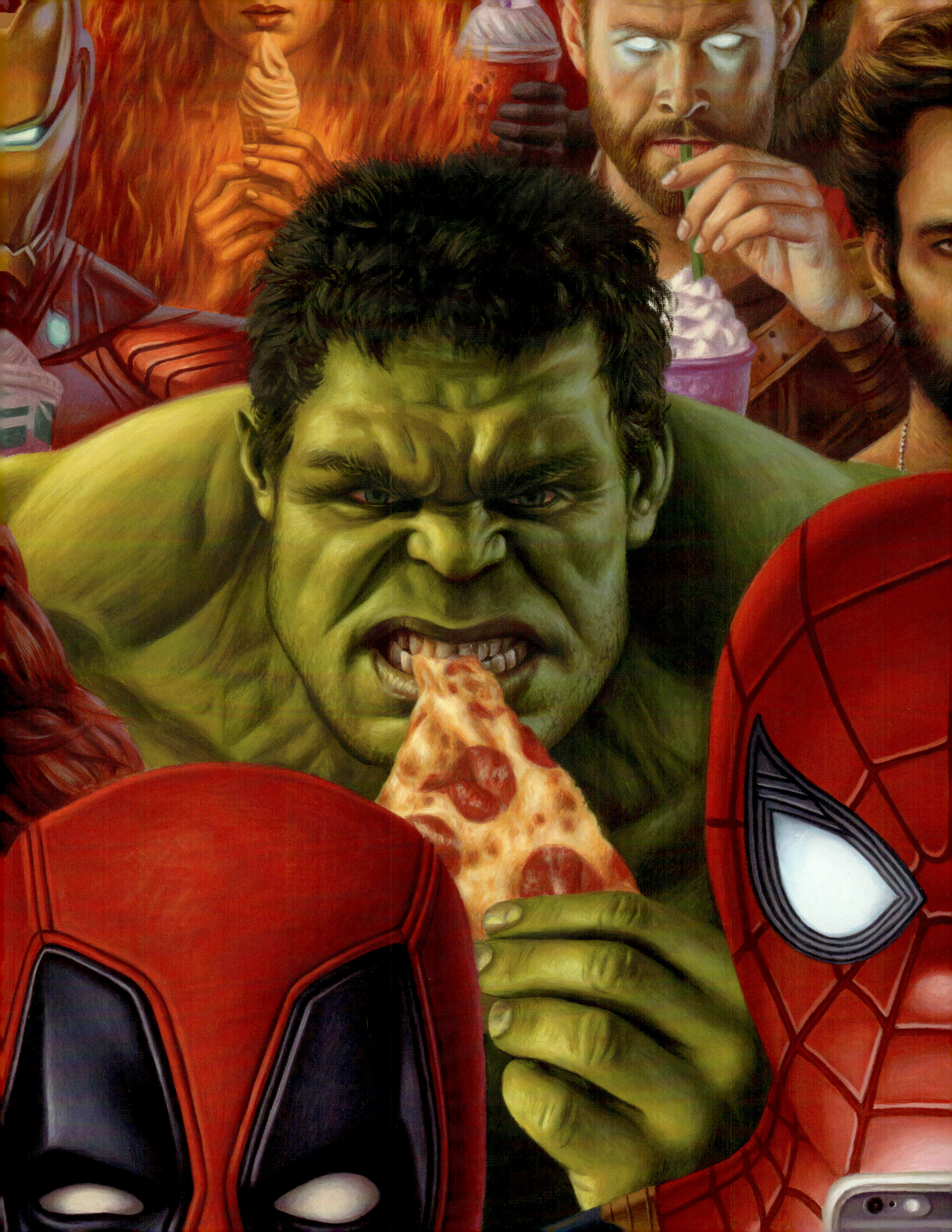

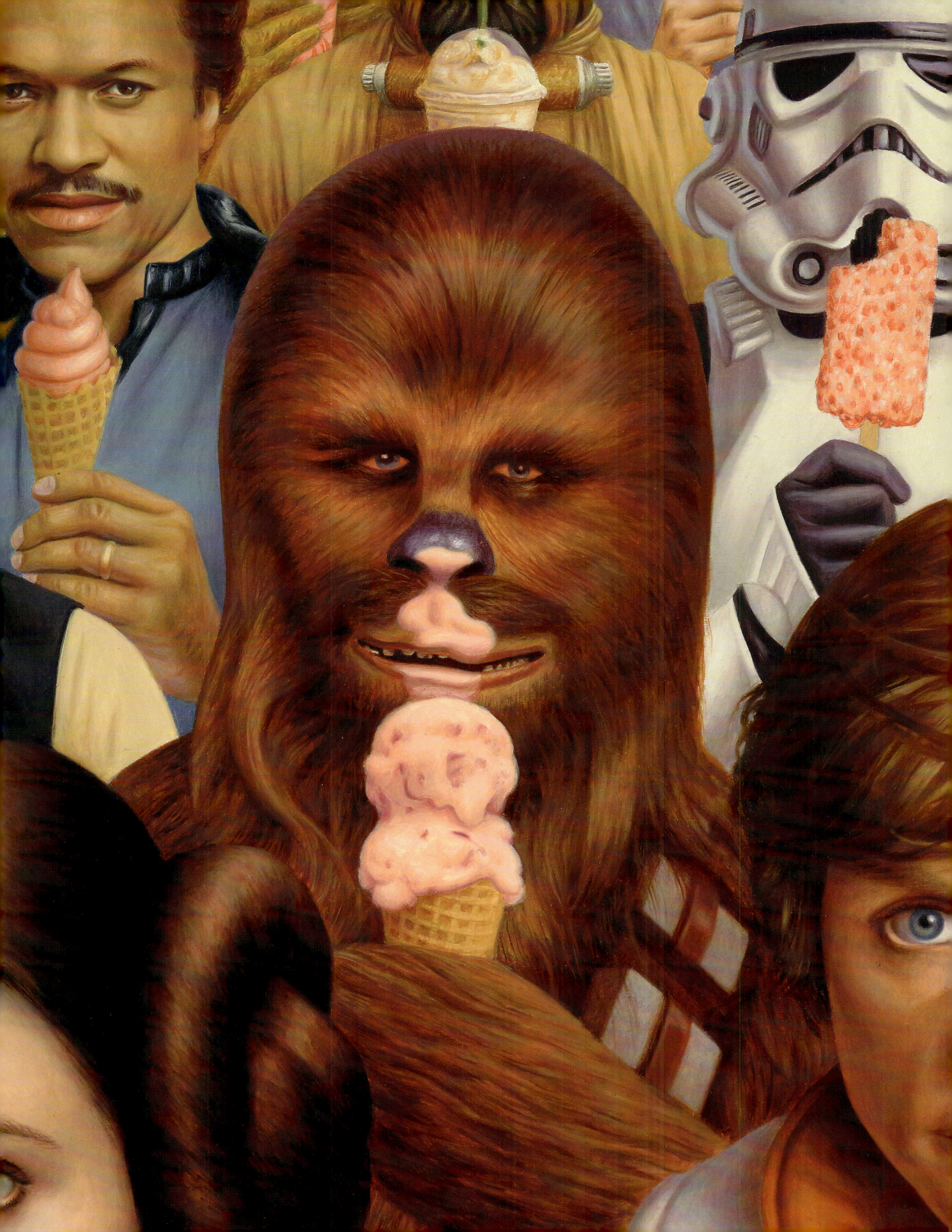

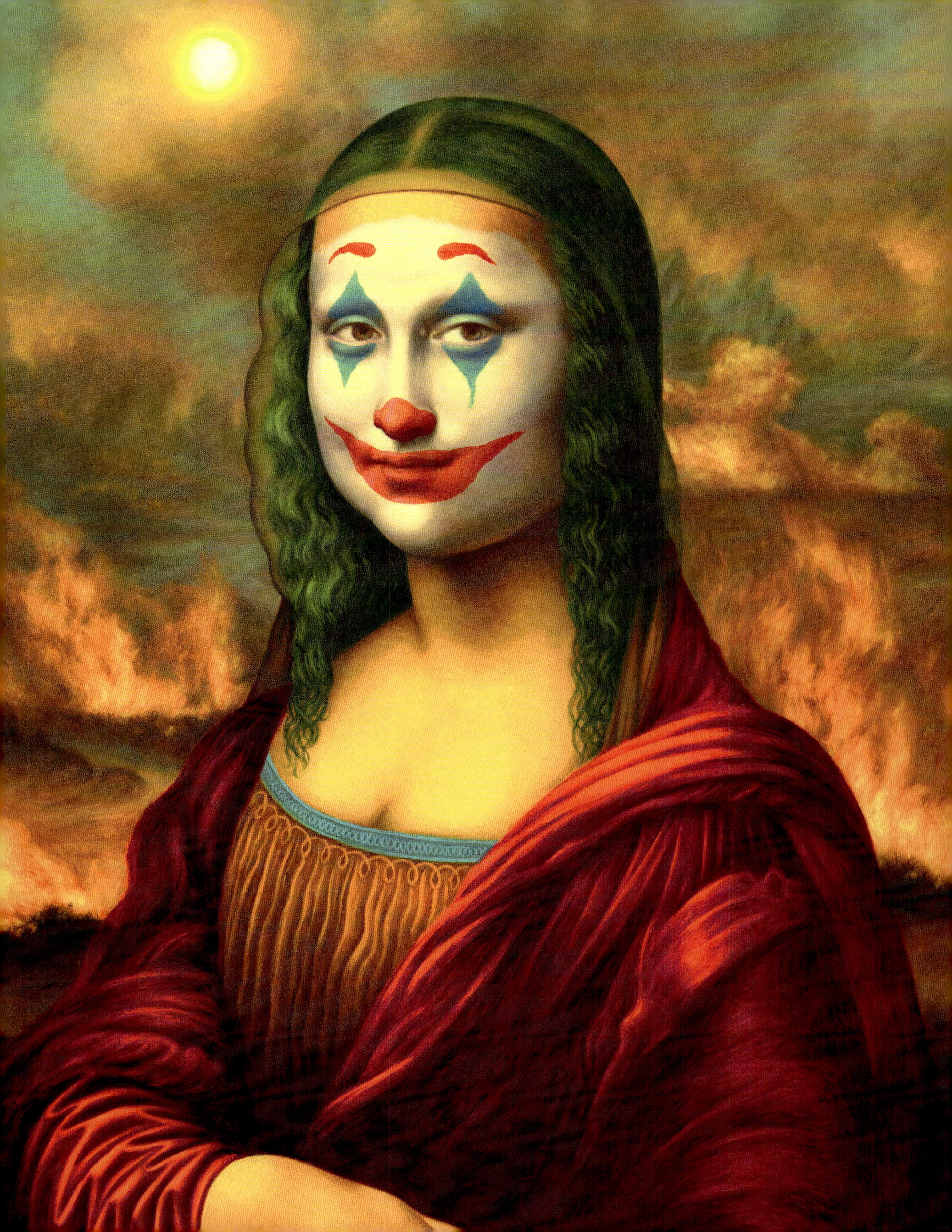

Beauty, Power & Branding

An interview with Alex Gross by John Seed

In 2014, art writer John Seed published an interview with artist Alex Gross in conjunction with his exhibition "Future Tense." Ten years later, Seed sat down with Gross for a fresh interview that explores the new characters, themes and developments that have appeared in his work over the past decade.

What is your primary motivation as an artist? Or to put it another way, what gets you up in the morning?

It's funny, I am not good at recalling things from my childhood. But one thing I remember clearly is the need to draw. If I was out all day with my family or doing something with friends, when I got home, I always felt this need to get to work on my art. I have no idea where that came from, but it was real, and it was powerful. At that time, it was mostly centered around making comic strips and beginnings of comic books that I never finished. I thought I would be a comic book artist when I got

older. So, as far as I can tell, I've just about always had a drive to create visual images. It is still there with me: I like to make pictures.

Your son Ronan has been growing up in the studio. How have his interests and his presence affected your work?

It's been wonderful sharing my workspace with my son. He's contributed to my work in many ways. For my painting entitled "Trash," he was the one who suggested that Darth Vader be drinking chocolate milk. He doesn't usually ask me what a painting means, unlike many other people in the art world. He seems to accept everything and is always curious. Any personal growth I might have achieved in the last few years is probably a result of being his father.

Since we last spoke ten years ago your work has added new pop culture characters and situations. How have the messages of your work evolved since then?

My recent themes are extensions of ideas I was working with at that time, but with the addition of more pop culture elements and characters than I was using previously. I have also been using some fresh settings—for example, the skate park in "Darth Skater"—and reaching back to the Renaissance when creating three separate homages to the "Mona Lisa" and the crucifixion in "The Revanchists."

A decade ago, I was painting a lot of people on phones, because I was seeing that everywhere and it disturbed me. Sad to say that now we all just expect everyone to be staring at their phones all the time, and the more exceptional thing is to see someone being present in the moment instead of absorbed by a screen.

Let's talk about some of your recent paintings. In "Batmania," a throng of characters enjoy sweet treats, facing outward as if the viewer is the show. What are some of the ideas behind this work?

This series began years ago with a painting of the same type but featuring anonymous people, and then a second piece where every character was myself. That one was called "Narcissism" and it appears in my FUTURE TENSE book. It just occurred to me that people might be more interested in seeing characters they like, rather than me, or some unknown faces. It also adds an element of social commentary that an image of anonymous people cannot.

Some have suggested that I am criticizing all of these properties for being essentially pop culture junk food for the masses. If this is so, then many people are not getting the joke, since these are some of the most popular images that I have ever released. It's certainly possible to interpret them in that way. But I think it is equally valid to take them as humorous twists on what are usually serious characters from typically solemn properties. It makes me smile to think of Cersei and Jaime Lannister, the villains from "Game of Thrones," sharing Tic-Tacs, as they do in my painting "Obsession."

The word revanchism refers to retaliating and recovering something that has been lost. In your 2022 canvas "The Revanchists" who are some of the figures and what revenges are they seeking?

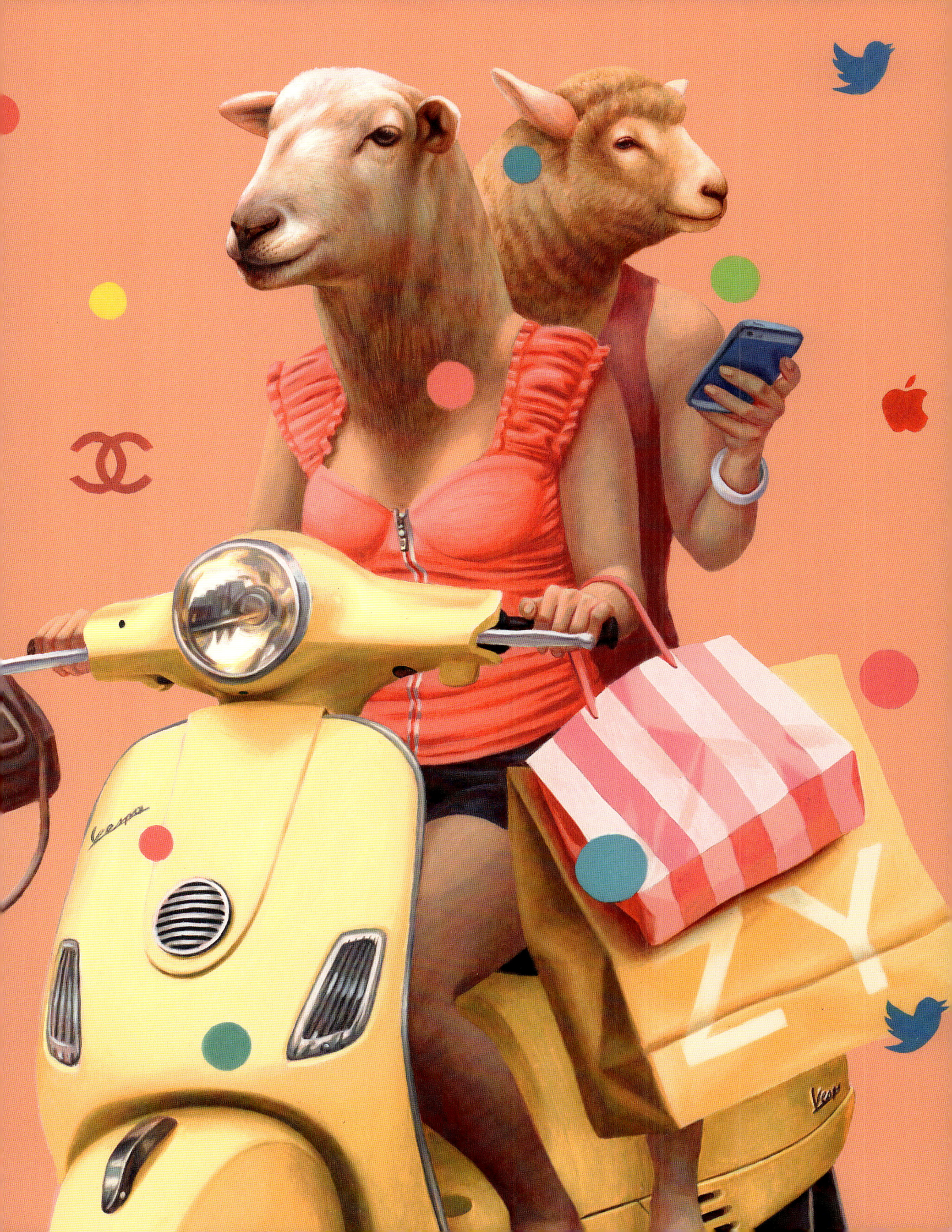

Vespa
ZY

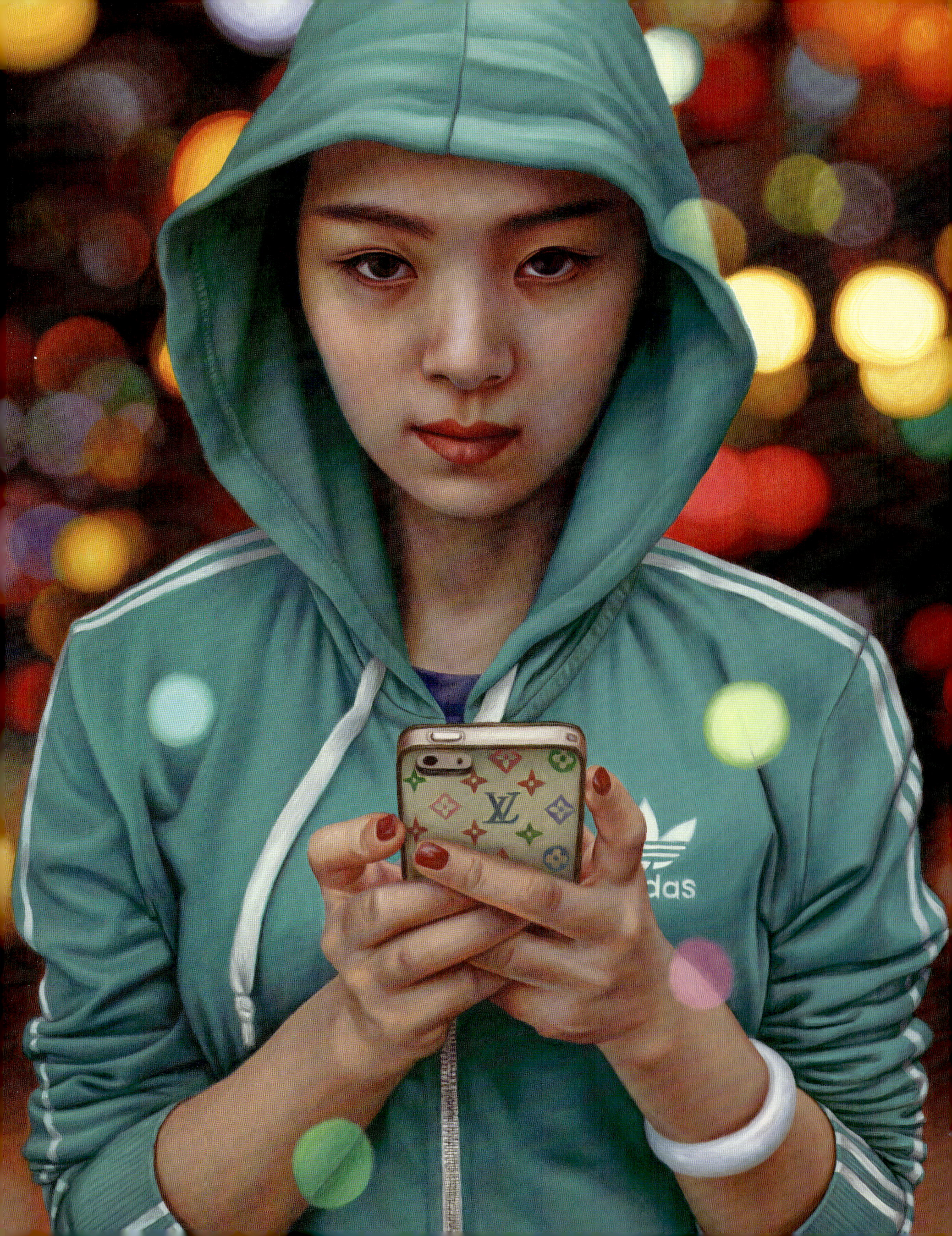

The setting for the image itself is directly based upon Rogier Van Der Weyden's "Descent From The Cross" from the early 1400s. In my version, the Christ figure being lowered is a semi-nude woman bedecked in jewelry. Additionally, the background of my image features dozens of chain-store brand freeway signs, including Starbucks, Walmart, KFC, etc.

Several of the figures in this painting are well known public personalities, such as Daft Punk, Lizzo, and Trixie Mattel. Others in the image are not celebrities. Lizzo is well known for both her music and her proud, plus-sized glamour. Trixie is probably the most famous drag model in the world right now with an HBO show, podcast, and hit songs. Daft Punk are musicians who used to dress as robots.

I rarely make an image with a distinct intellectual or political agenda in mind. It's more of a flow state inspired by a variety of ideas and images. Ultimately, I think that my take on the Crucifixion raises issues of power, beauty, femininity, branding, and politics. That's why I named it "The Revanchists." We only ever hear the term revanchism in reference to political revenge, often in terms of reclaiming territory. I felt that it was a stimulating title for an image that deals with the political undertones of femininity, changing norms of womanhood, beauty and power. But like much of my work, I also think it is very open to interpretation by the viewer.

How did you develop the ideas for "Prison of the Mind" which features two Joker figures standing in room filled with pharmaceutical capsules alongside a flaming monkey toy and stuffed unicorn?

This piece is probably the ultimate example of my process and what I consider success. I began with an old photo of two men shaking hands. I knew I wanted at least one of them to be one of the Joker characters from recent films. I tried different combinations of characters but was not happy. At some point, it occurred to me to make them both different iterations of the Joker, particularly the two significant ones, Joaquin Phoenix and Heath Ledger. As soon as I had them, the rest of the image flowed from my unconscious in a way that was kind of remarkable to me.

Often, the setting of an image will be a big question mark for me. But in this case, I knew right away that they would be in a tiny, cramped and crooked room. As soon as I tried it, I realized that the visual space could represent the interior of their minds. The pills came next. It was not a conscious idea that there should be pills. It just felt right. These are incredibly unhinged people, of course they would be medicated, or not taking their meds. Each element flowed in sequence like this until I had the whole composition.

I haven't asked about your cabinet card paintings. Do you want to say anything about how they began and what part they play in your art and process?

I have been doing them for around 15 years now. They are usually a separate realm from my oil paintings on canvas and panel, though sometimes they do influence one another. In fact, the "Prison Of The Mind" painting that we discussed earlier emerged from a cabinet card painting that I did of the two Jokers together in a scene. It occurred to me later that they would also make a good subject for a large oil painting.

I generally do the cabinet card paintings once or twice a year, in a group of around ten pieces, and I have fun transforming these antique cabinet card photographs into pop culture characters. I always enjoy doing them, and they are quick. I can finish two or three in two days or so, compared with a month or two for a large oil painting on canvas. So they are sort of a palette cleanser for me. There is a group of around 25 of them in the Delta SkyLounge at LAX, where people regularly discover them. It's a cool spot for my work and has given the cabinet card paintings greater exposure than anything else of which I am aware.

What concerns do you have about AI apps like Midjourney and Dall-E and how they will affect art and artists?

Maybe it's just me, but I find much of it boring and the results appear similar in style. I am aware that many people do many different things with it, and that it can have a broad range visually. But so far I can only recall seeing one person's AI creations that I found really compelling and unique.

I think it could be a useful tool for people like me to generate compositions and visual solutions to creative ideas. I have experimented with it minimally. It is another tool, and when used appropriately, it can be a great addition to an artist's repertoire. But ultimately as we get more and more saturated by AI created imagery, I feel that it will only lessen people's overall interest in the non-moving image, which already has to compete with video.

Do you think of your art as anti-elitist?

Like many artists now, I do not follow the old rules / model of the gallery and museum world of the recent past. I have taken control of most of my business and sales and do not have solo gallery exhibitions anymore. In my experience, and in that of many other artists, galleries do less and less, but still take far too big a piece of an artist's income.

Social media has been helpful for us to take things into our own hands. This model of course only really works if you have a large audience.

I have never been interested in what a small number of museums have decided is the most significant and elite artwork, since little of it is representational, and almost none of it even involves painting. I have always been a representational painter. Most people seem to prefer representational art to abstract or installation artwork. But these people are not the art world elite, who tend to ignore or demean that kind of work in general. So, in that respect, yes, I am anti-elitist.

———————————————————————

John Seed is an artist, writer and curator based in California. His writings on art and artists have appeared in Arts of Asia, The Huffington Post, Hyperallergic and Sotheby's Magazine. Seed is the author of "Disrupted Realism: Paintings for a Distracted World" and "More Disruption: Representational Art in Flux."

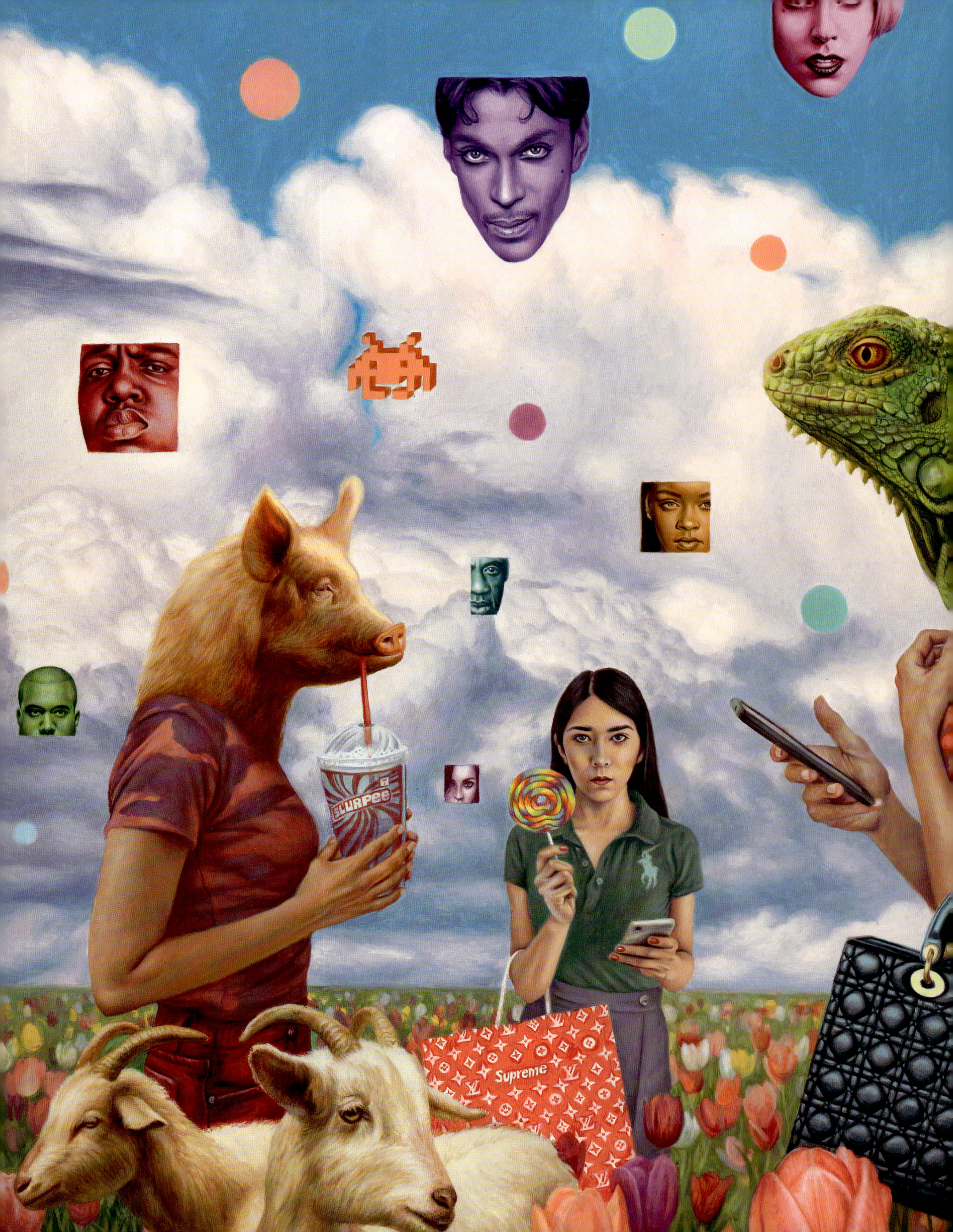

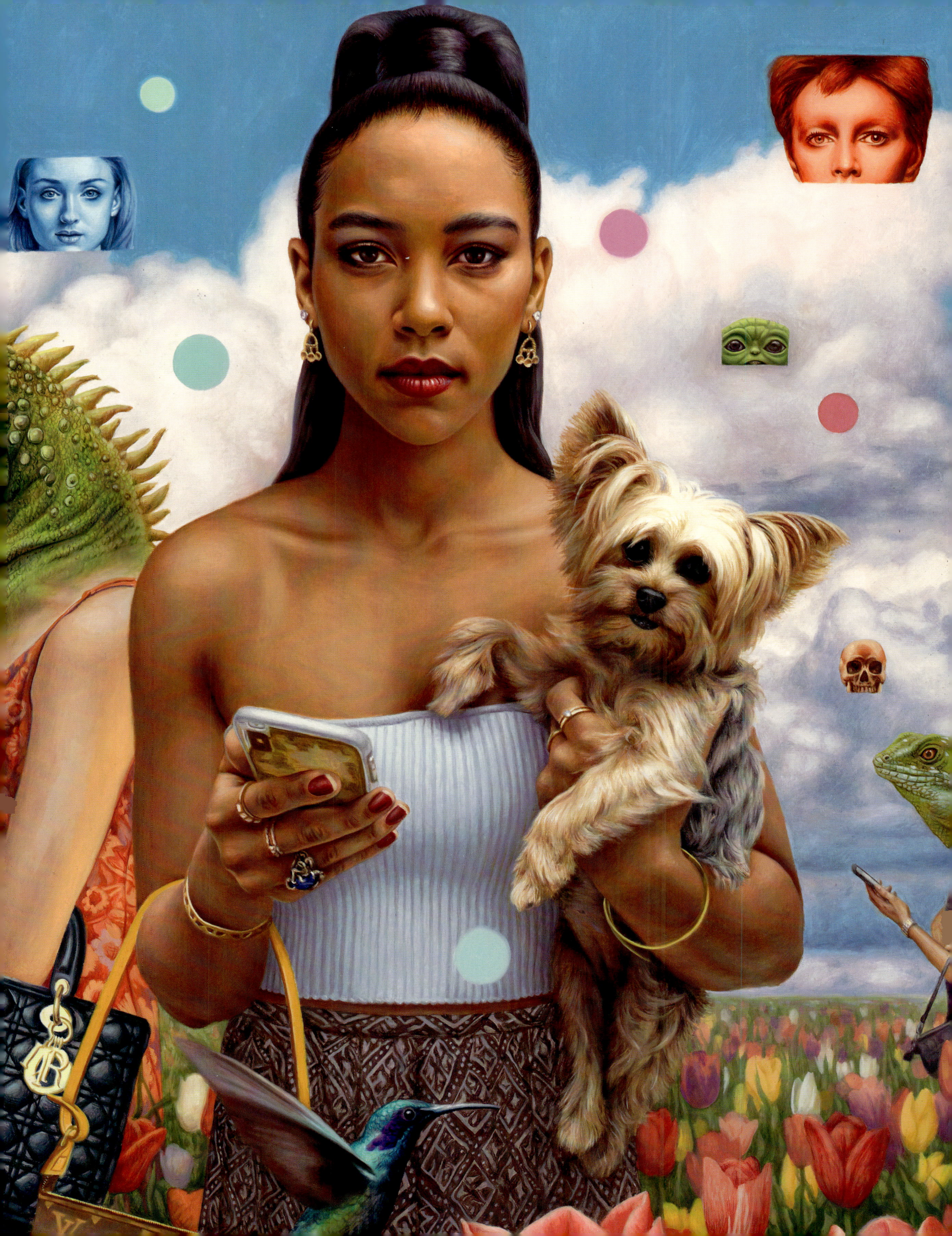

REVERIE

Oil on Canvas / 40" x 63" / 2020

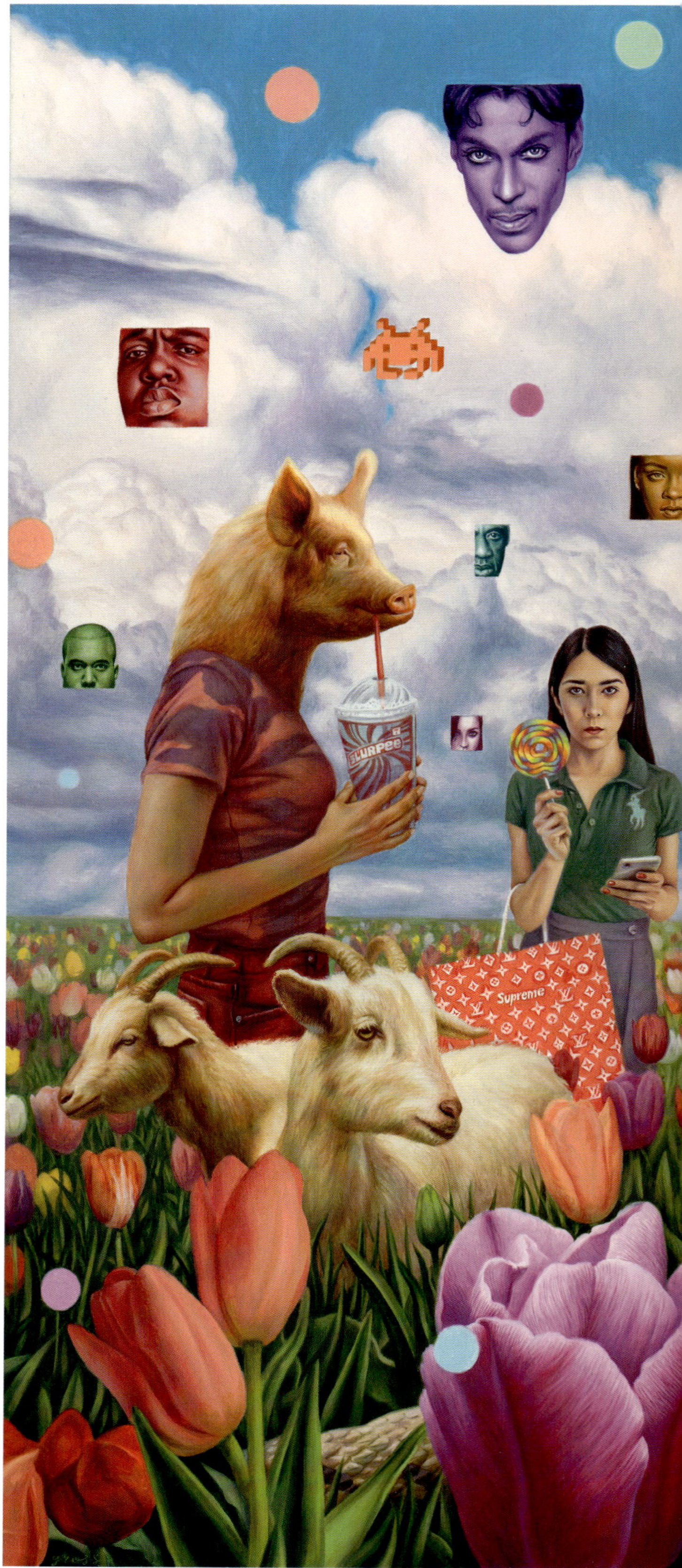

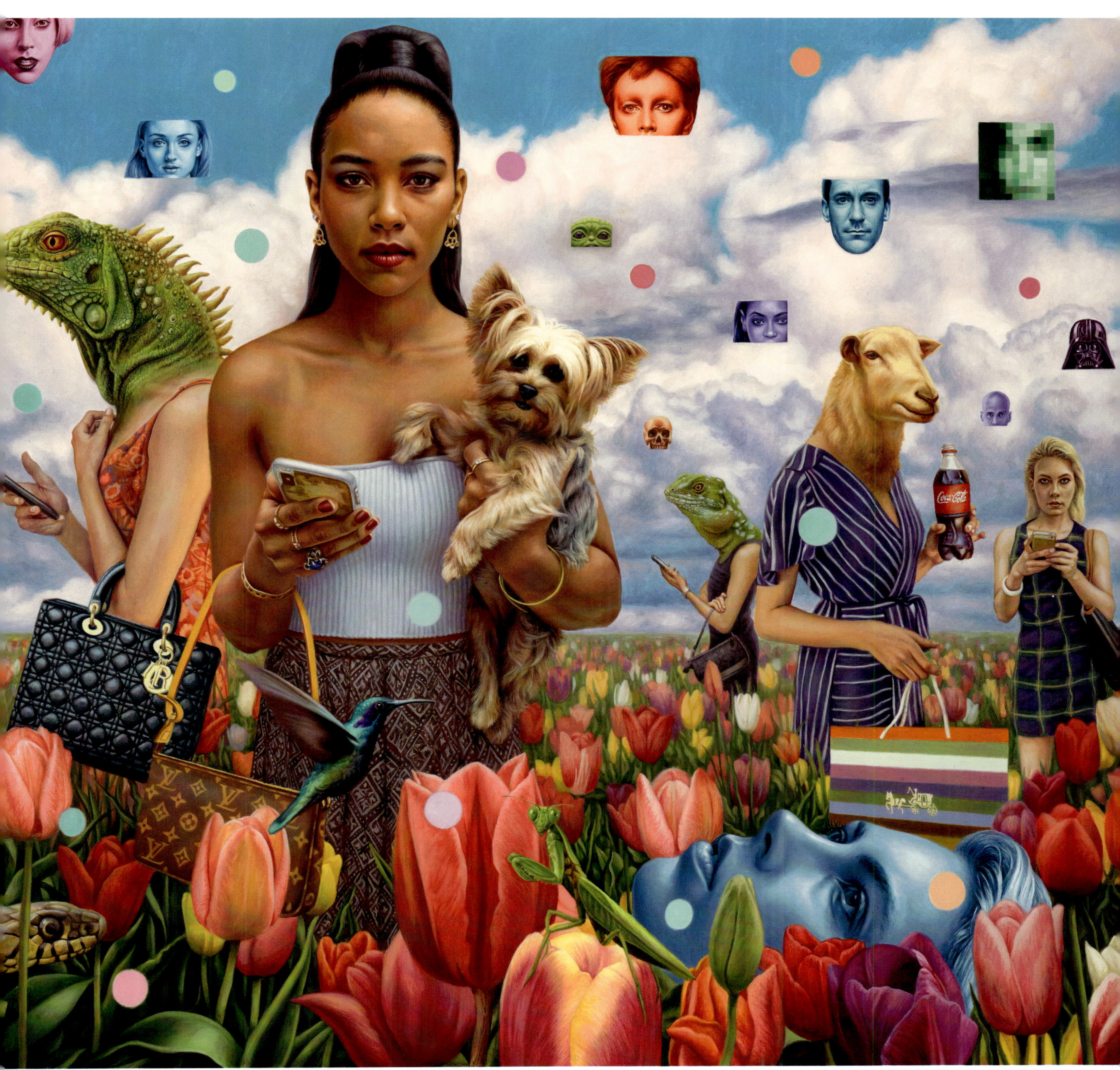

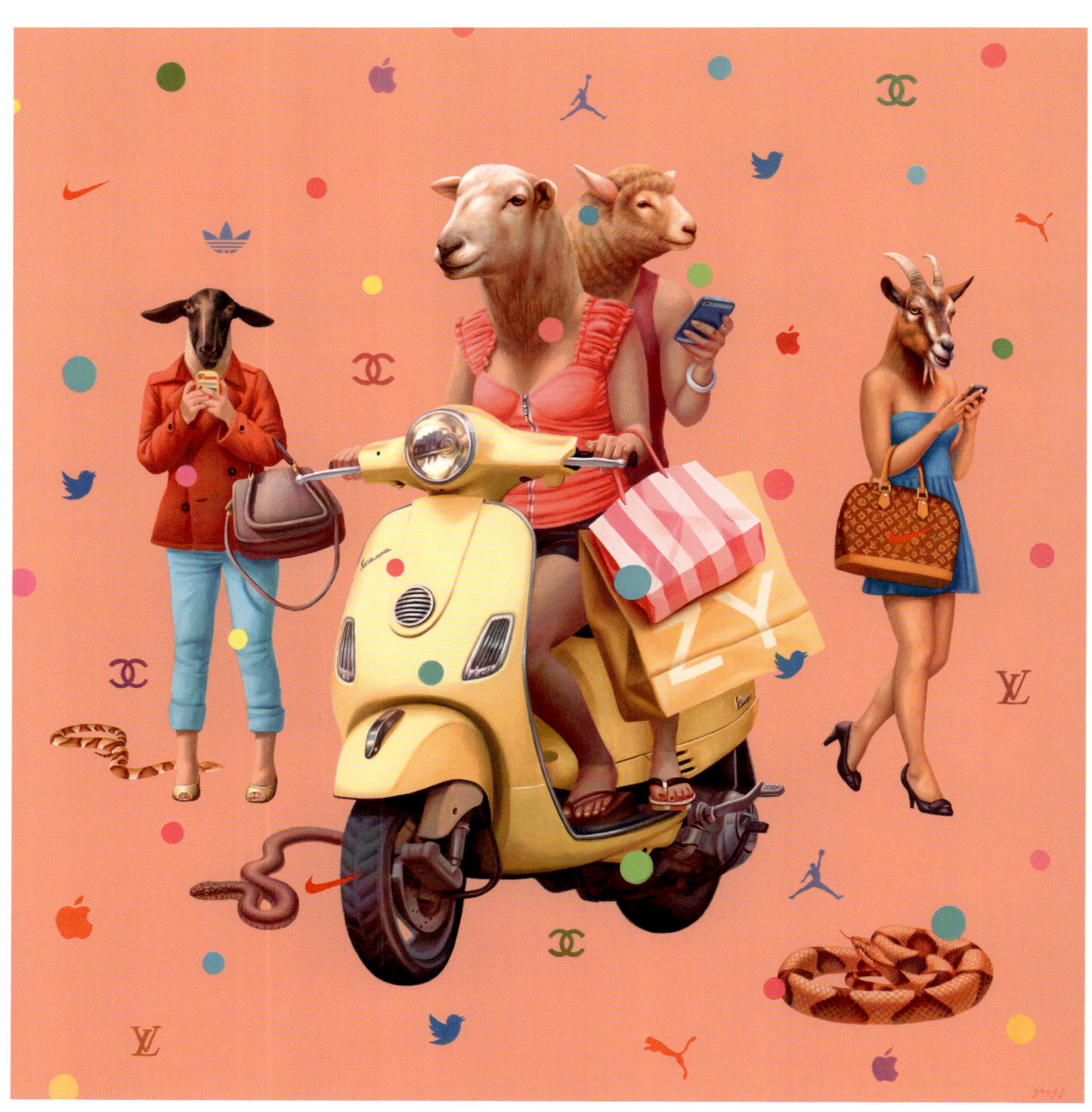

SHOPAHOLICS II
Oil on Canvas / 42" x 42" / 2016

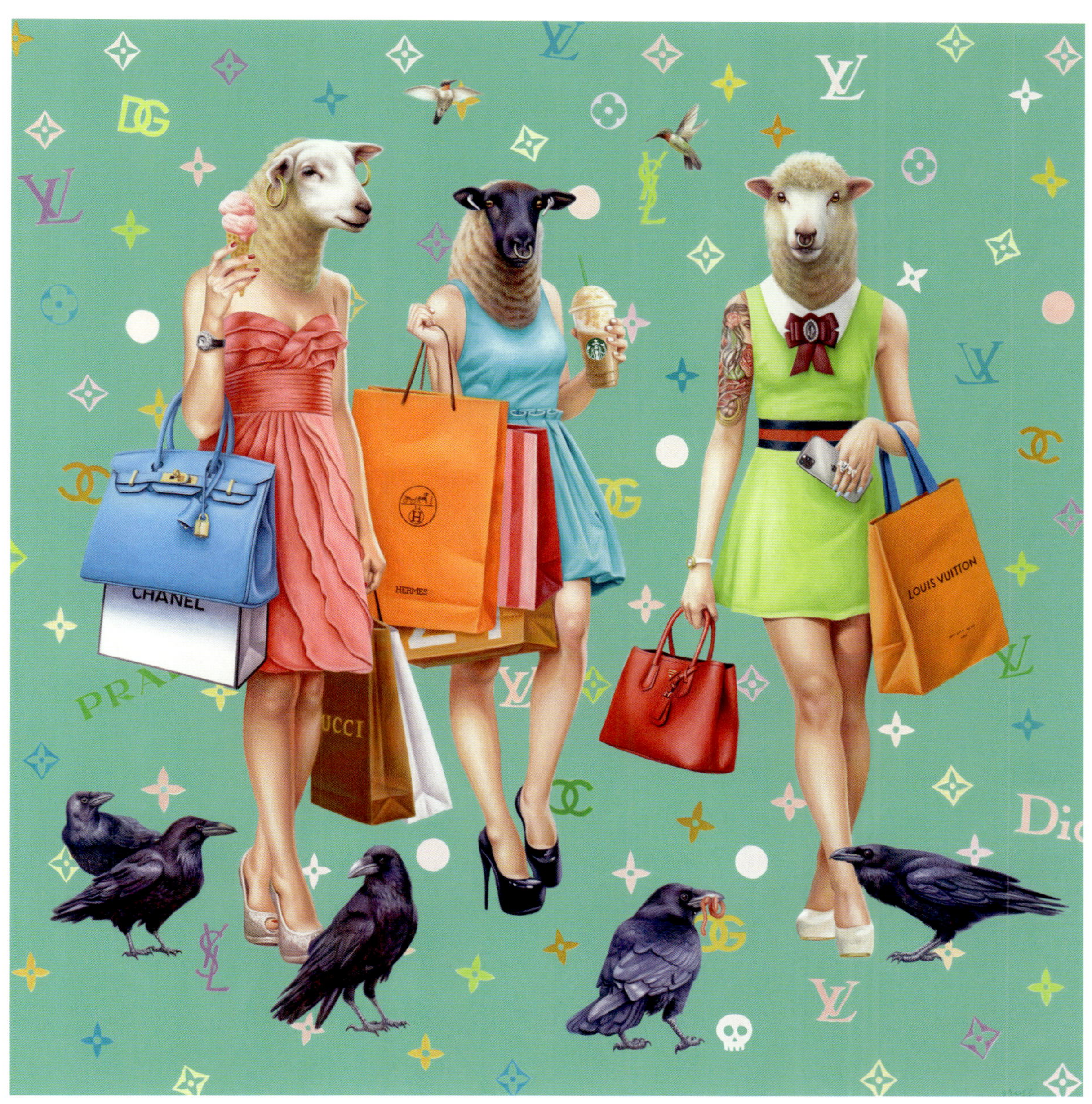

SHOPAHOLICS IV

Oil on Canvas / 42" x 42" / 2024

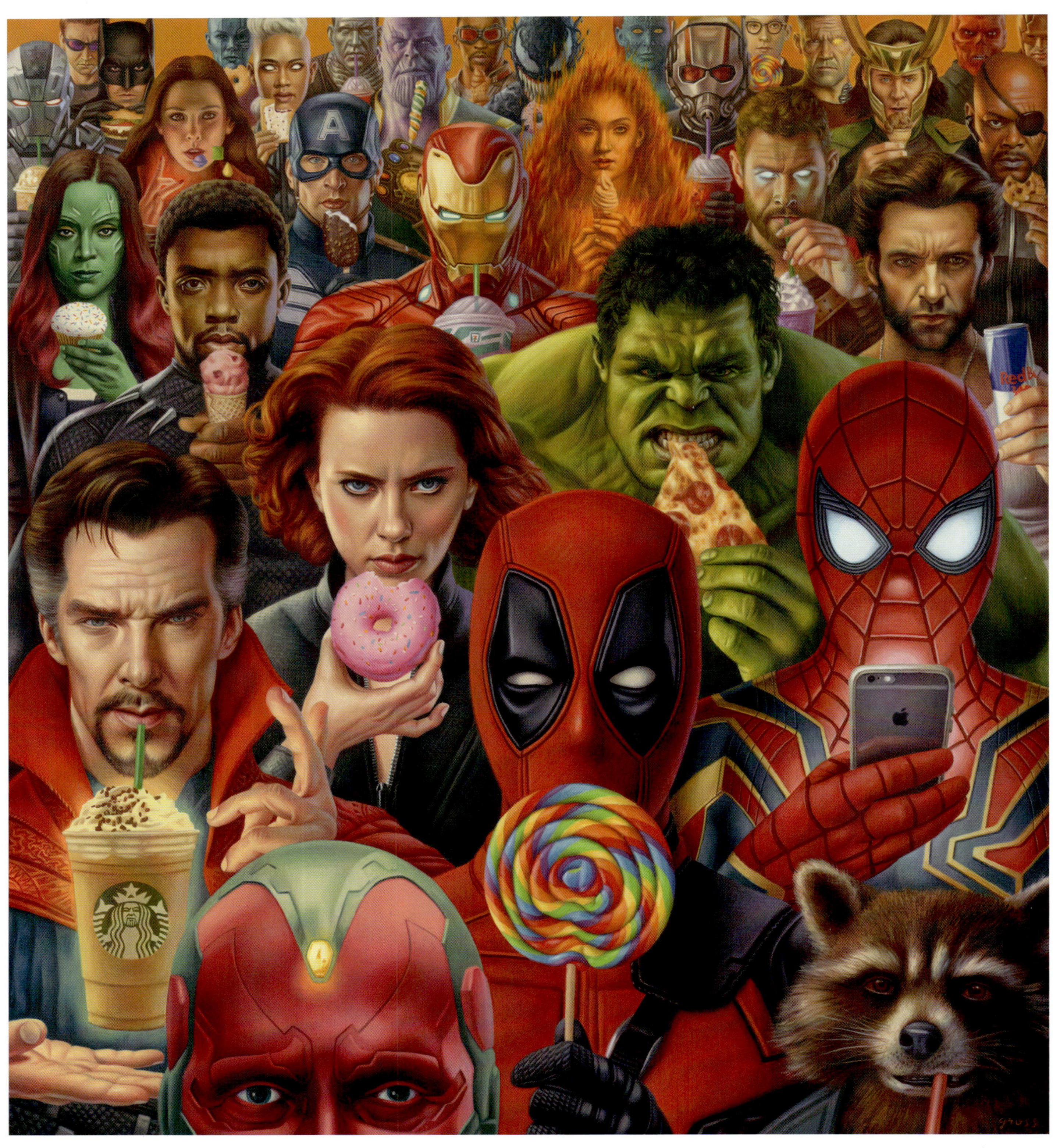

DIVERSIONS

Oil on Canvas / 38.5" x 36" / 2018

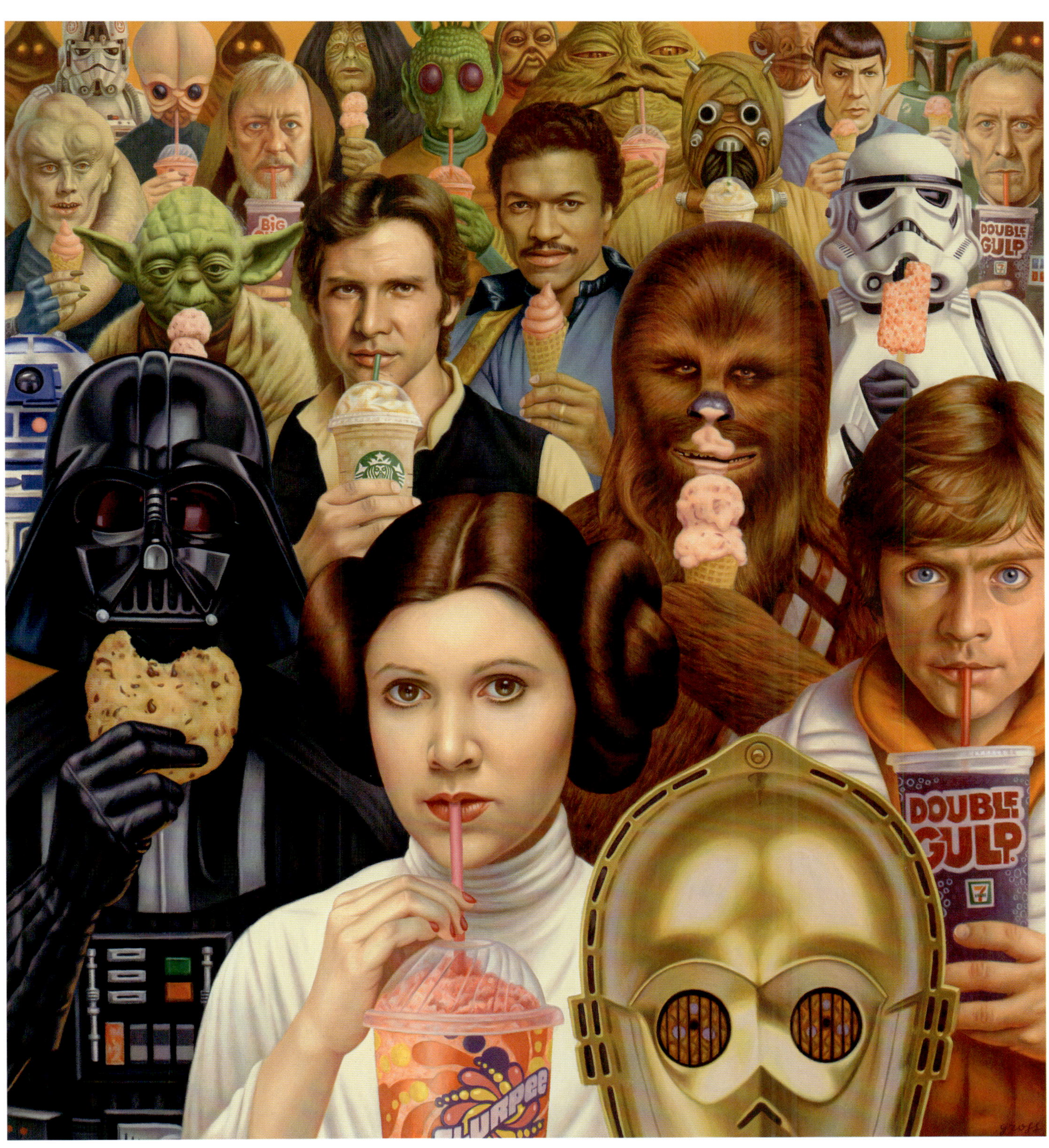

COMPULSION

Oil on Canvas / 38.5" X 36'" / 2018

MONA LEIA
Oil on Canvas / 36" x 24" / 2022

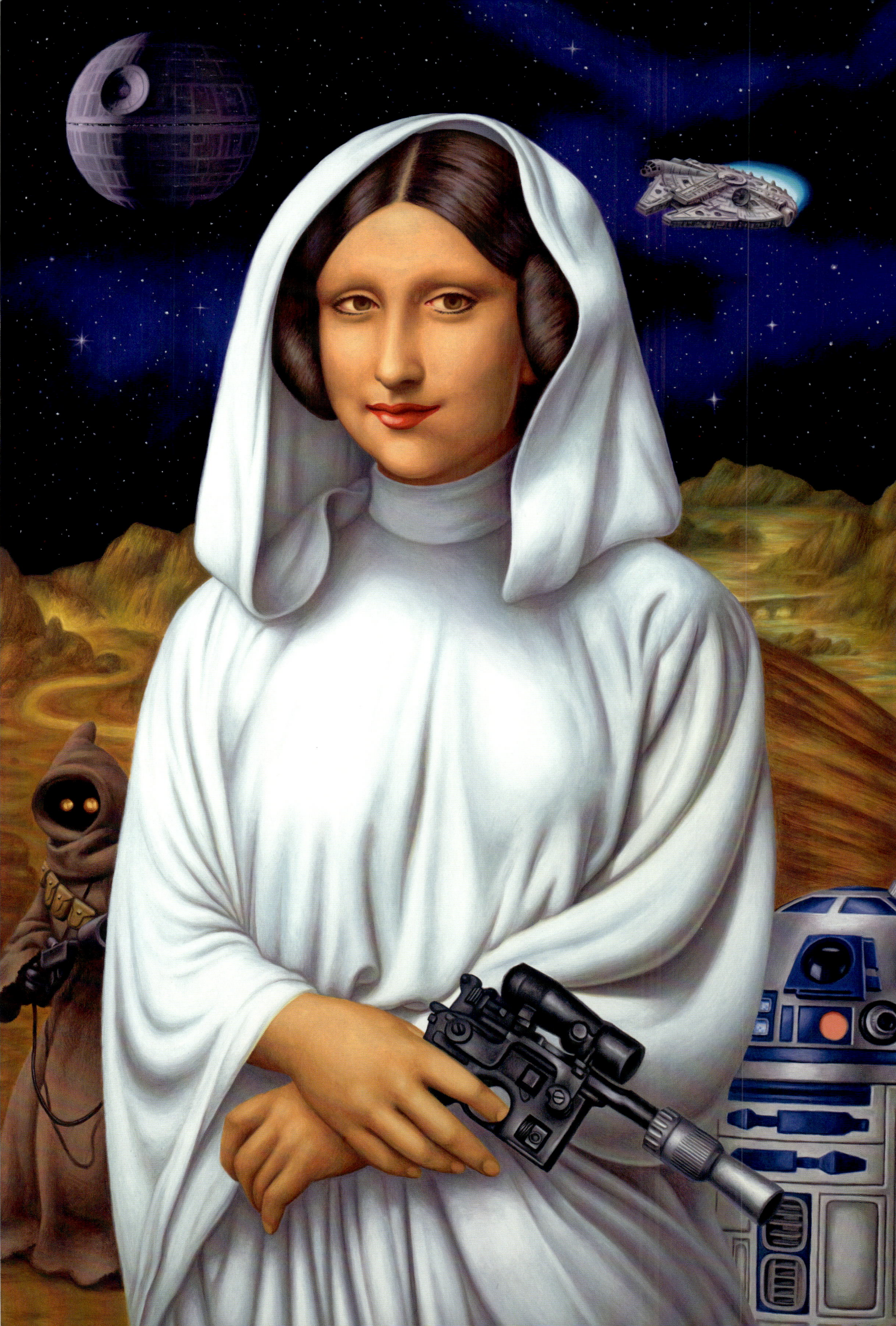

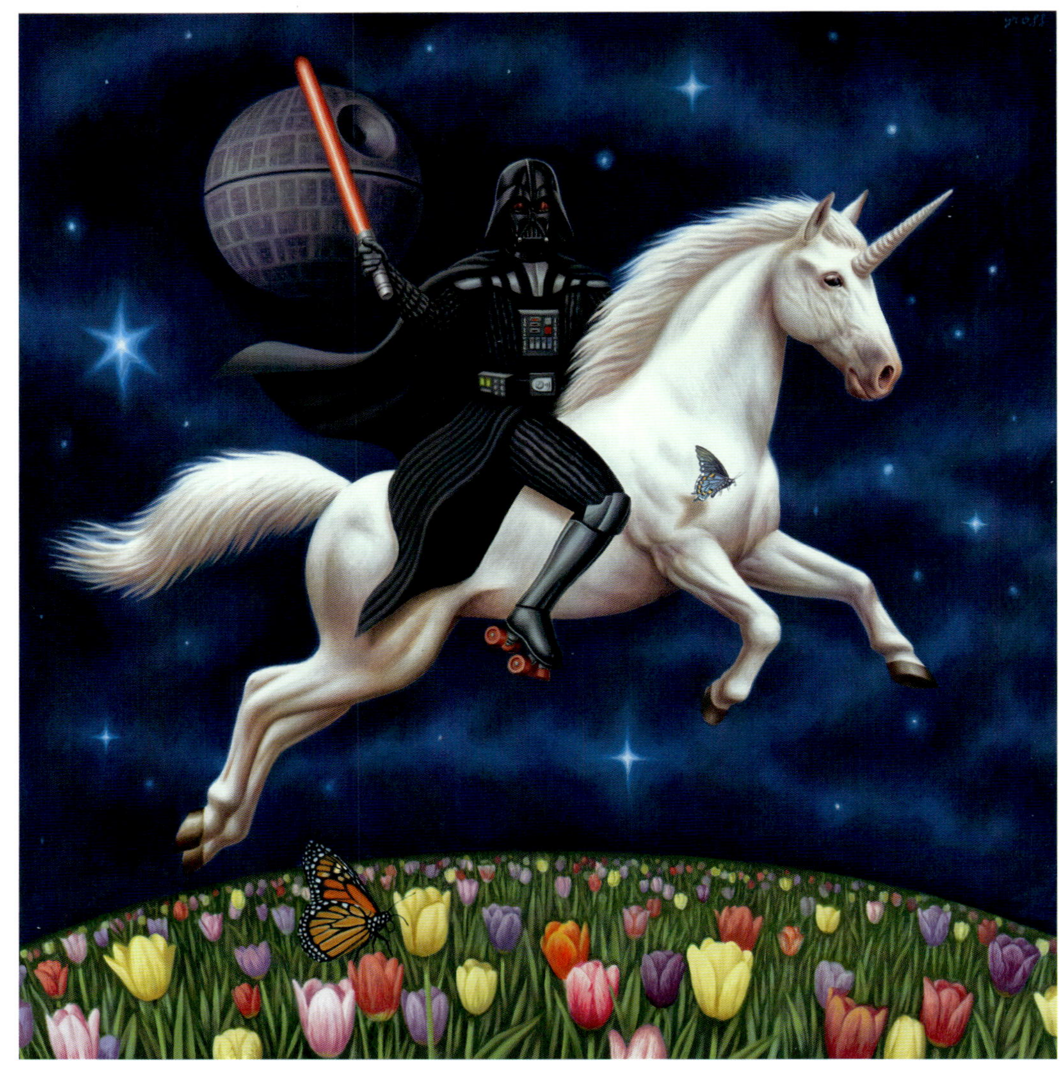

DV UNICORN

Oil on Canvas / 32" x 32" / 2017

DARTH SKATER

Oil on Canvas / 36" x 29.5" / 2023

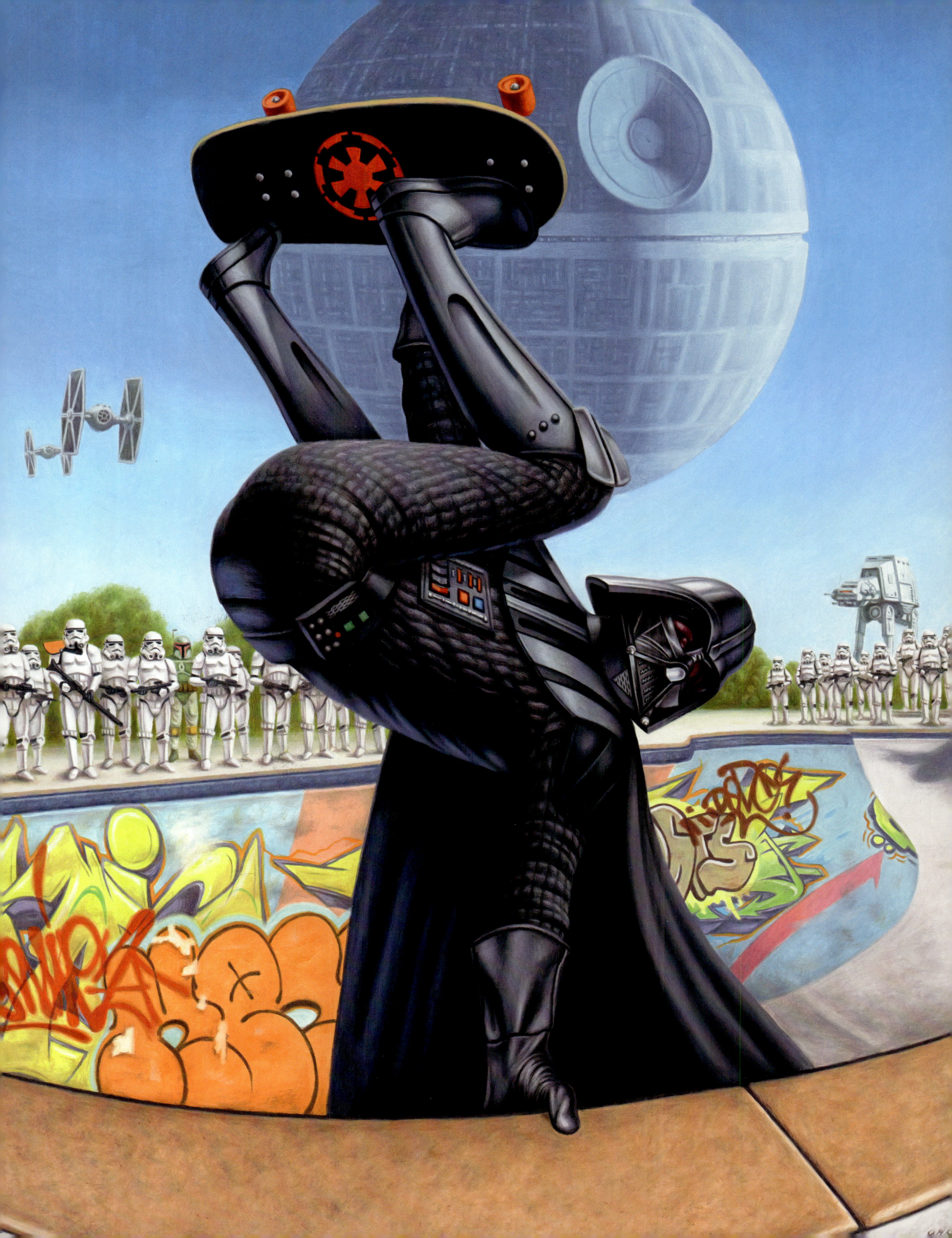

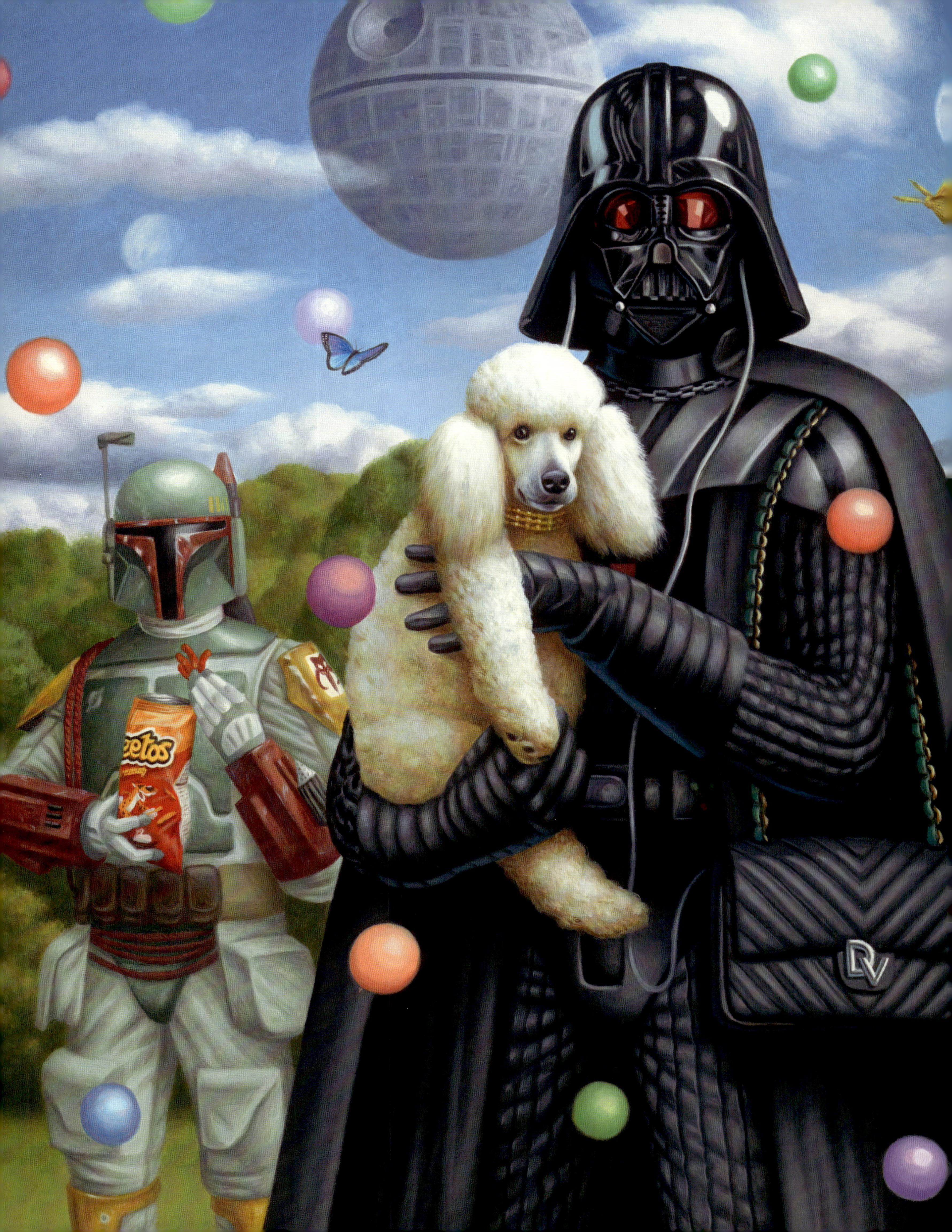

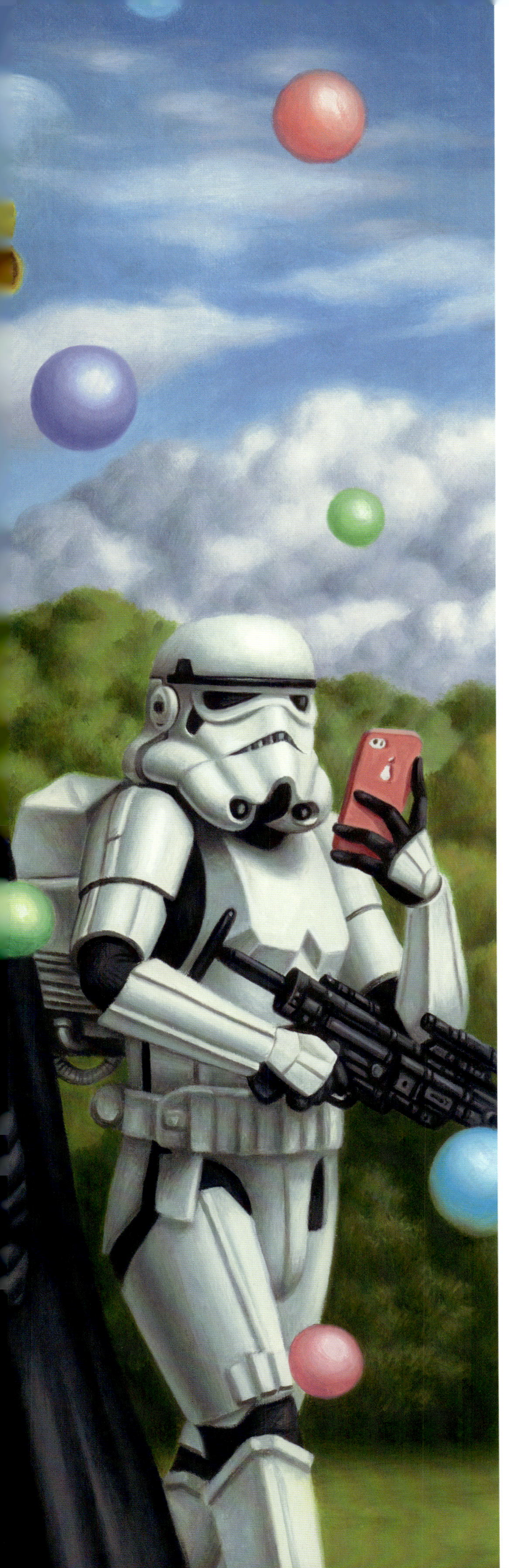

DV POSSE

Oil on Canvas / 24" x 26.5" / 2017

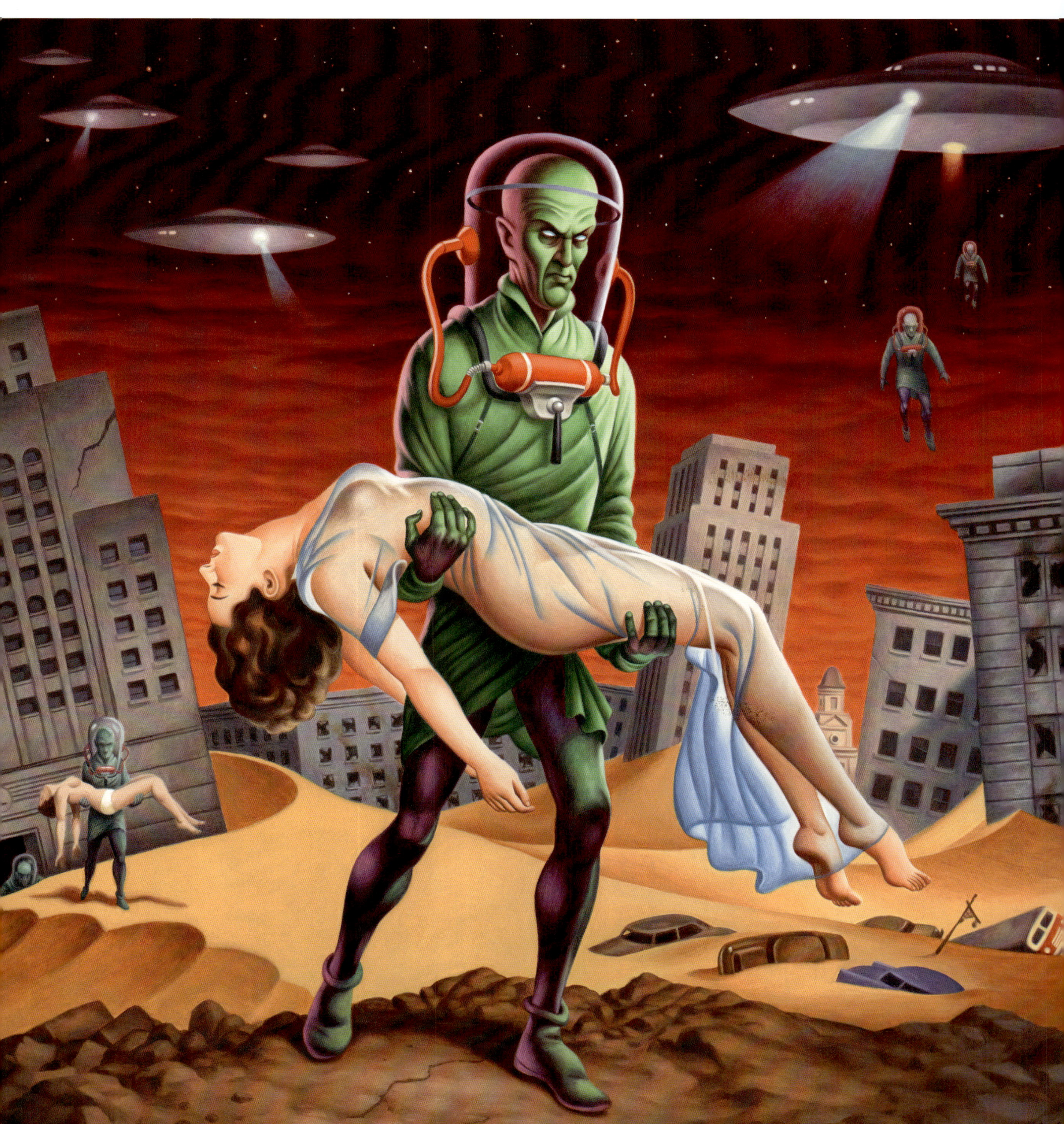

FANTASTIC STORY (*after Schomburg*)

Oil on Canvas / 36"x 36" / 2022

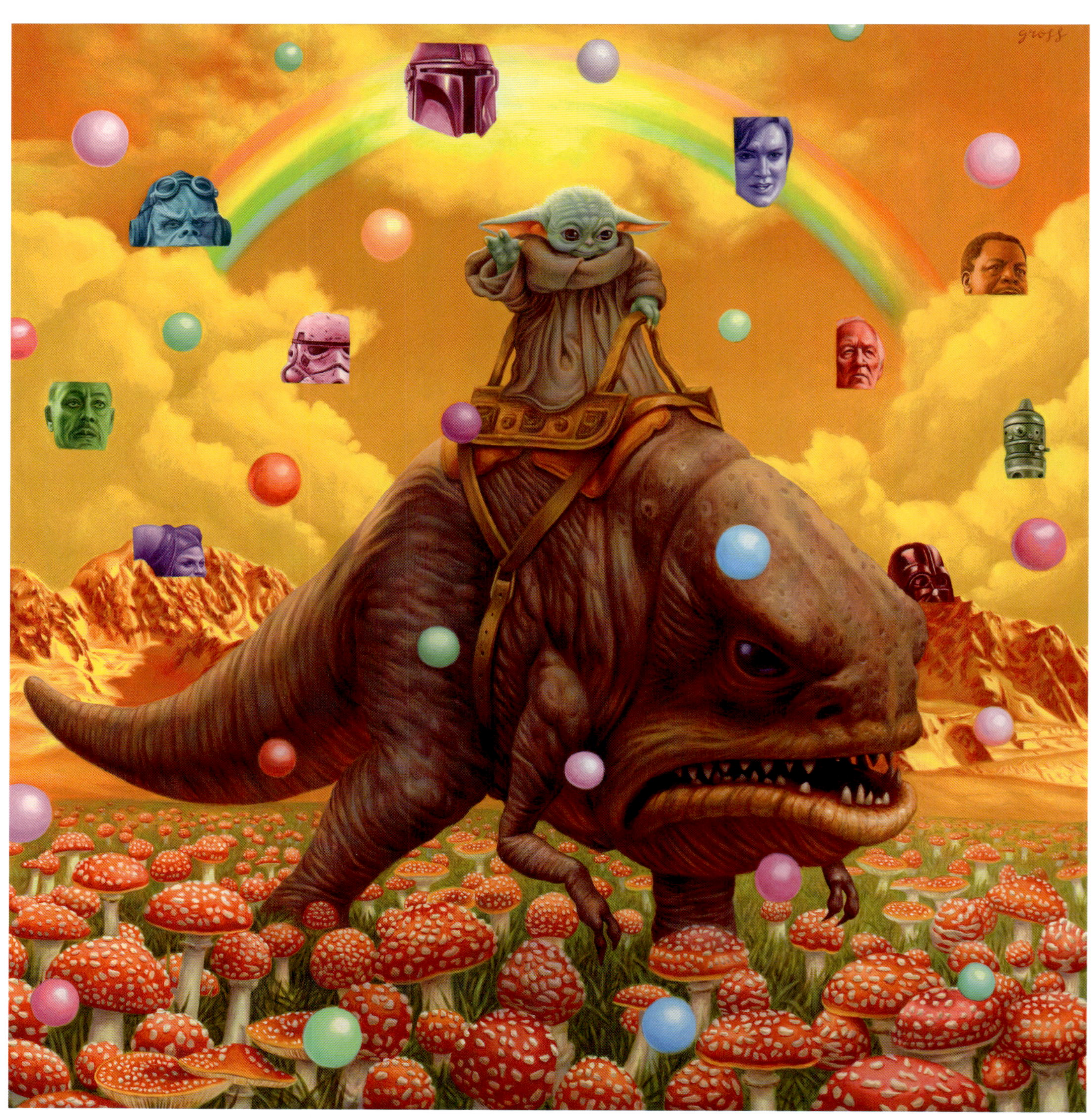

THE CHILD

Oil on Canvas / 30″ x 30″ / 2020

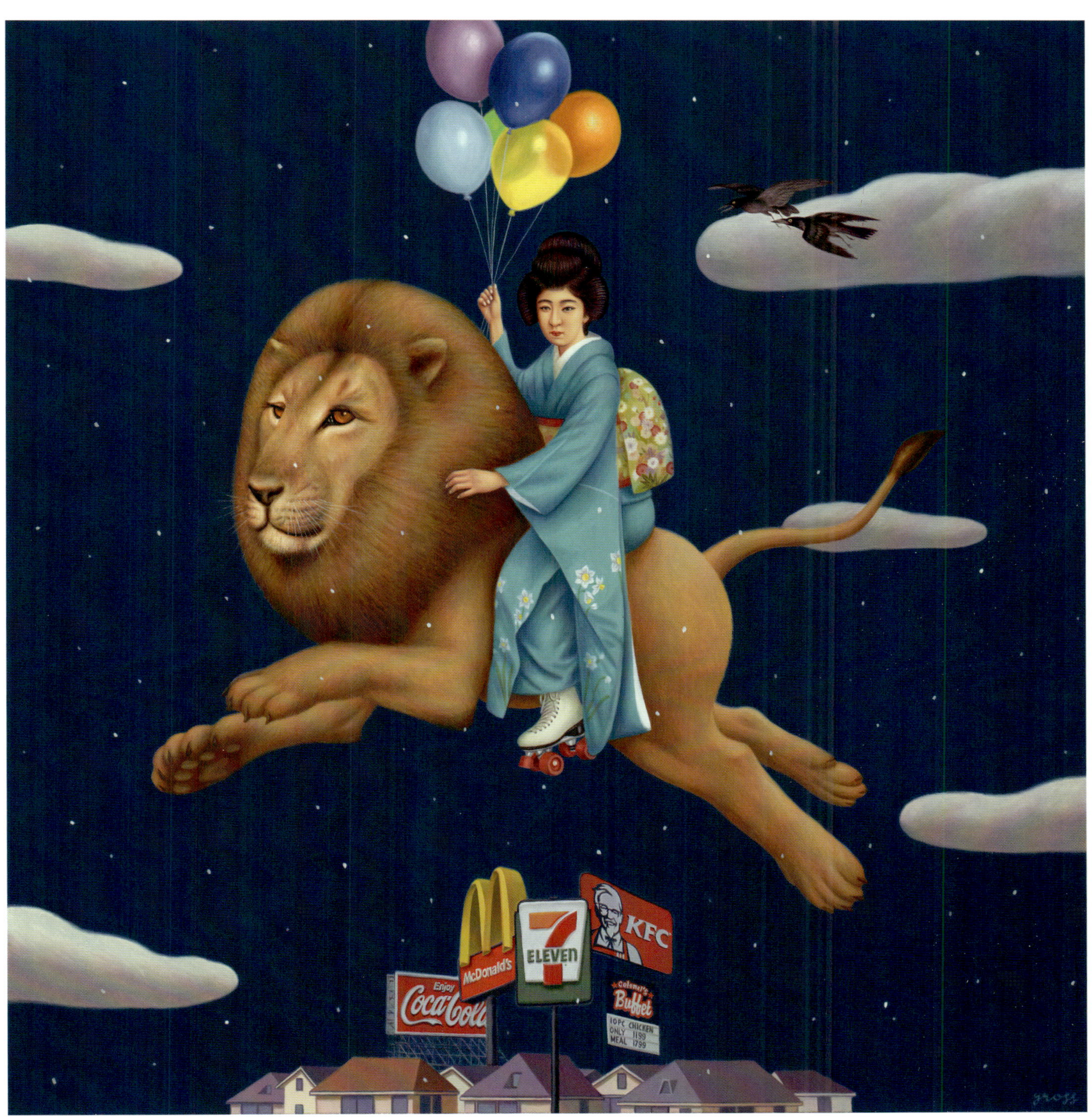

MONOGATARI

Oil on Canvas / 41" x 42" / 2015

INEVITABILITY
Oil on Canvas / 32" x 35" / 2020

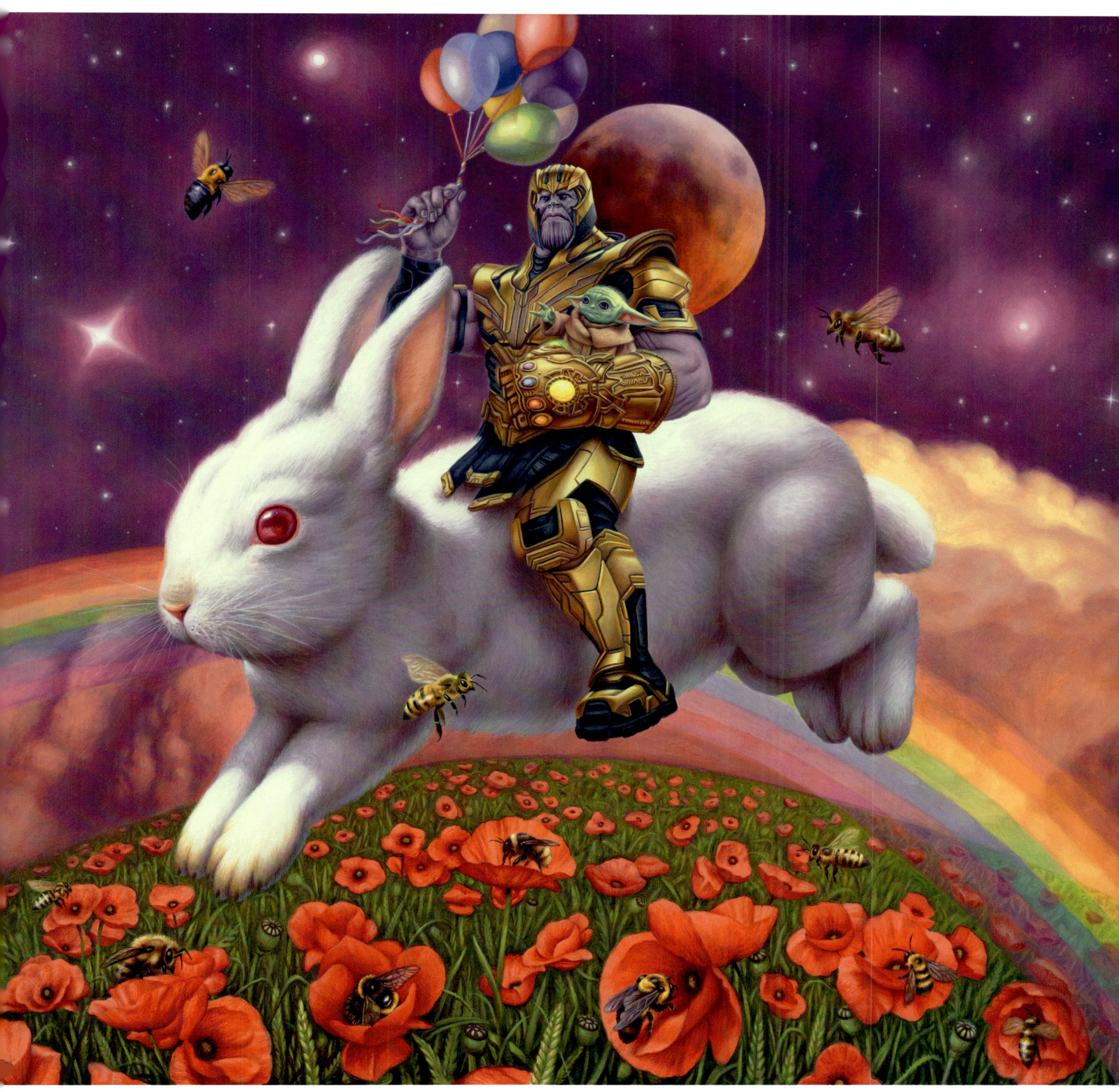

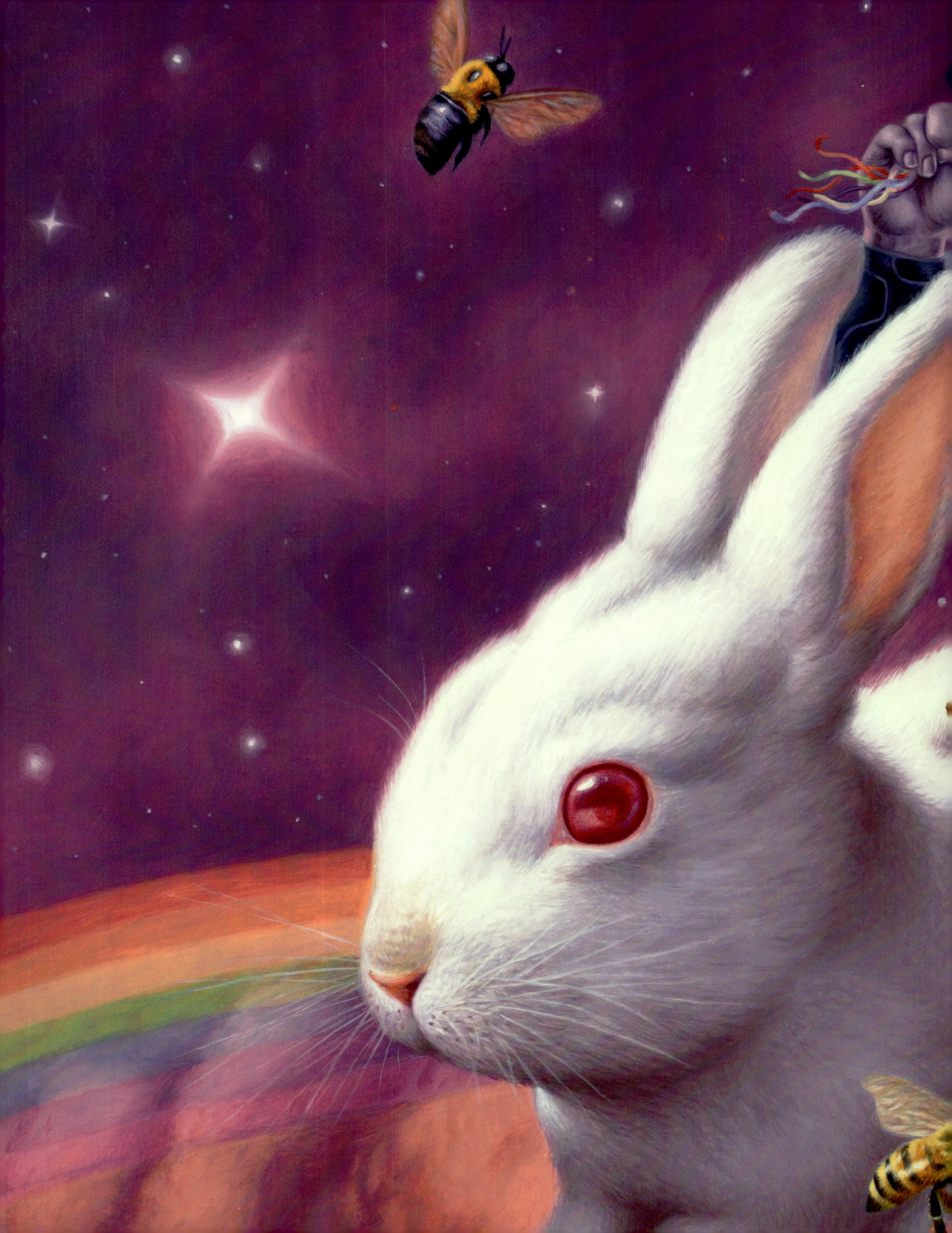

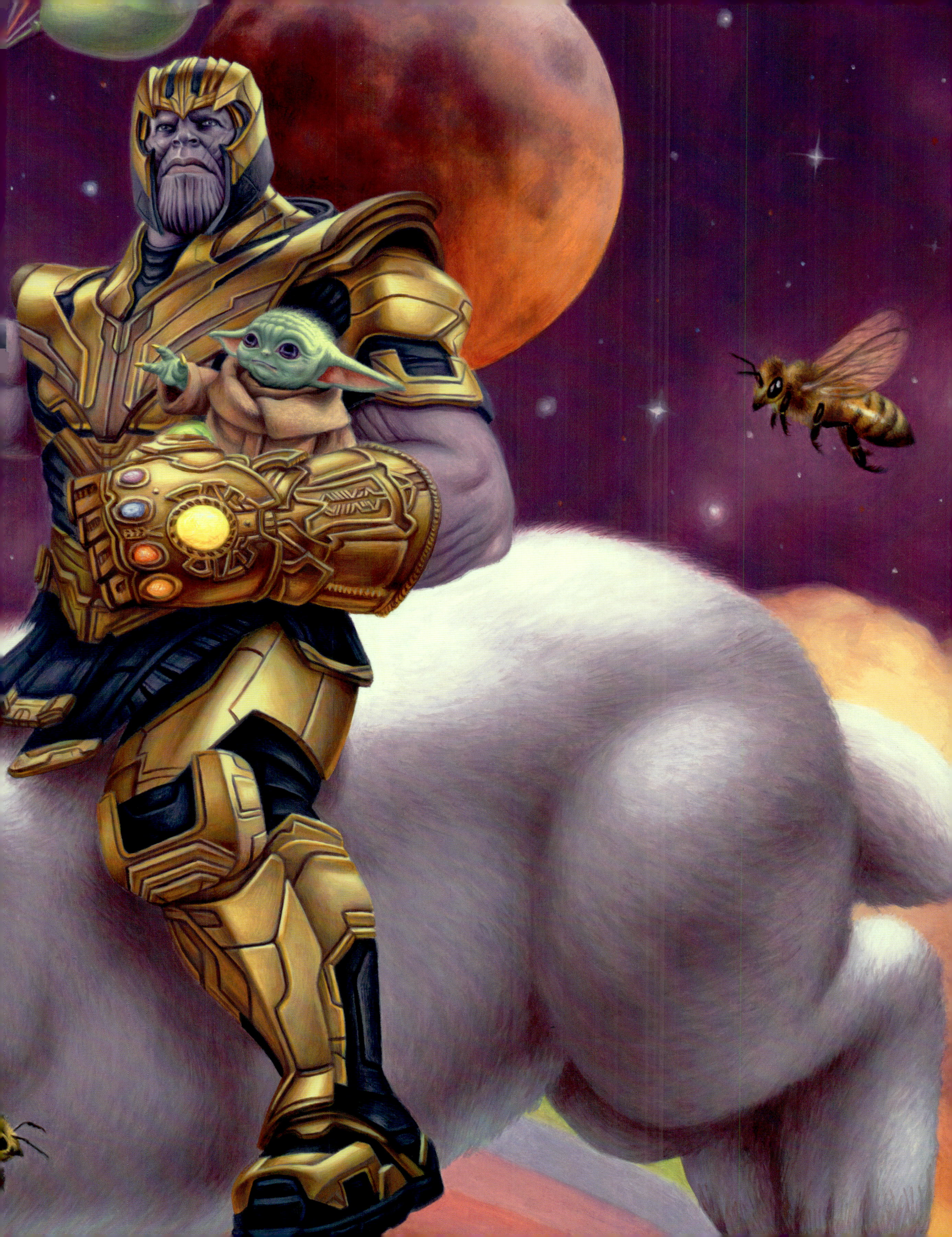

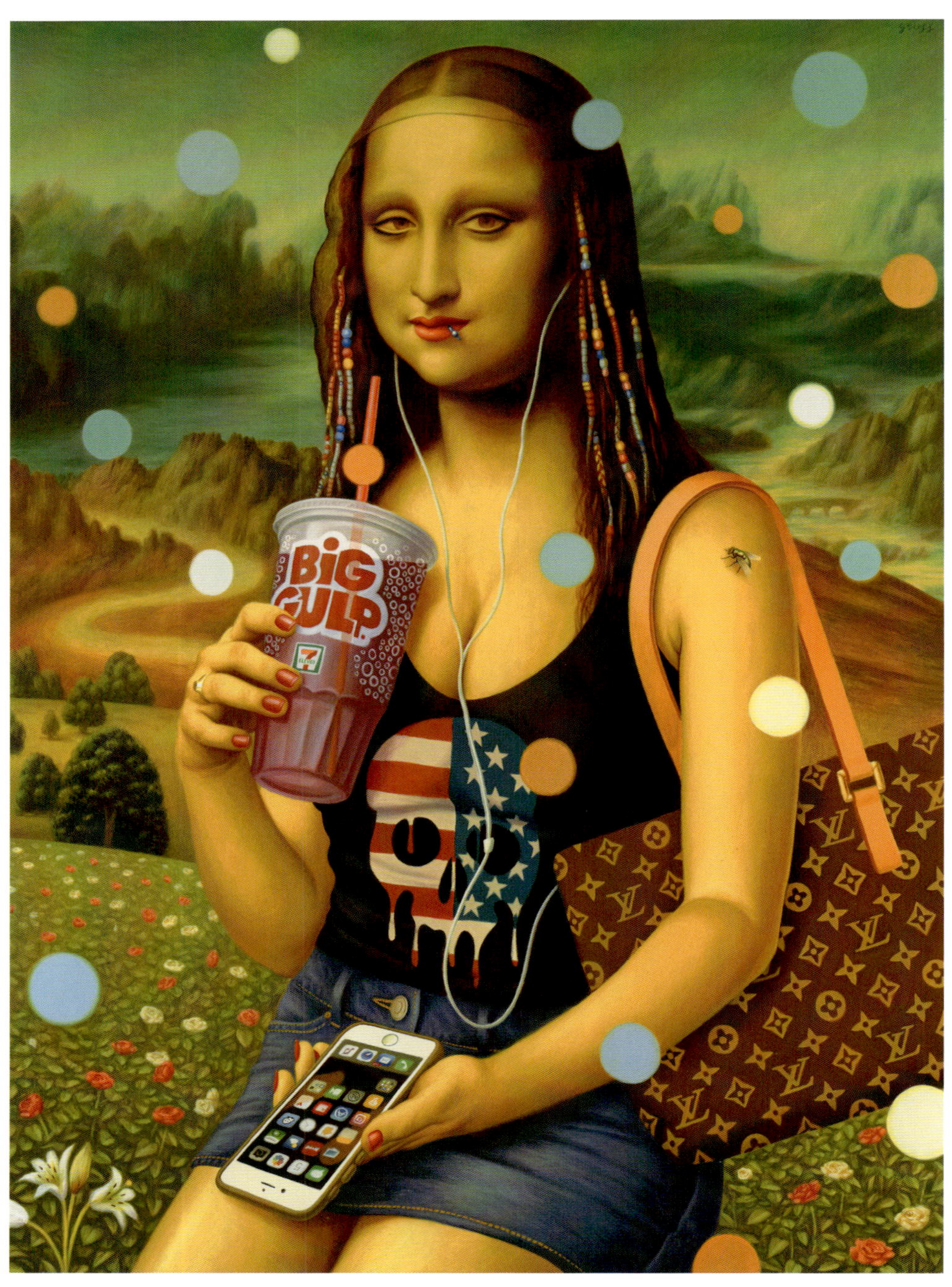

#MONALISA2018

Oil on Canvas / 48" x 36" / 2018

MONA LISA JOKER

Oil on Canvas / 36" x 24" / 2020

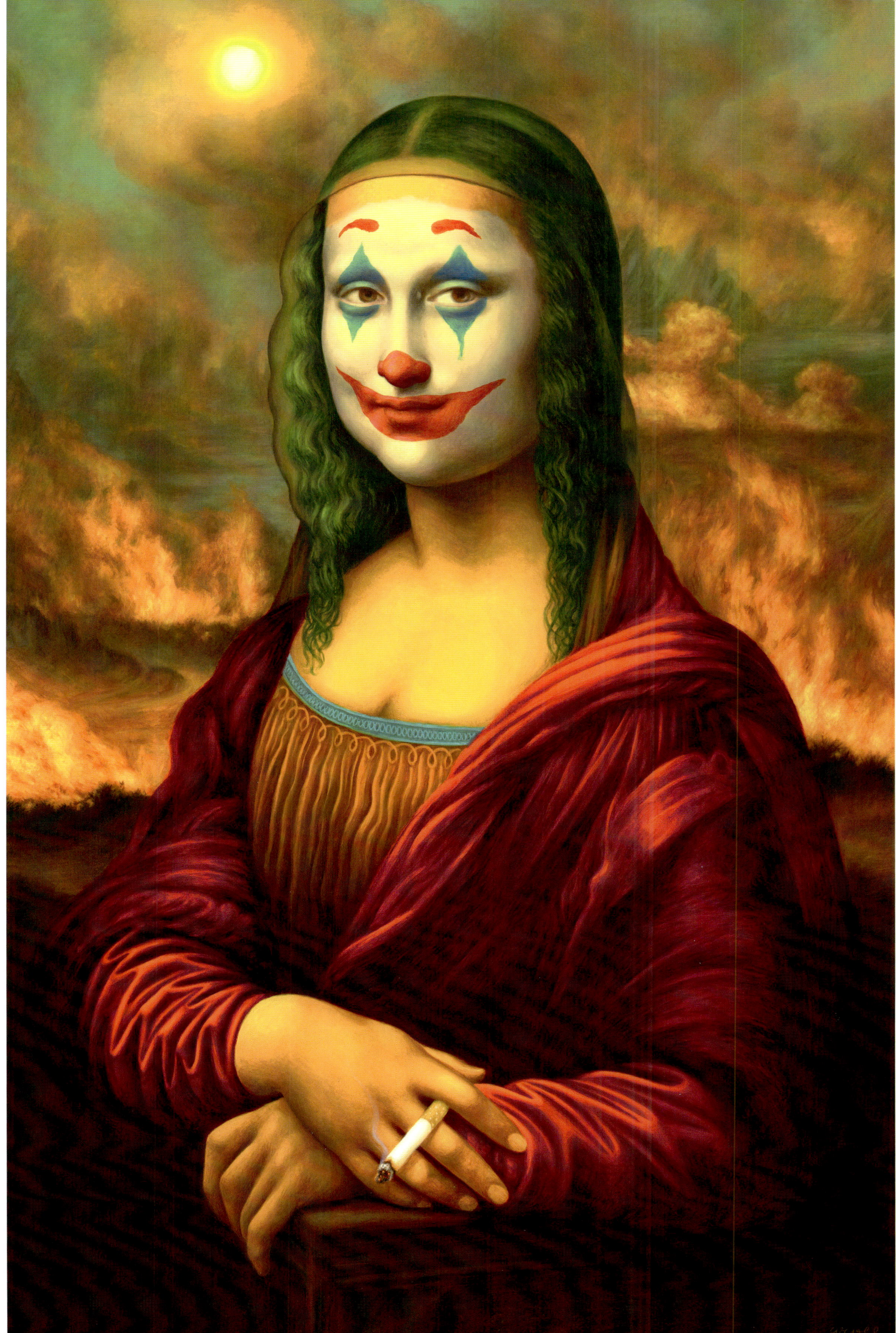

PRISON OF THE MIND

Oil on Canvas / 45.5" x 36" / 2021

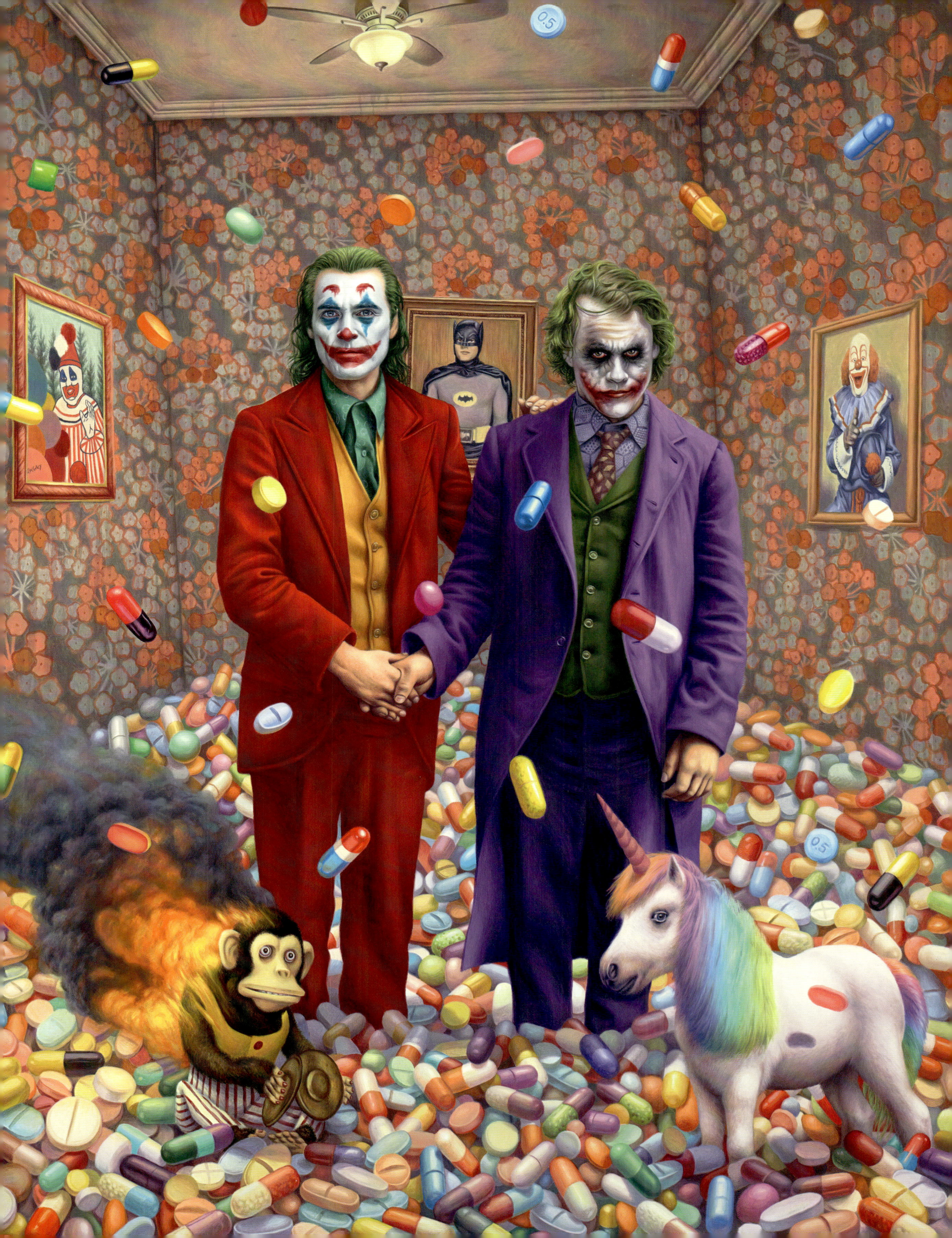

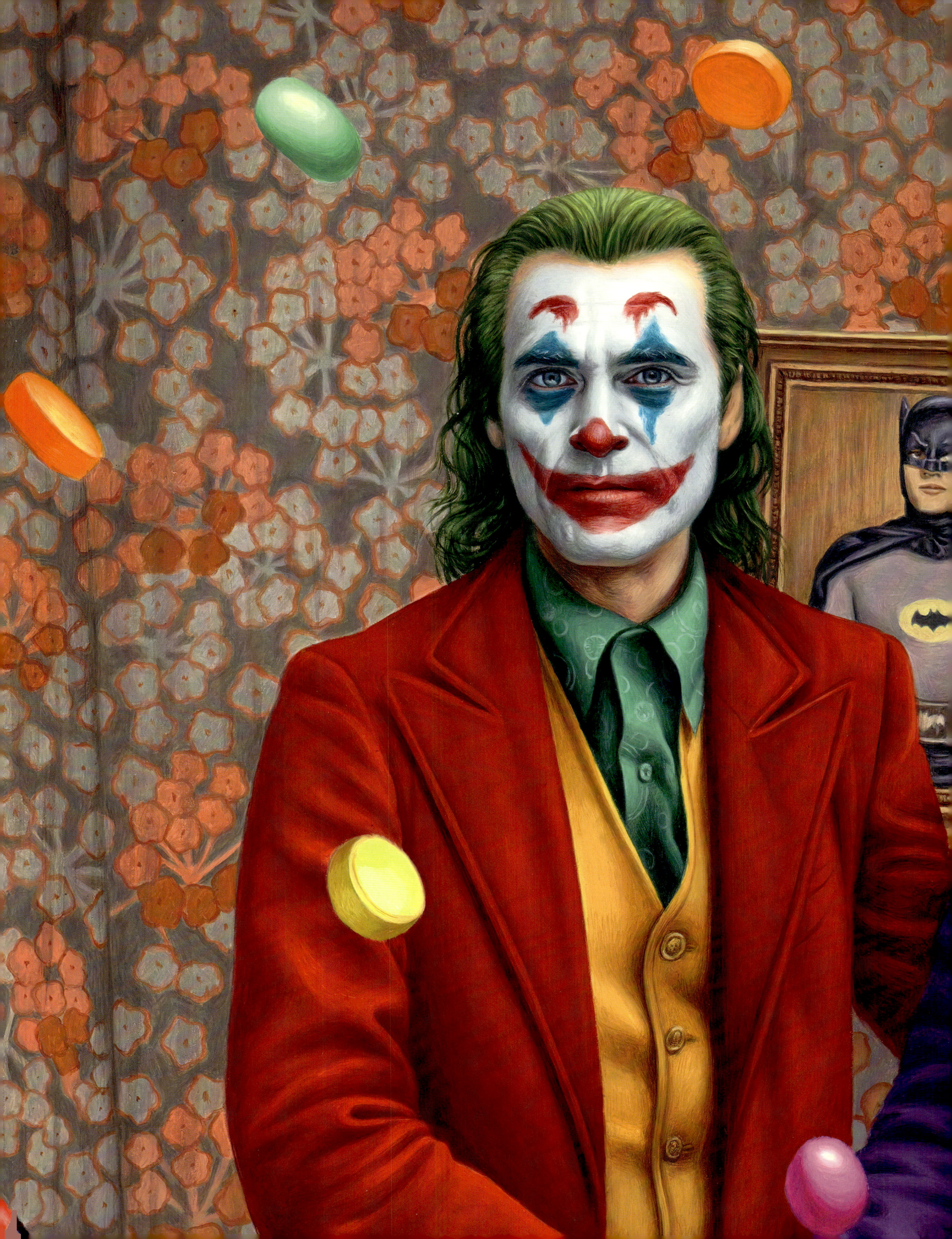

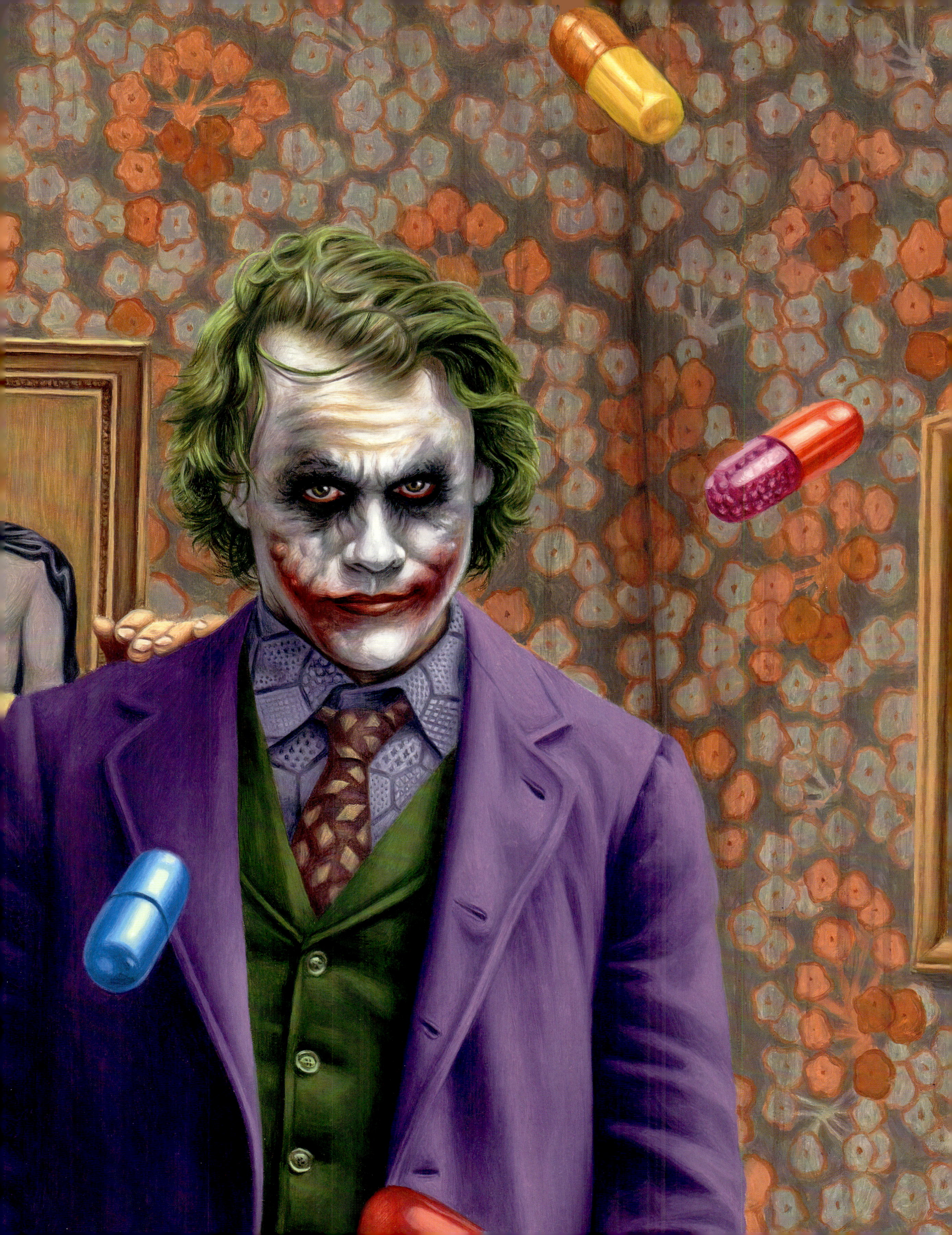

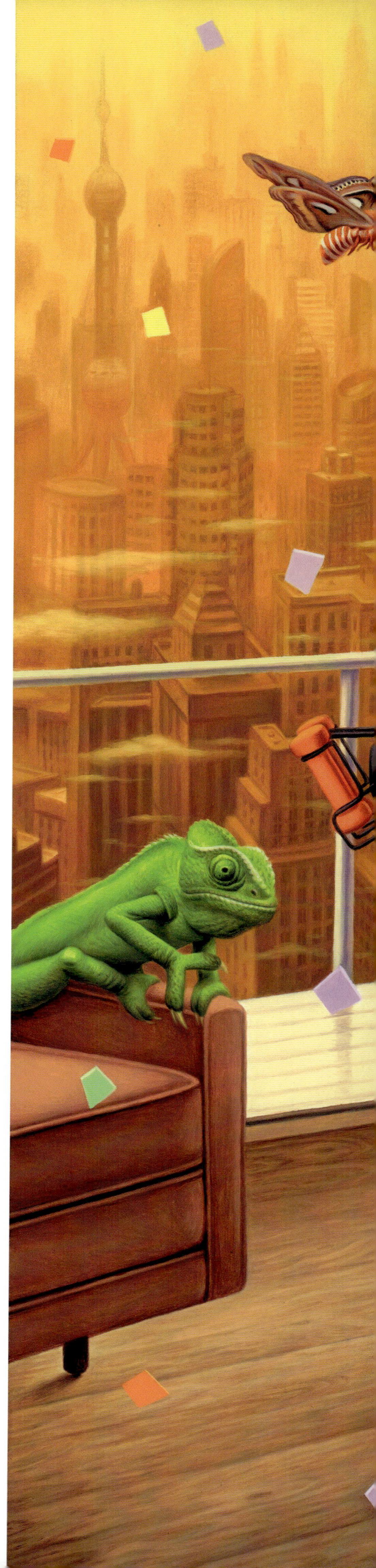

REPTILOTON

Oil on Canvas / 36" x 36" / 2021

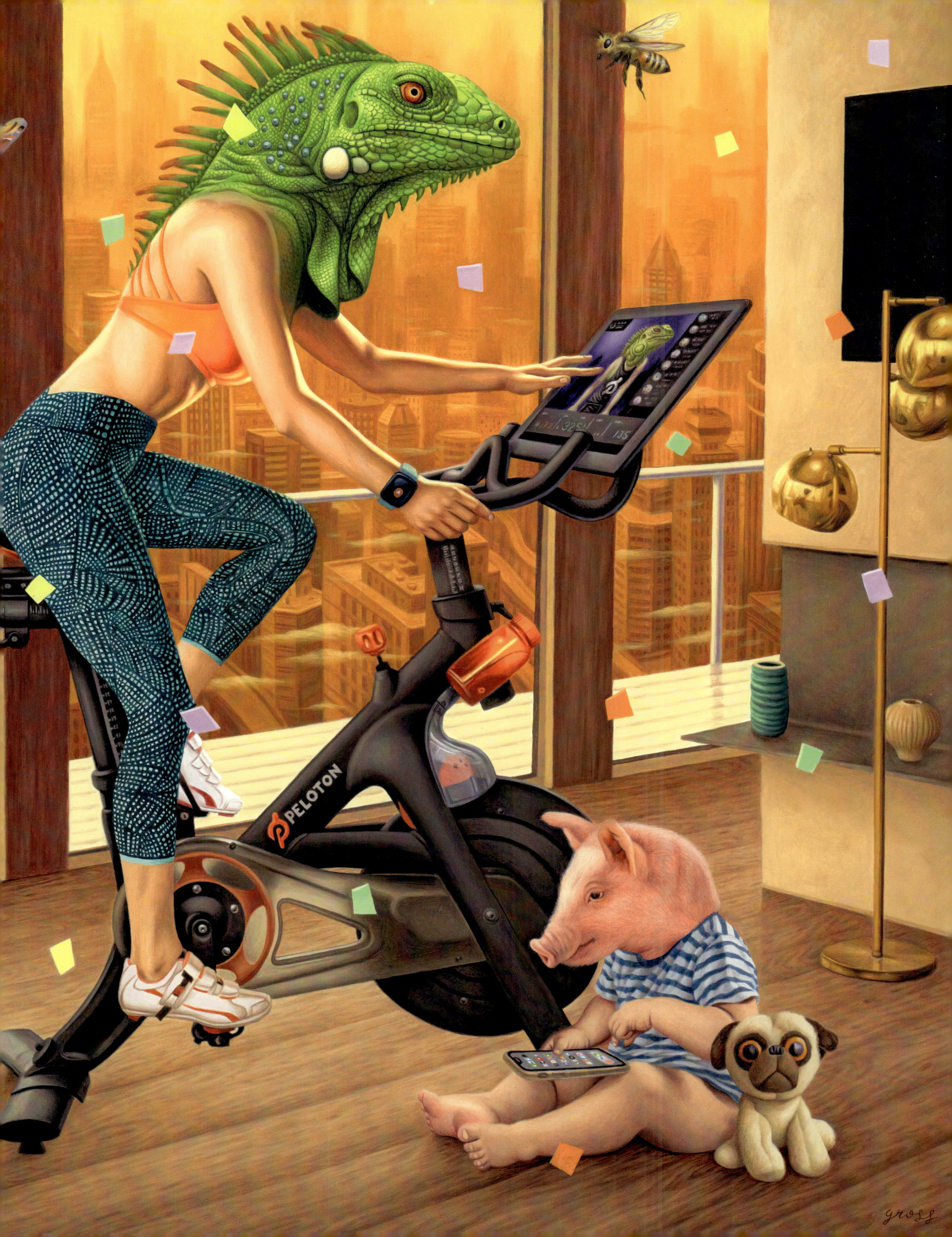
PELOTON

SUNDAY IN THE PARK WITH REPTILIANS
Oil on Canvas / 67.5" x 50" / 2016

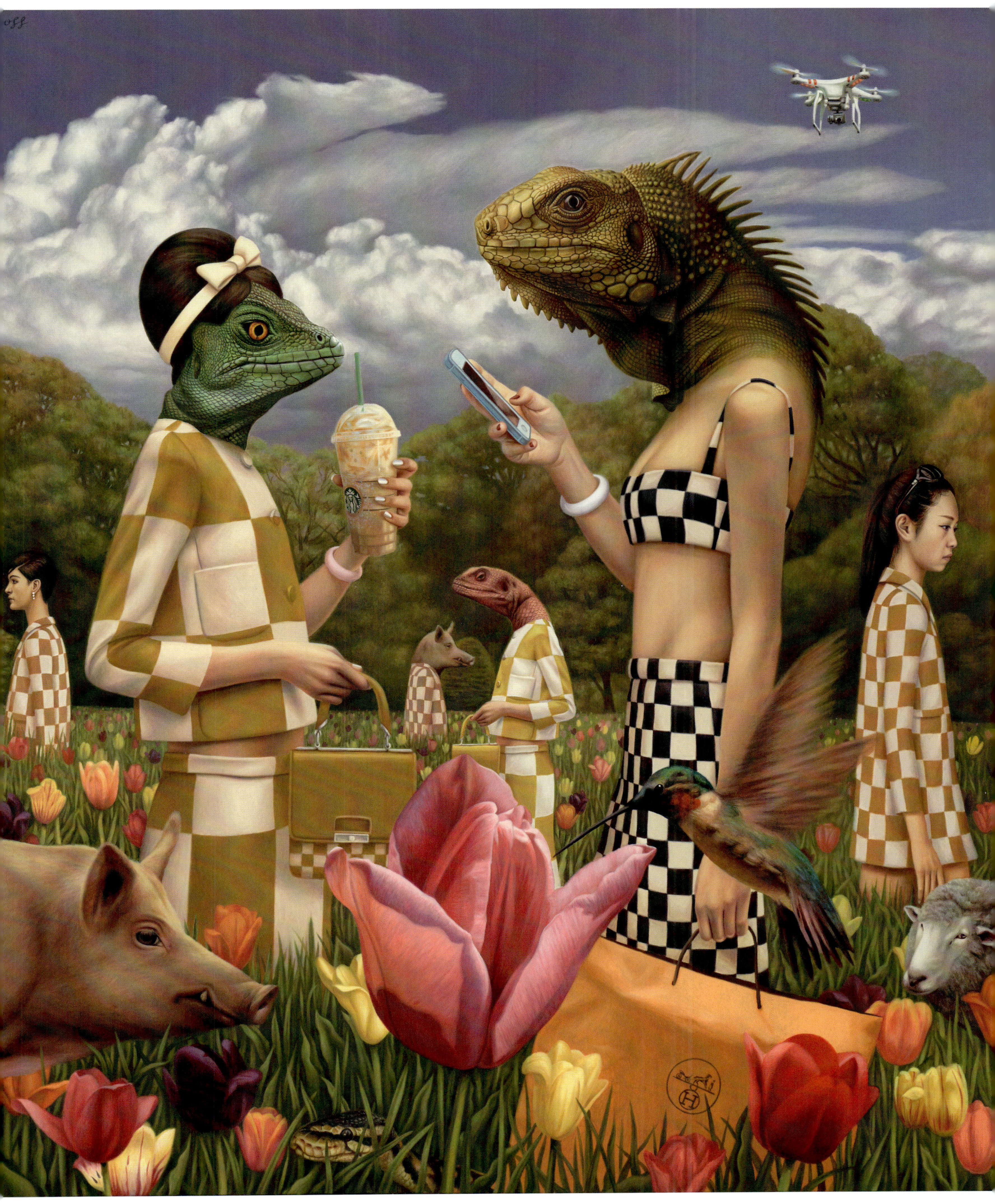

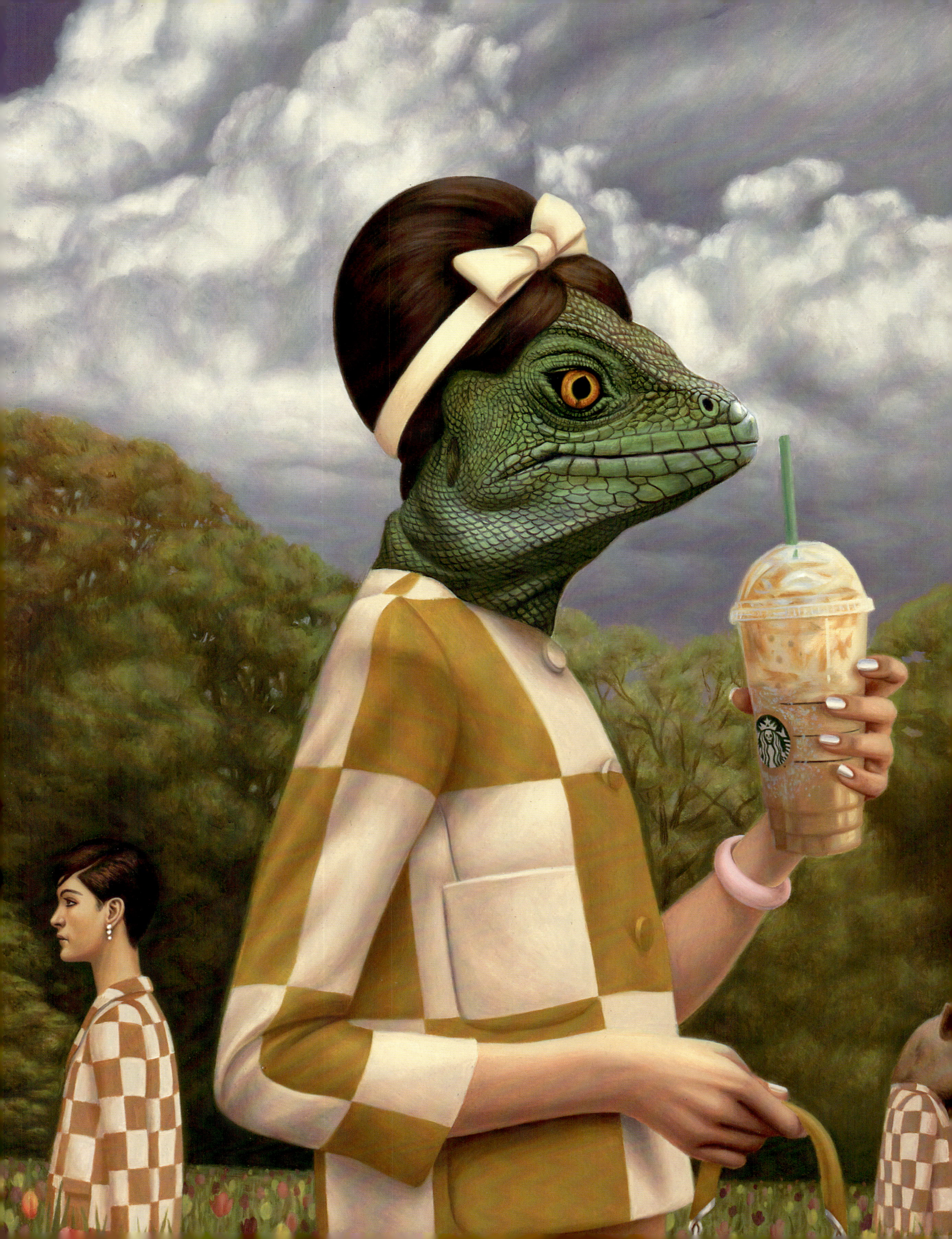

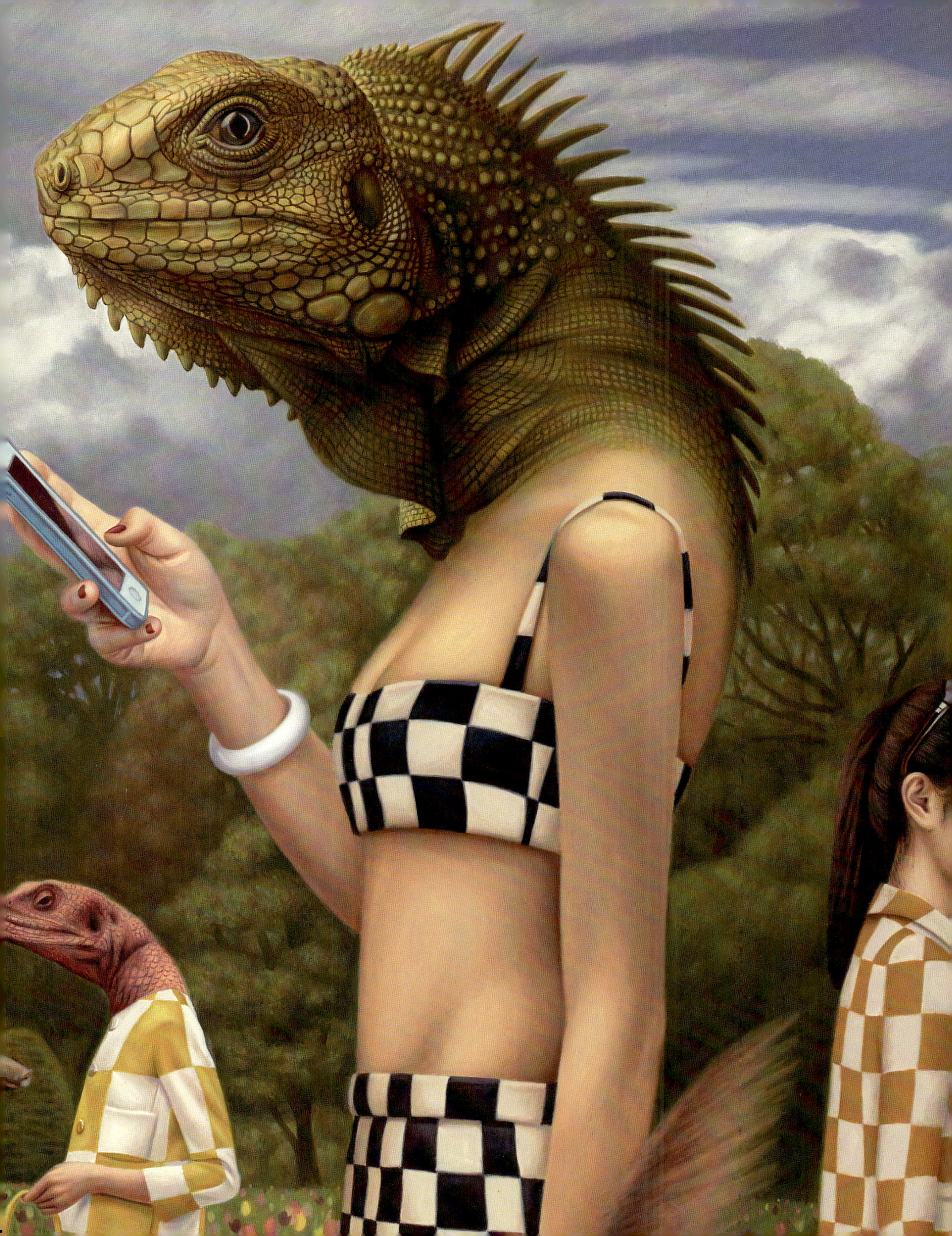

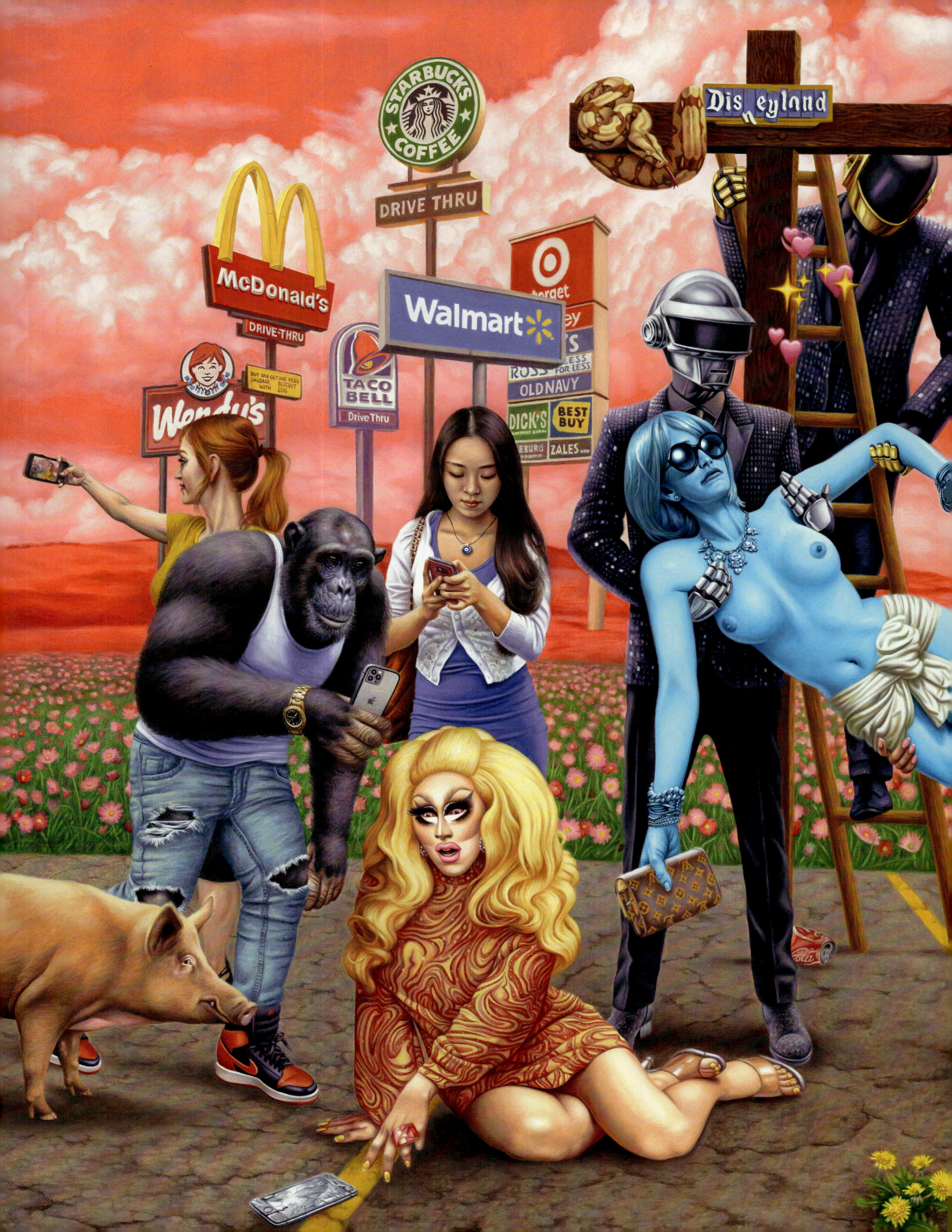

STARBUCKS COFFEE
DRIVE THRU
Disneyland
McDonald's
DRIVE-THRU
Walmart
target
Wendy's
BUY ONE GET ONE FREE
SAUSAGE BISCUIT
WITH EGG
TACO BELL
Drive Thru
ROSS
DRESS FOR LESS
OLD NAVY
DICK'S
BEST BUY
ZALES
Coca-Cola

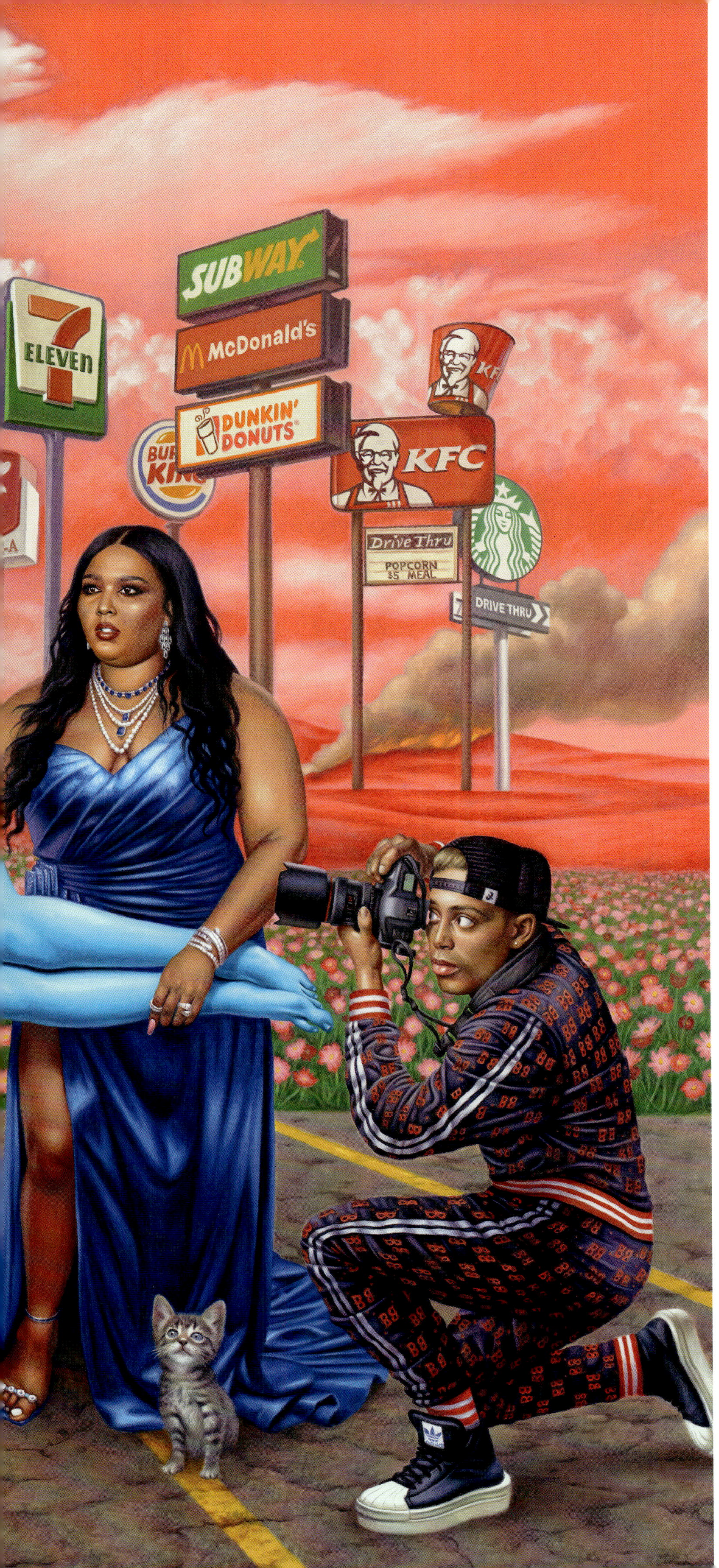

THE REVANCHISTS
Oil on Canvas / 50.5" x 63" / 2023

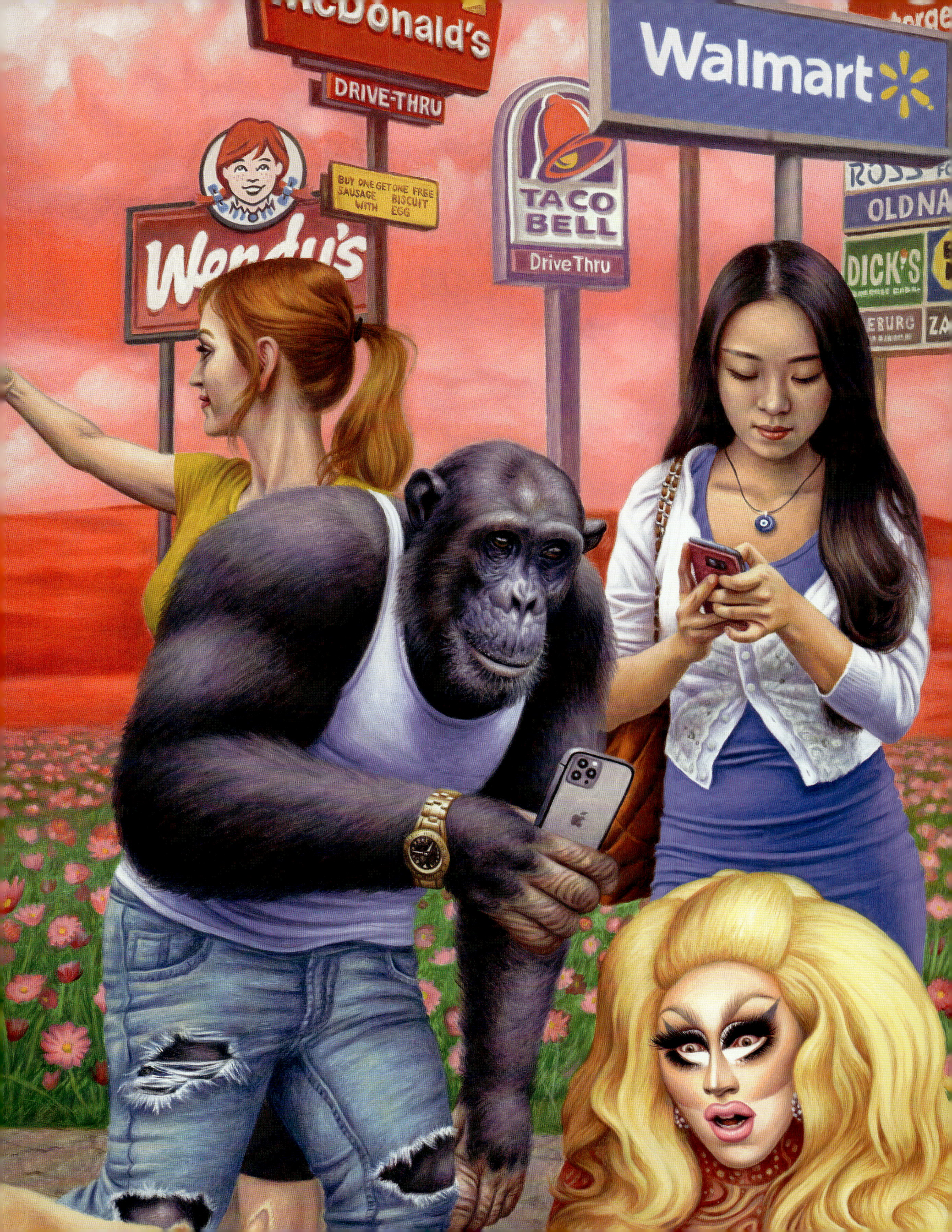

McDonald's
DRIVE-THRU
Walmart
Wendy's
BUY ONE GET ONE FREE
SAUSAGE BISCUIT
WITH EGG
TACO BELL
Drive Thru
ROSS
OLD NA
DICK'S

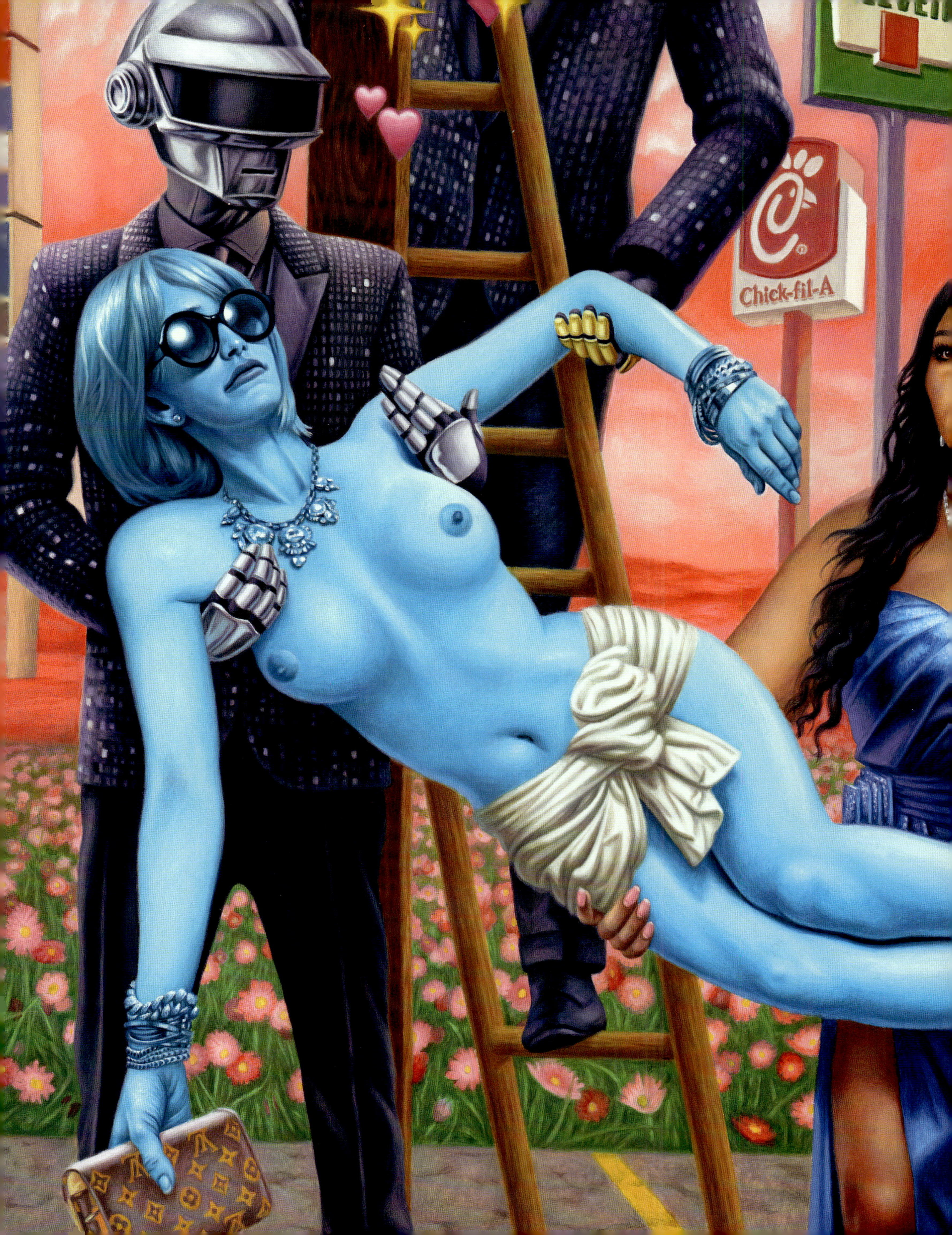
Chick-fil-A

IRIS FLOWER

Oil on Canvas / 61" x 47" / 2016

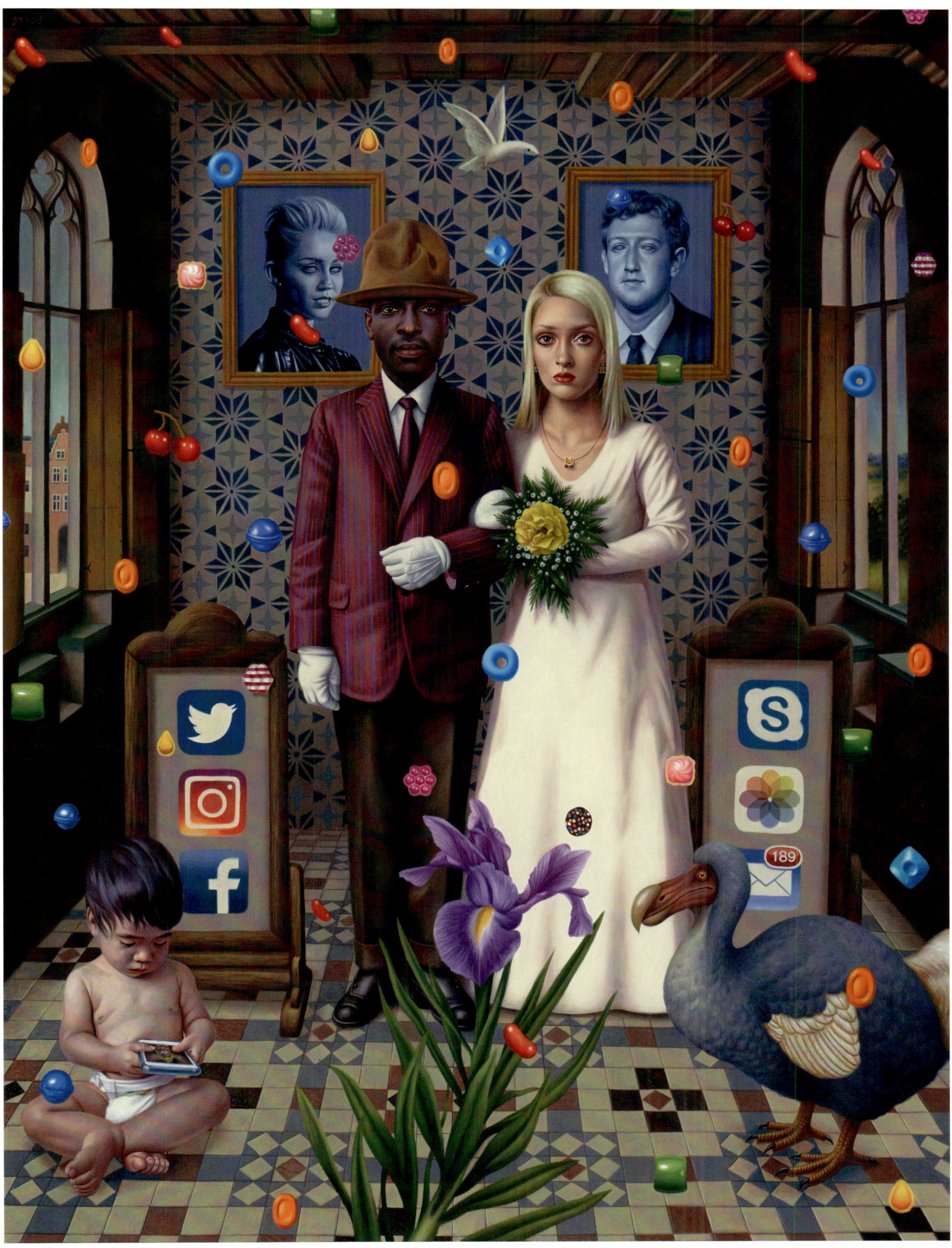

CANDY CRUSH

Oil on Canvas / 48.25" x 33.5" / 2014

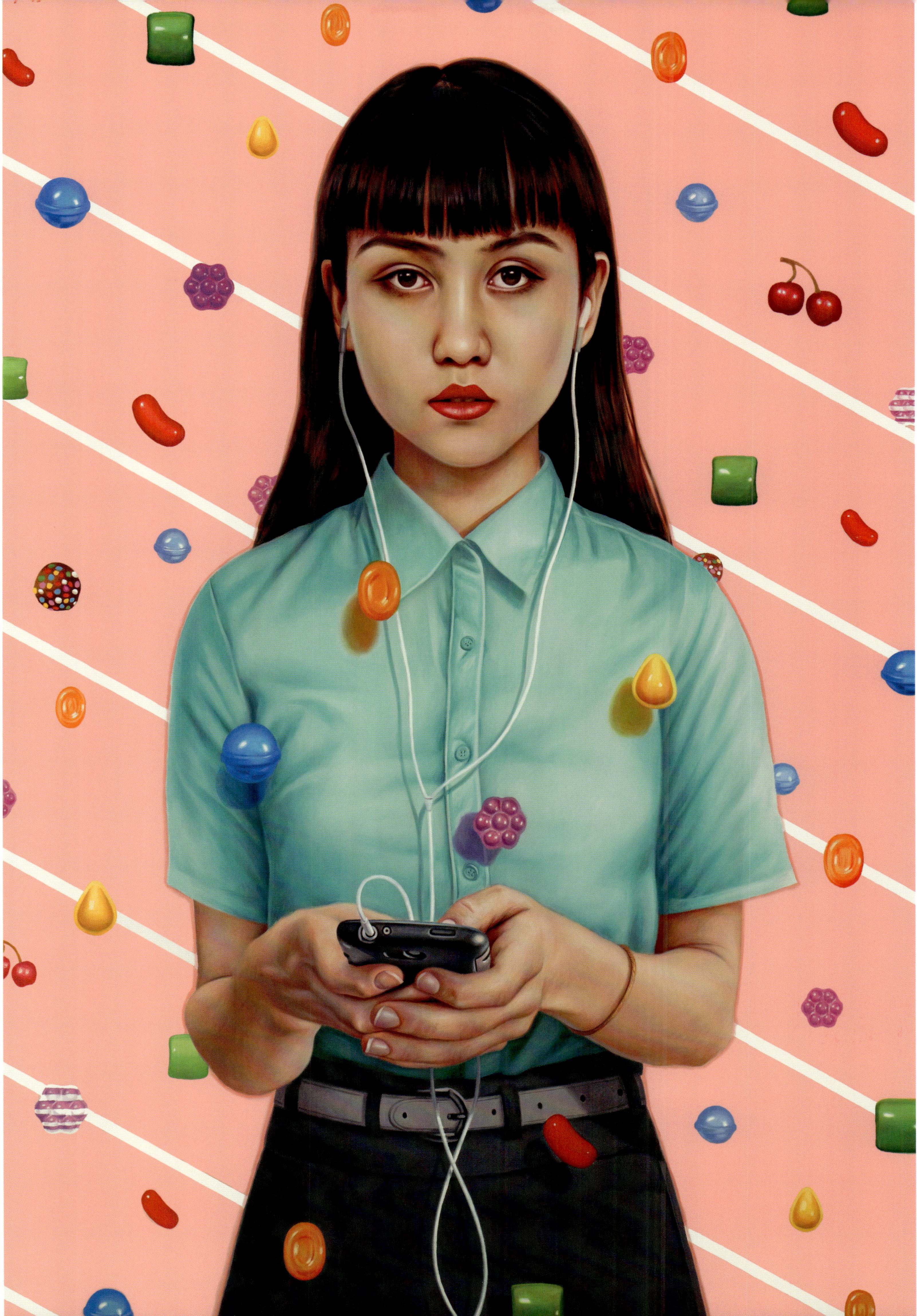

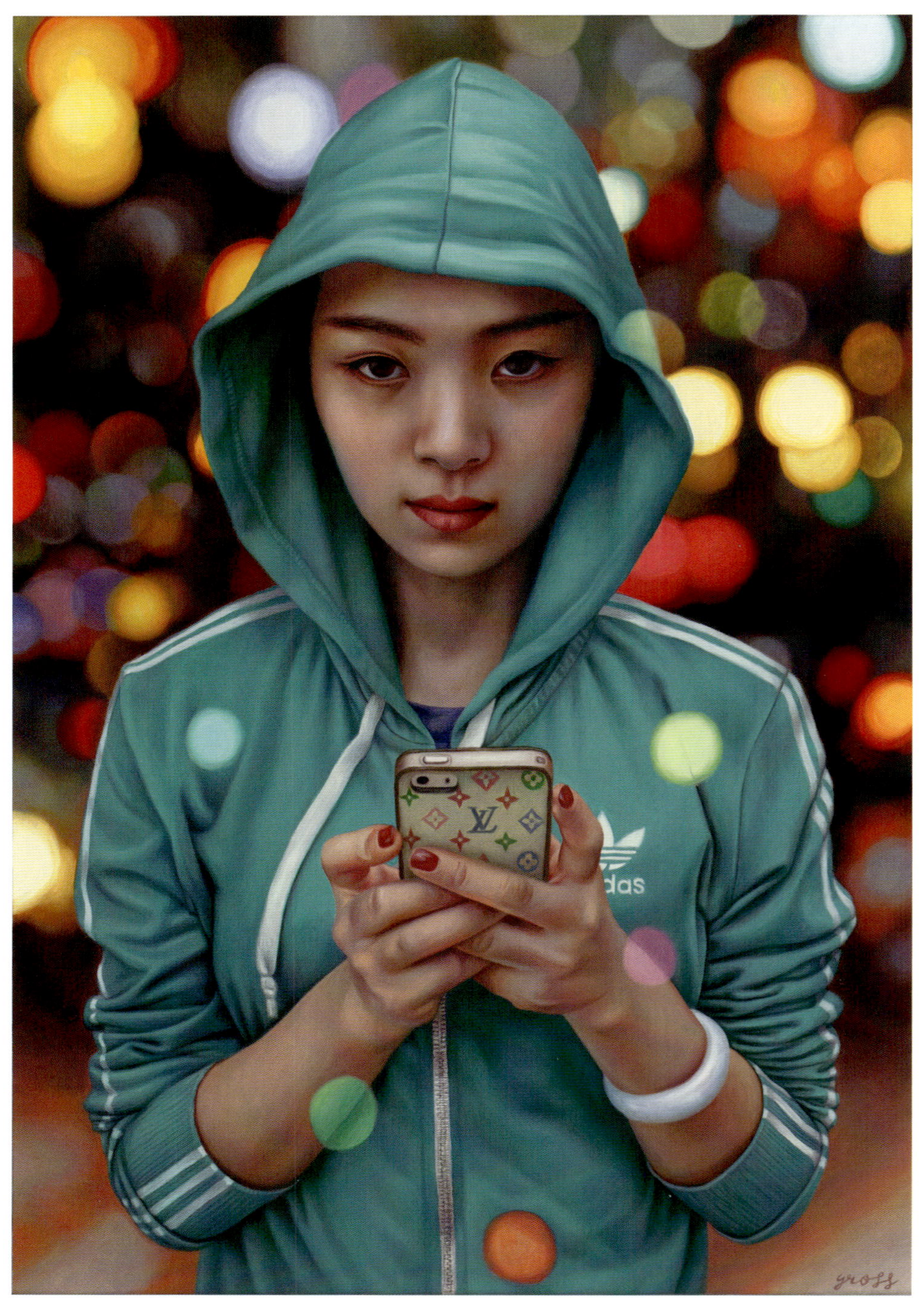

THE MESSAGE
Oil on Canvas / 26.25" x 18.5" / 2015

CONTEMPLATION (SLURPEE)
Oil on Canvas / 42" x 32" / 2016

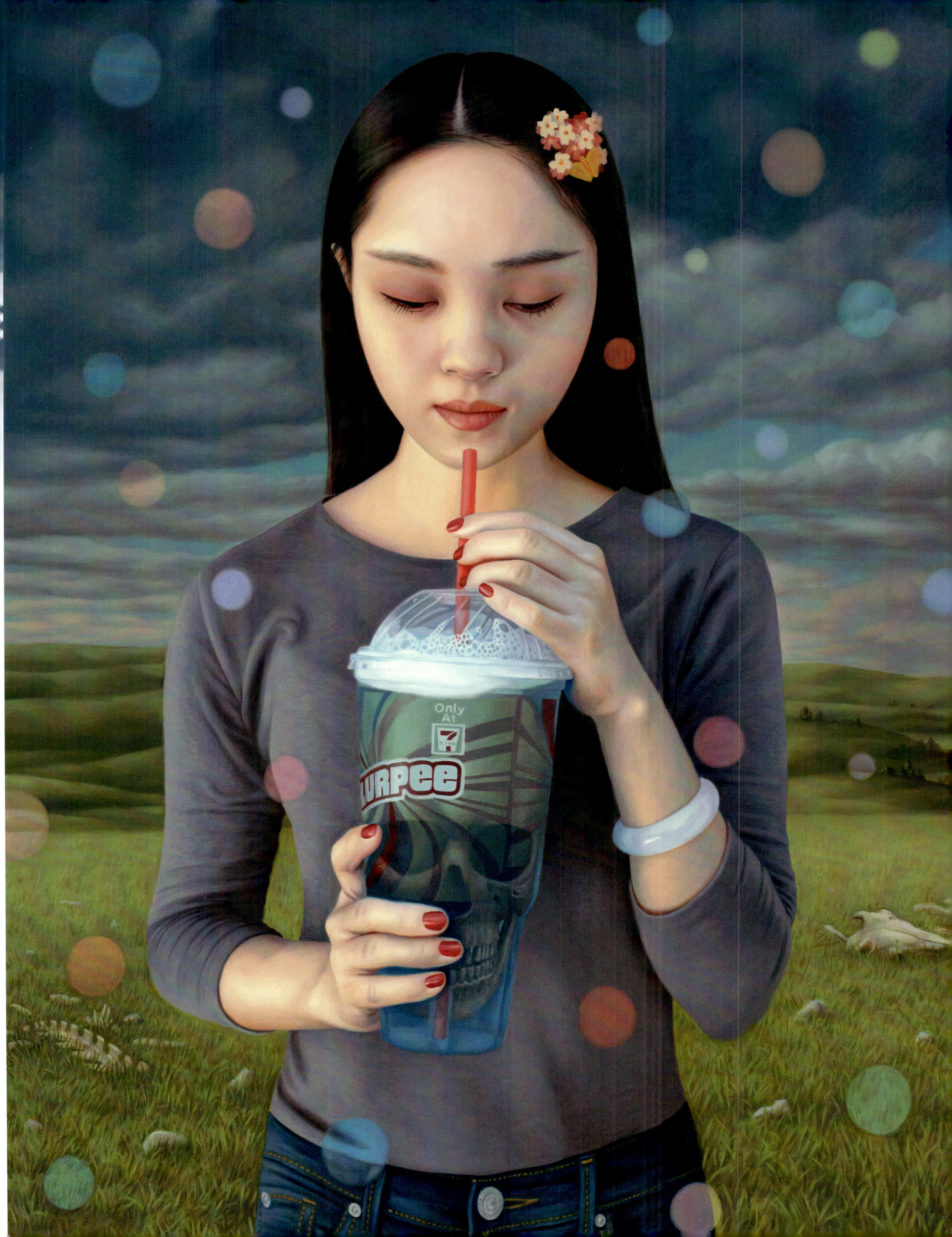

Only
At
7-ELEVEN
SLURPEE

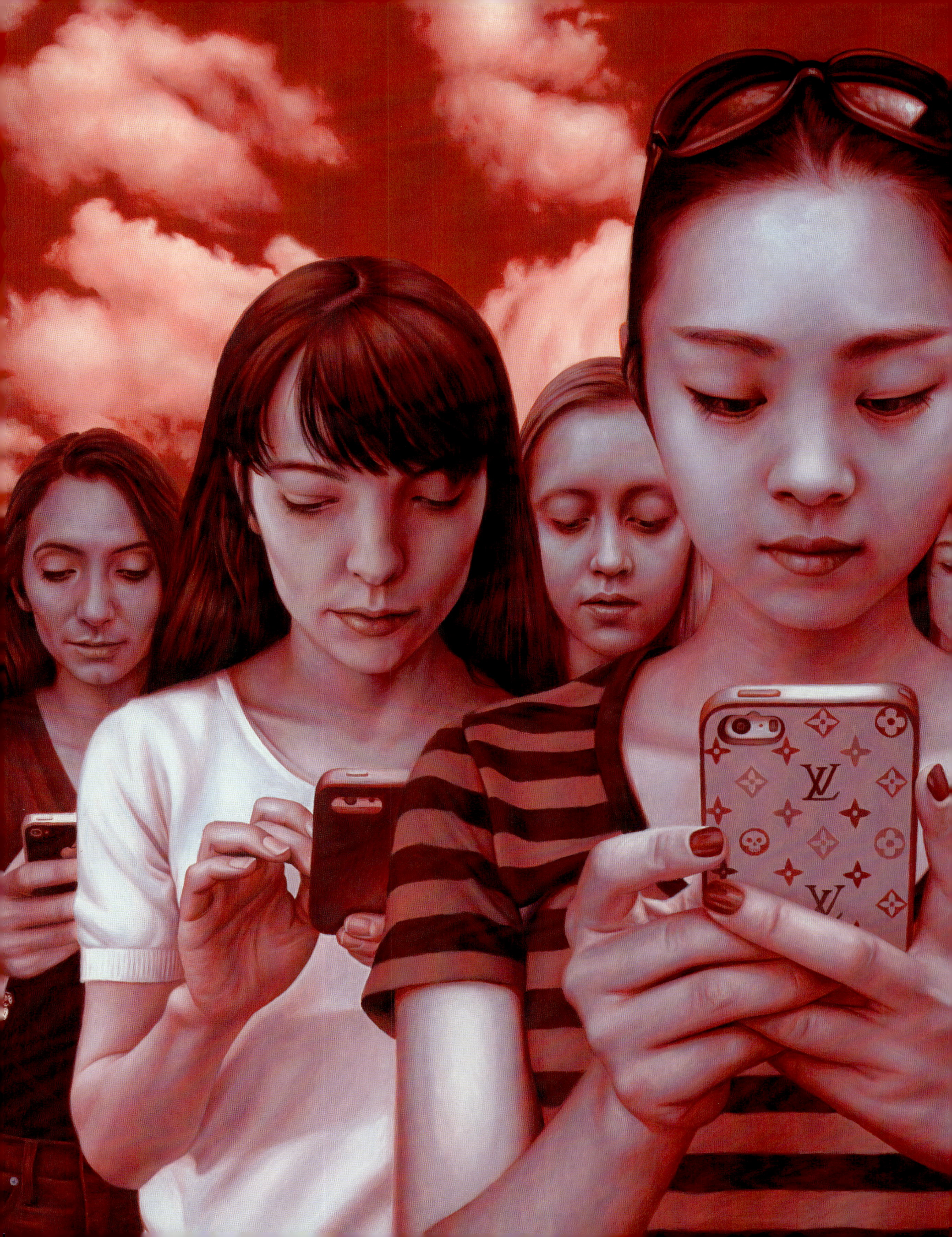

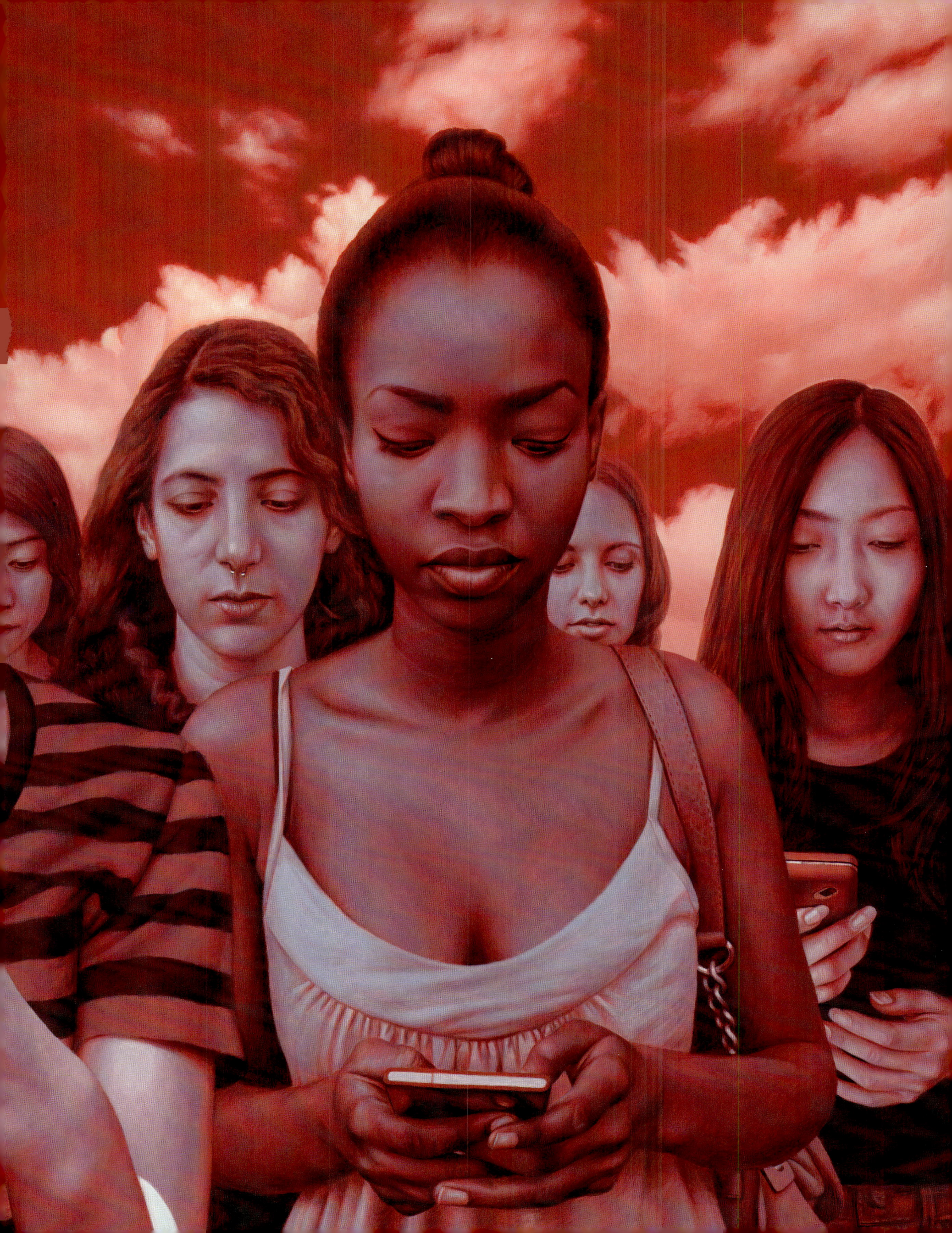

(previous spread) **ZEITGEIST**
Oil on Canvas / 37.5" x 60.5" / 2015

YESTERDAY
Oil on Canvas / 26" x 26" / 2015

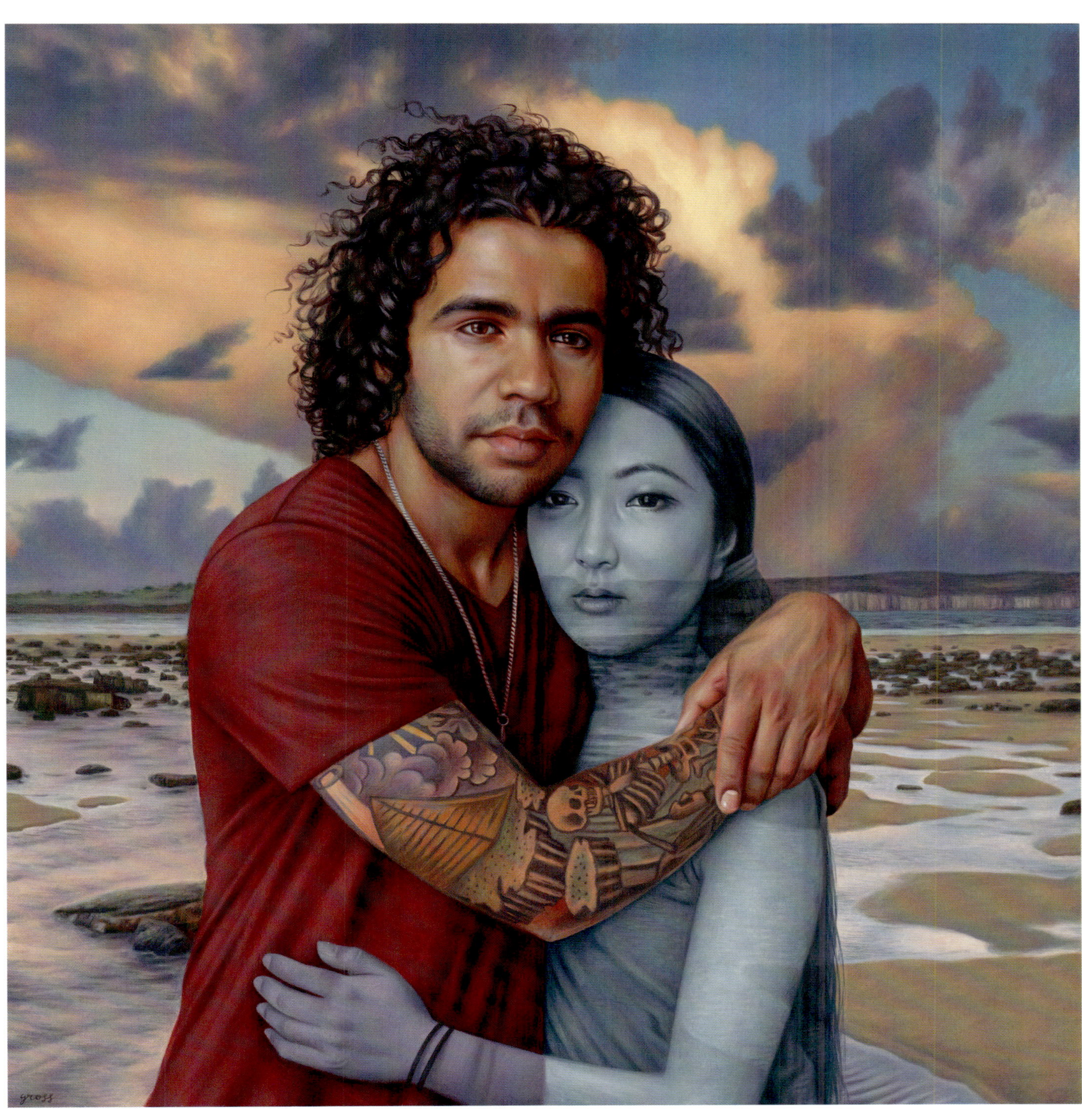

THE MEAL
Oil on Canvas / 29" x 33" / 2016

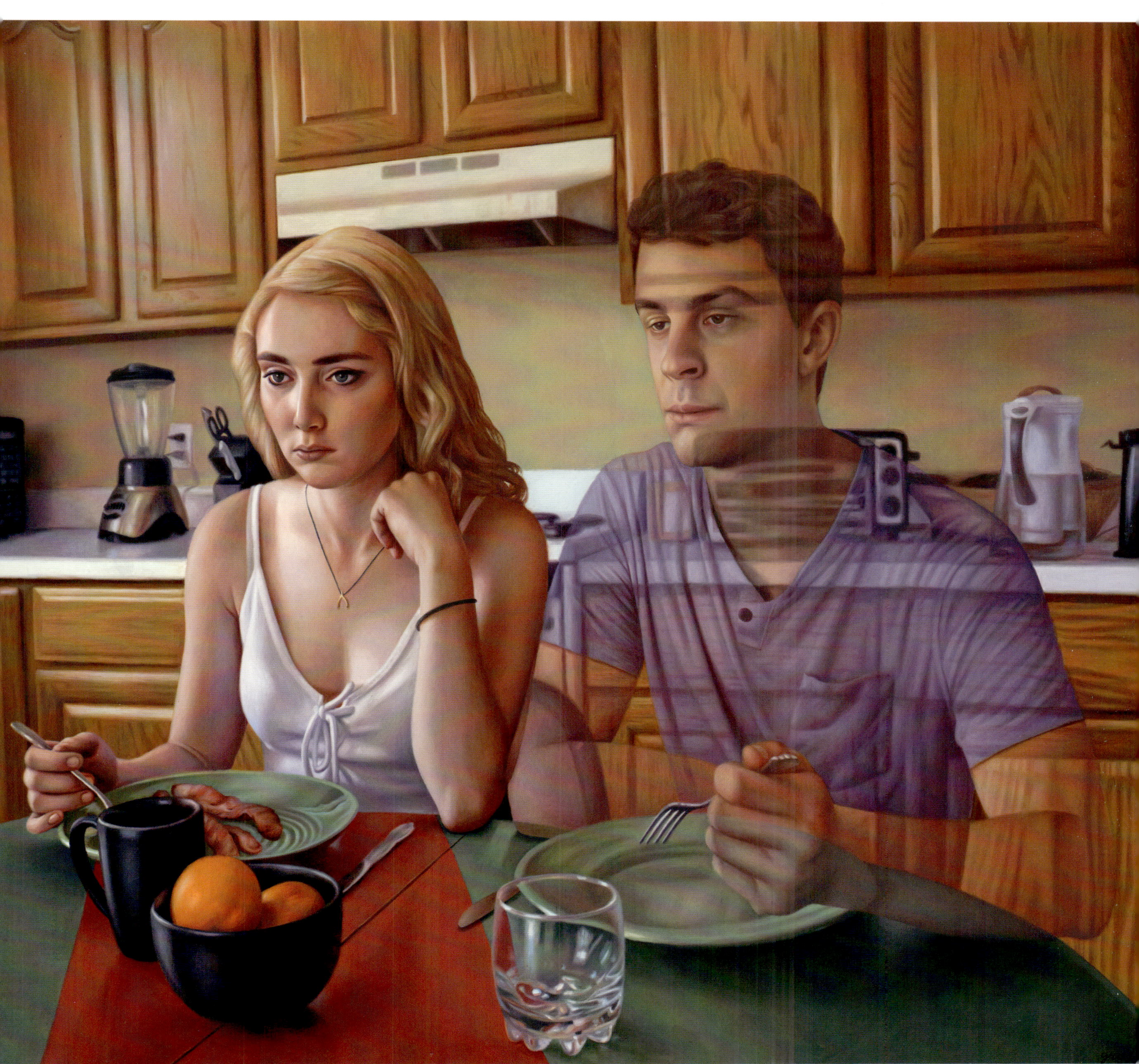

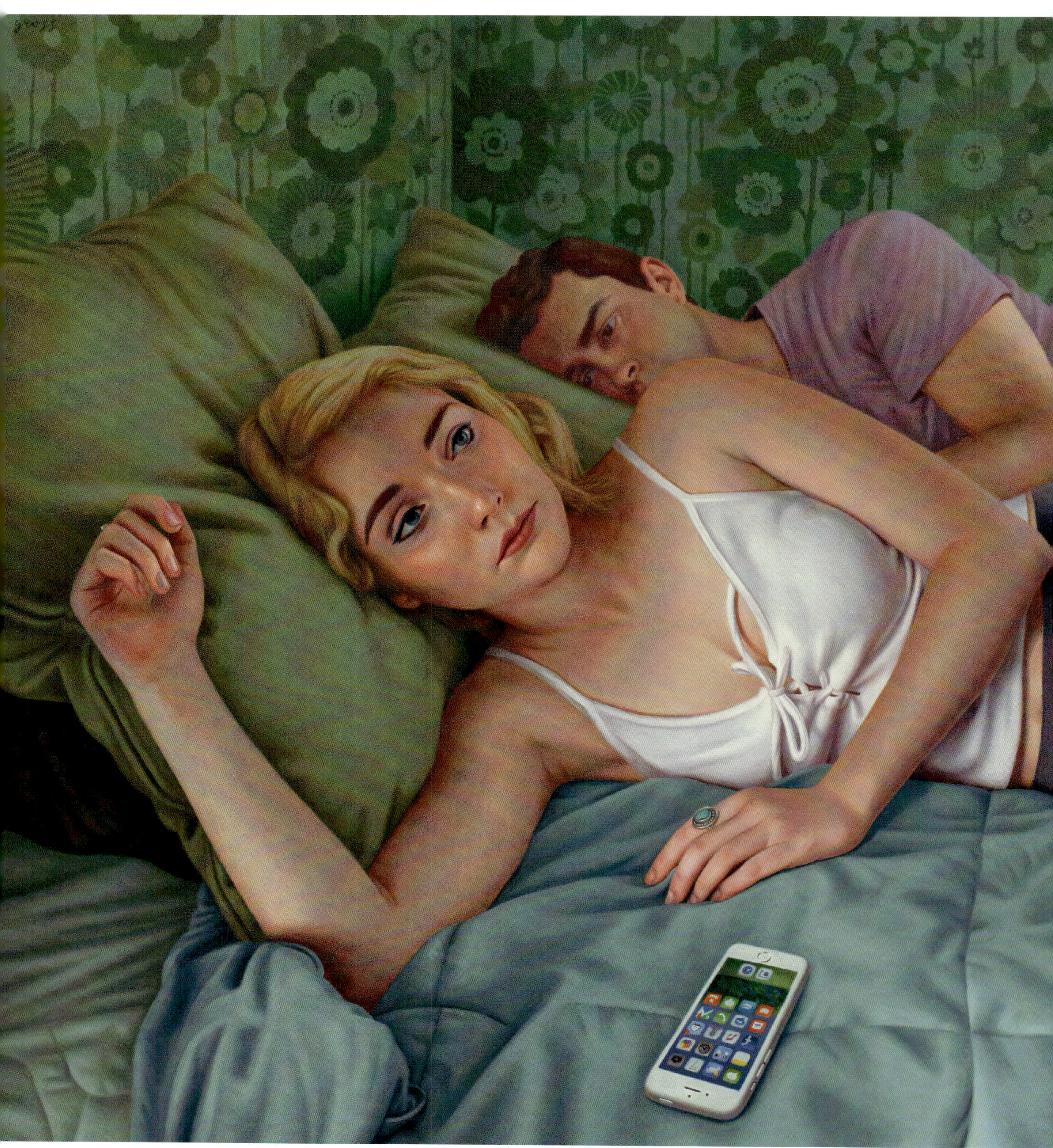

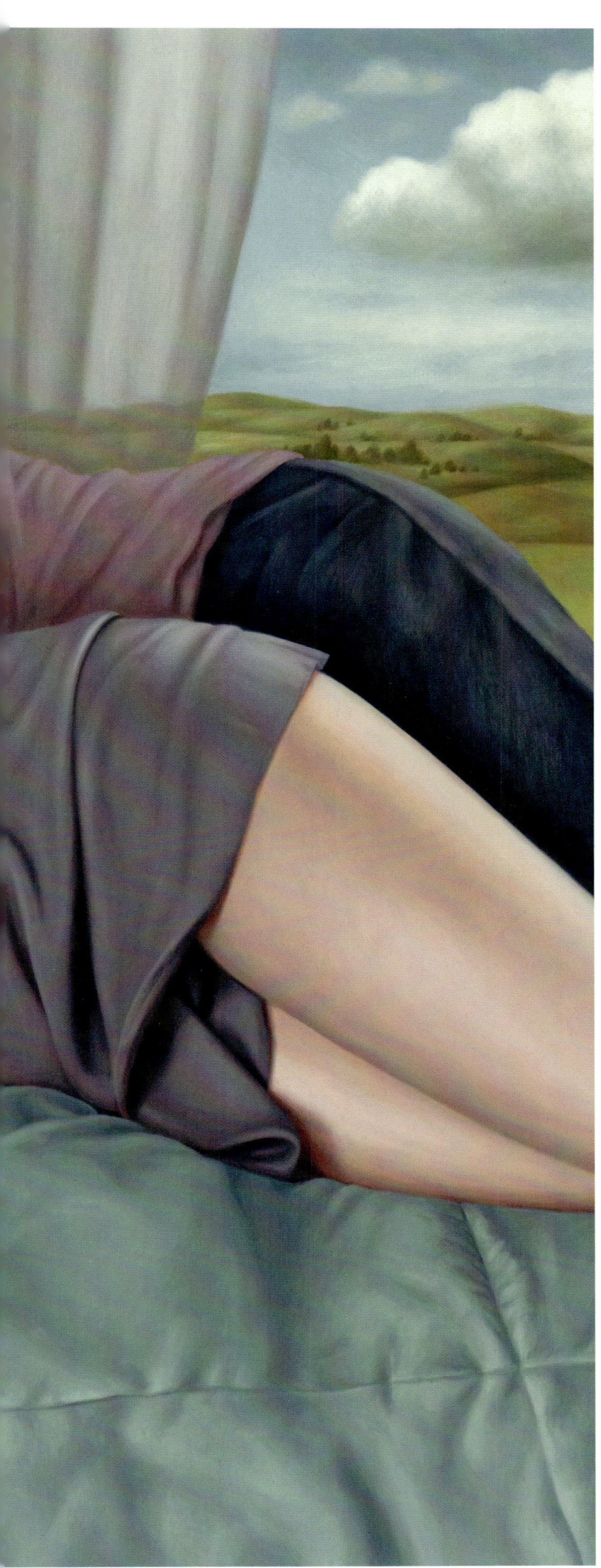

SUSPICION
Oil on Canvas / 35" x 48" / 2016

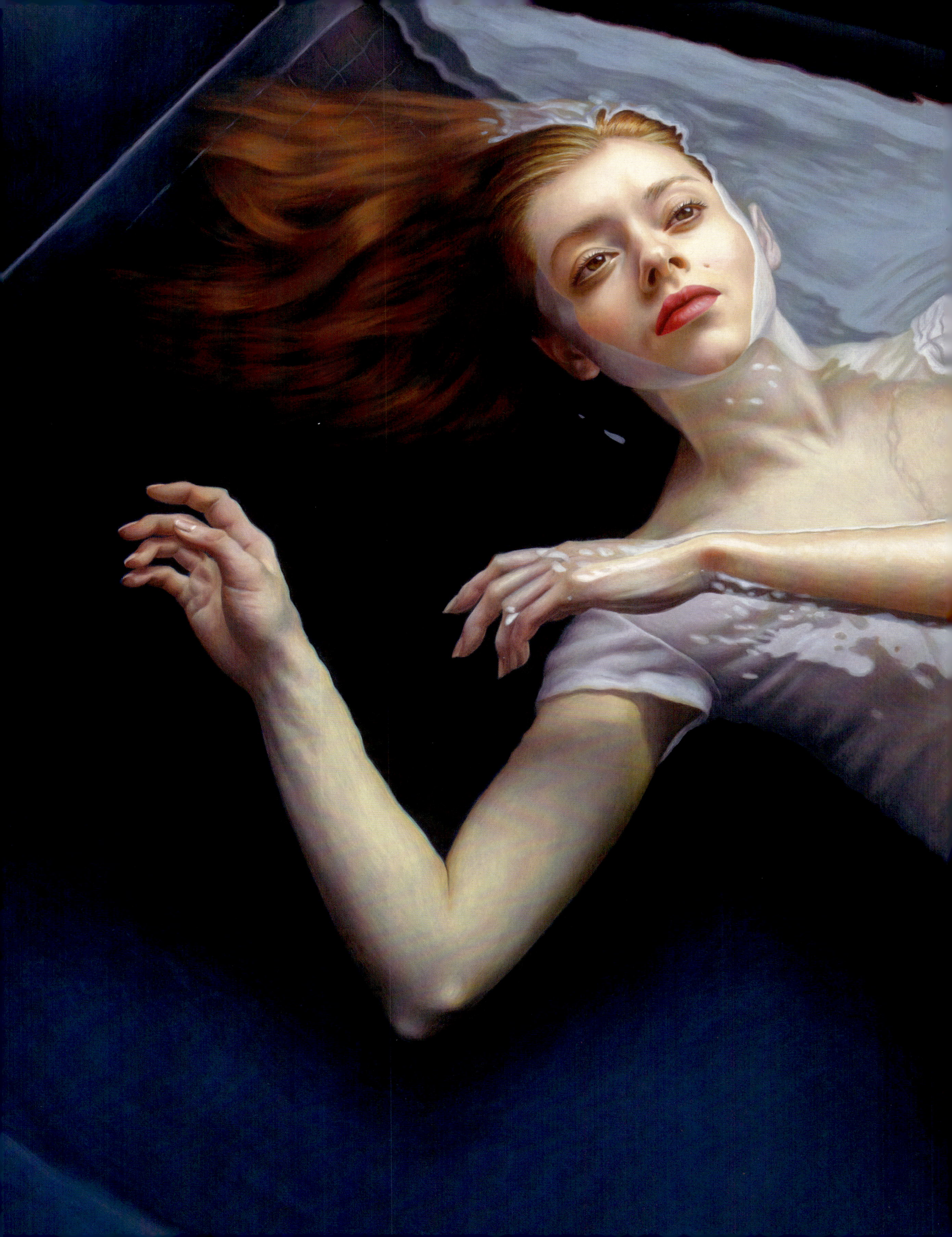

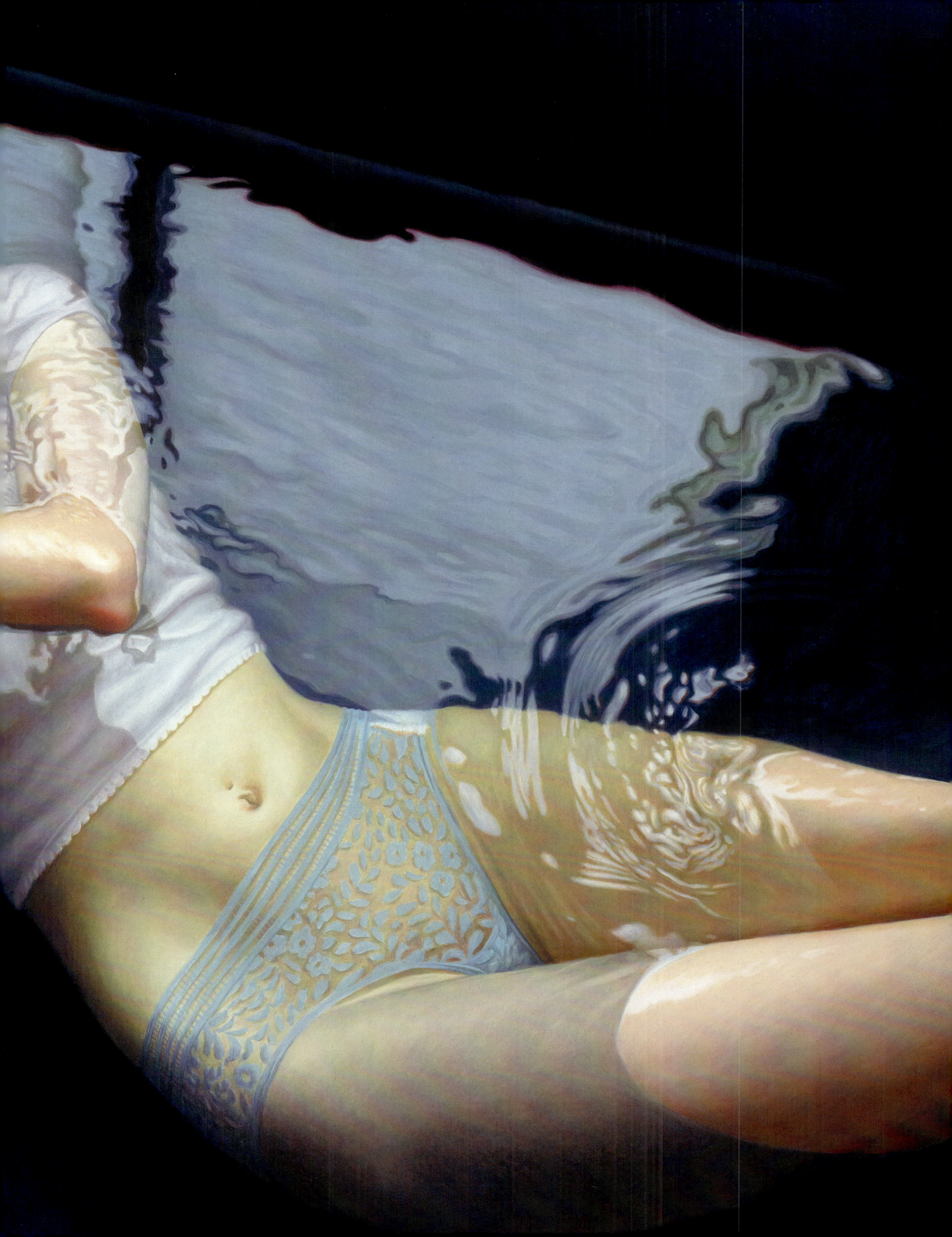

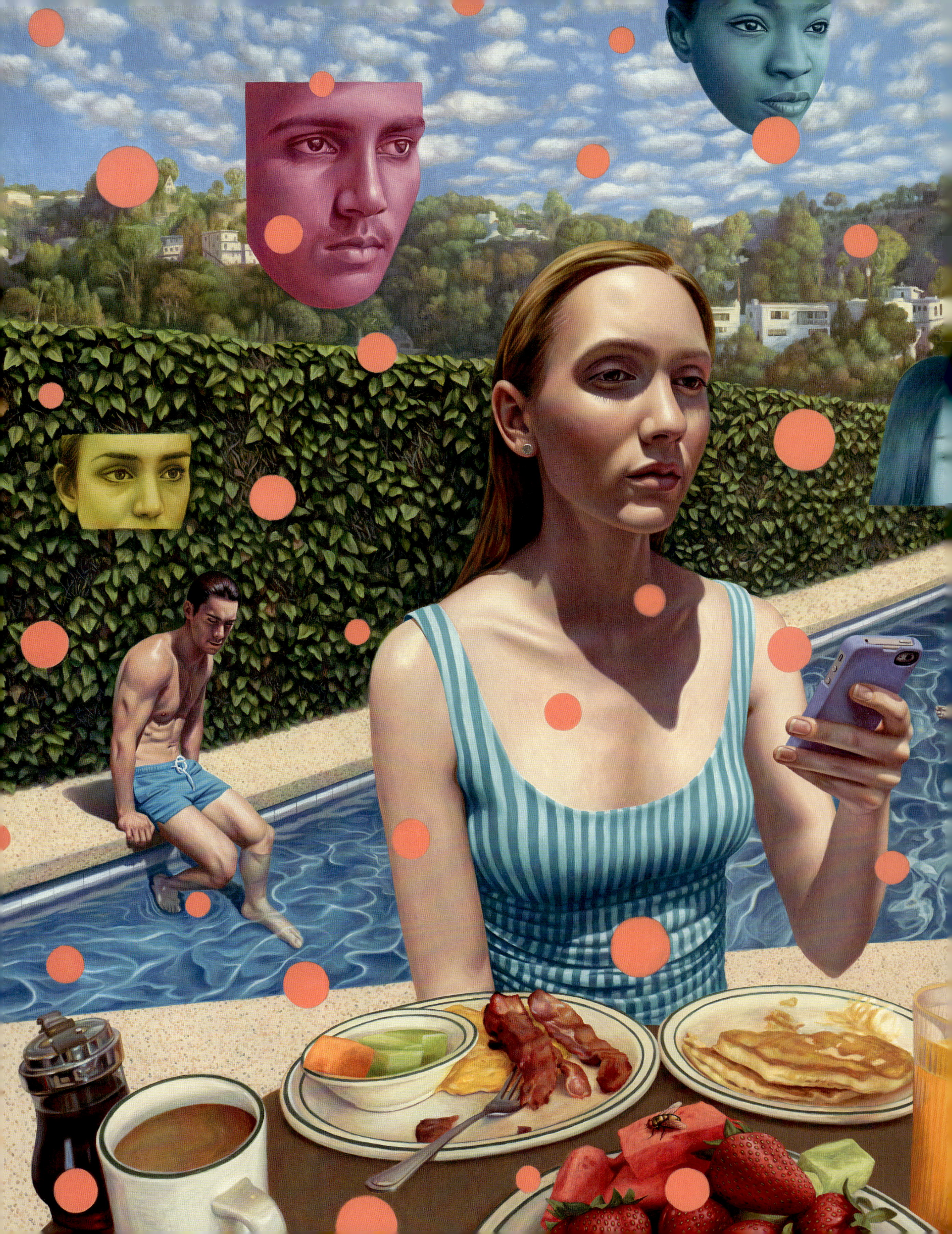

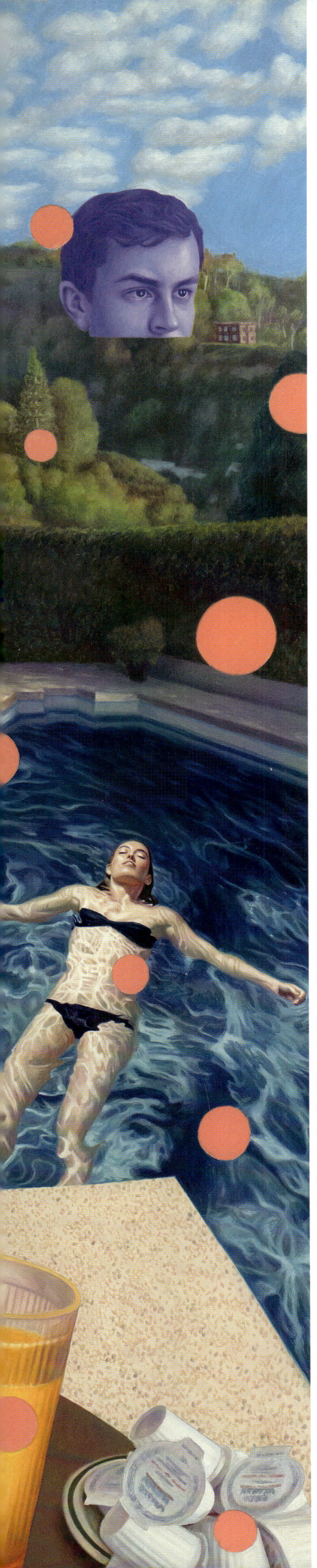

(*previous spread*) BATH II
Oil on Canvas / 34.5" x 49" / 2019

LAUREL CANYON SOCIAL NETWORK
Oil on Canvas / 60" x 60" / 2017

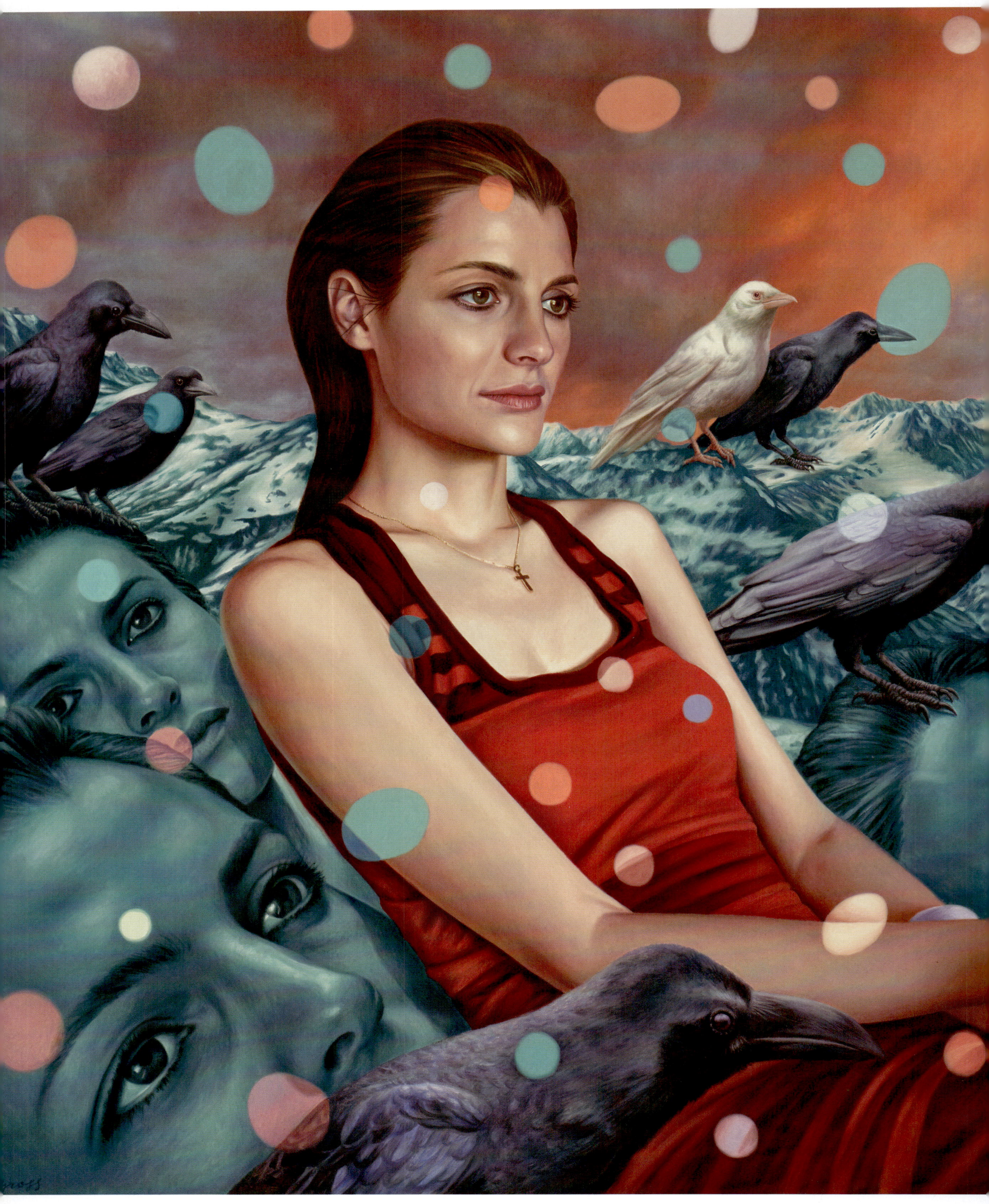

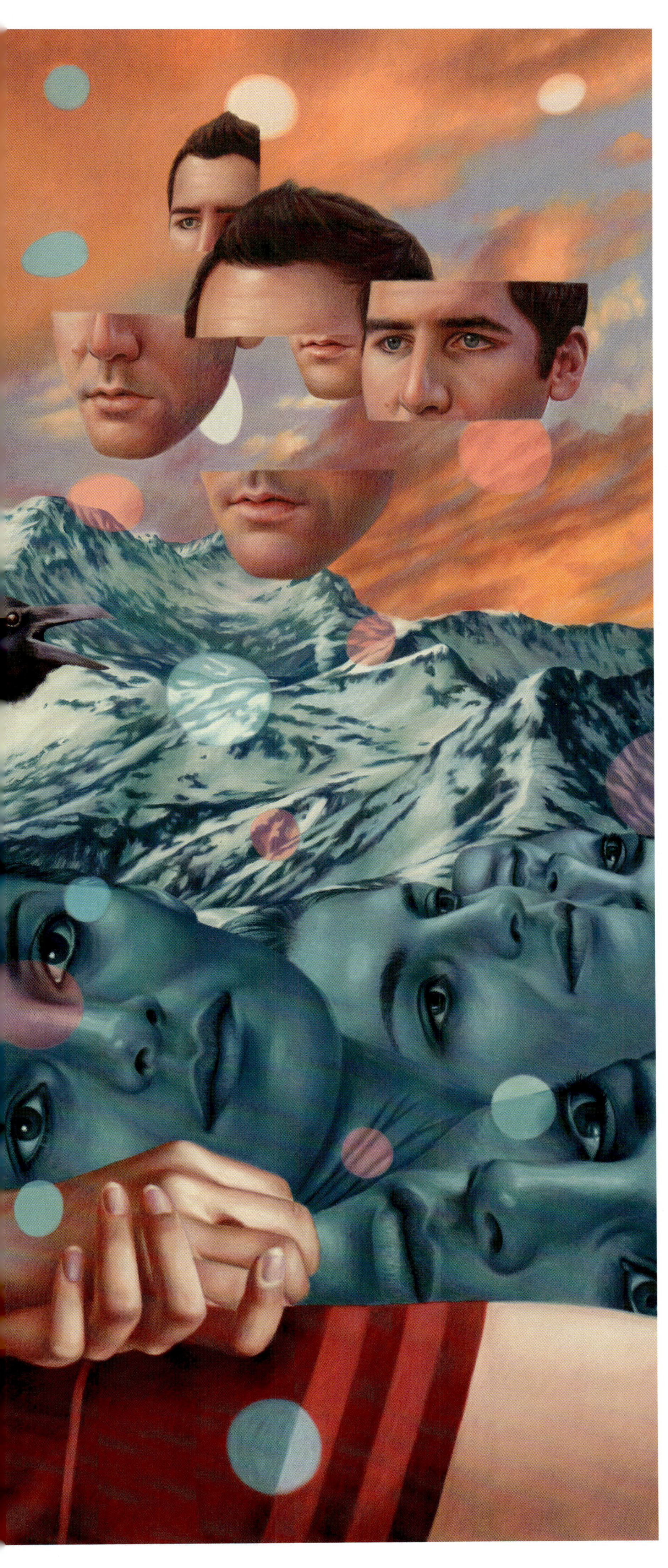

MEMORY FRAGMENTS
Oil on Canvas / 40.25" x 53.5" / 2015

Cabinet Card Paintings

The following are a series of paintings done directly upon antique Victorian era cabinet cards. Cabinet cards are early photographs mounted on heavy card stock, and they first appeared in the 1860s. Photo studios in every city existed largely to shoot portraits of customers for use as cabinet cards. You can see their logos in elegant script or Old English style fonts on the bottom of many of these cards, along with the city where they were located.

Most of the cabinet card photos that I use come from the period between the 1880s and the 1900s. I also paint on CDVs, which are smaller cards produced from about 1850 to 1885. Occasionally, the photo will have the name of the person or people on the back of the card, and every now and then, a dedication, such as *"From Your True Friend, Robb Wilson, June 16th, 1878."* Finding cabinet cards is easy between the internet, flea markets and antique stores. What is tougher is finding the right card for a specific idea. Many of the men back then had moustaches and beards, which can be extremely limiting in terms of what character they might become. Cards with young, clean-shaven men tend to work much better.

Sometimes I will have a specific character in mind, and seek someone who resembles that person. Other times, it's more about the facial expression, such as the amused look on the Wonka card, which is uncommon in cabinet card photographs. Groups of people can be most fun in choosing who they are going to become. Having done many straightforward combinations of characters, it is rewarding to come up with an idea like the one at top right, combining antagonists and protagonists in one scene, which I call *"Frenemies."*

Sometimes a card sparks an idea, such as the Hobbits card later in this section, which occurred to me as soon as I saw how vertically challenged these gentlemen all appear to be in the original cabinet photo. Painting these is some of the most fun I ever have as an artist. I hope you enjoy looking at them as much as I do making them!

– Alex Gross, February 2024

All pieces:
Mixed media on antique photograph, usually 6.5" x 4.25,"
before and after images pictured

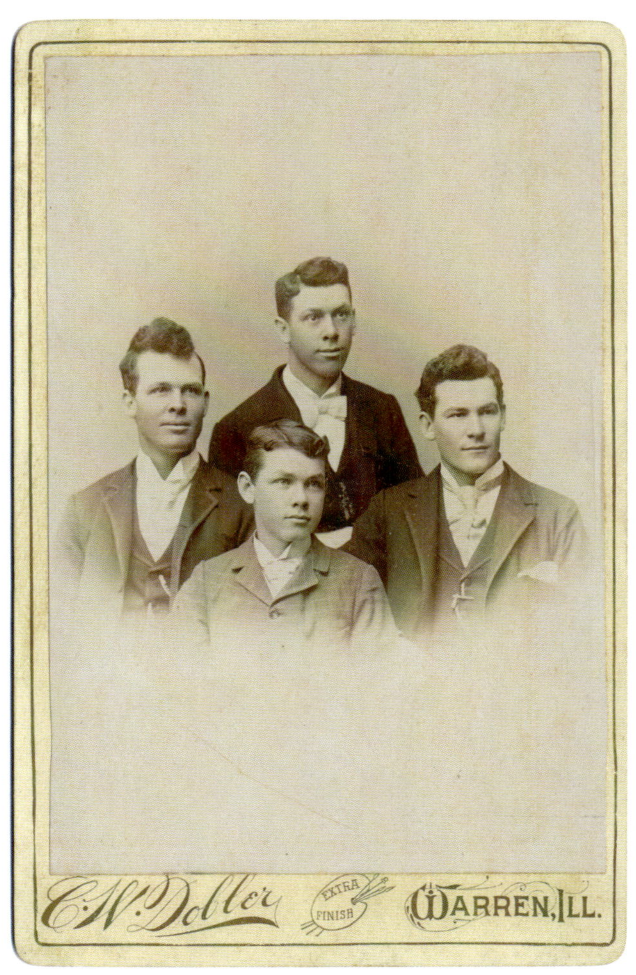

C. N. Doller
EXTRA FINISH
WARREN, ILL.

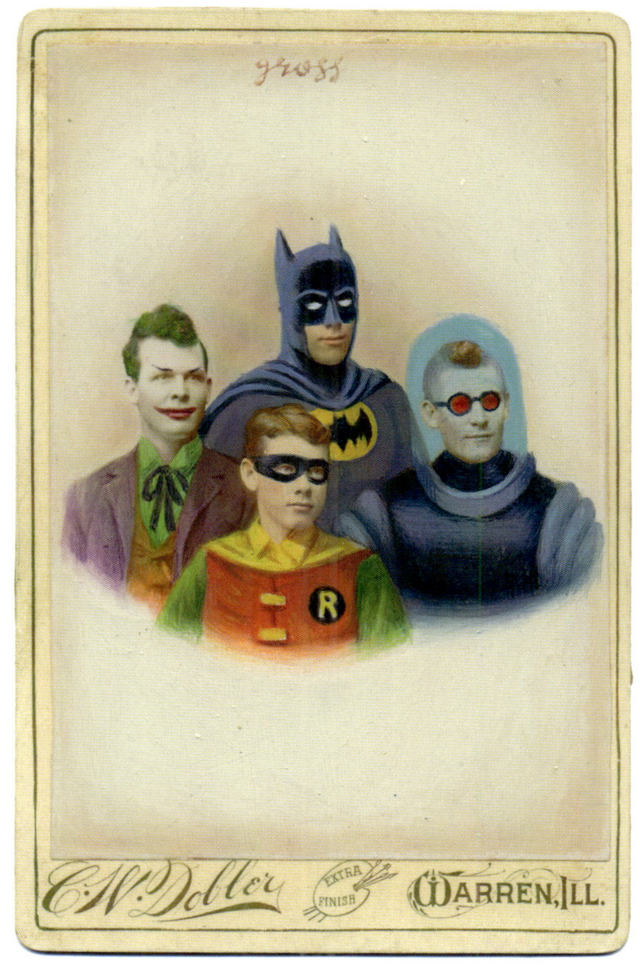

gross
C. N. Doller
EXTRA FINISH
WARREN, ILL.

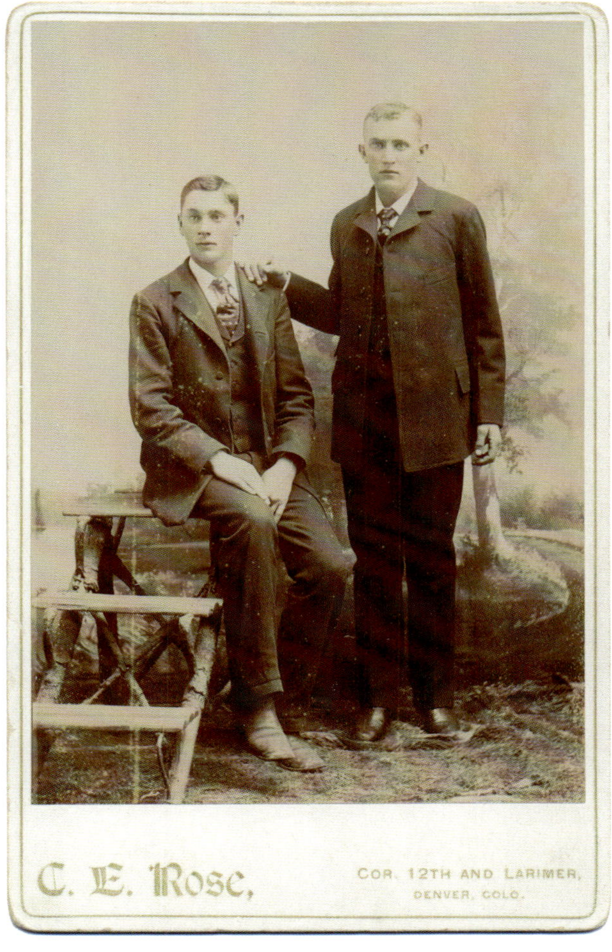

C. E. Rose,
COR. 12TH AND LARIMER,
DENVER, COLO.

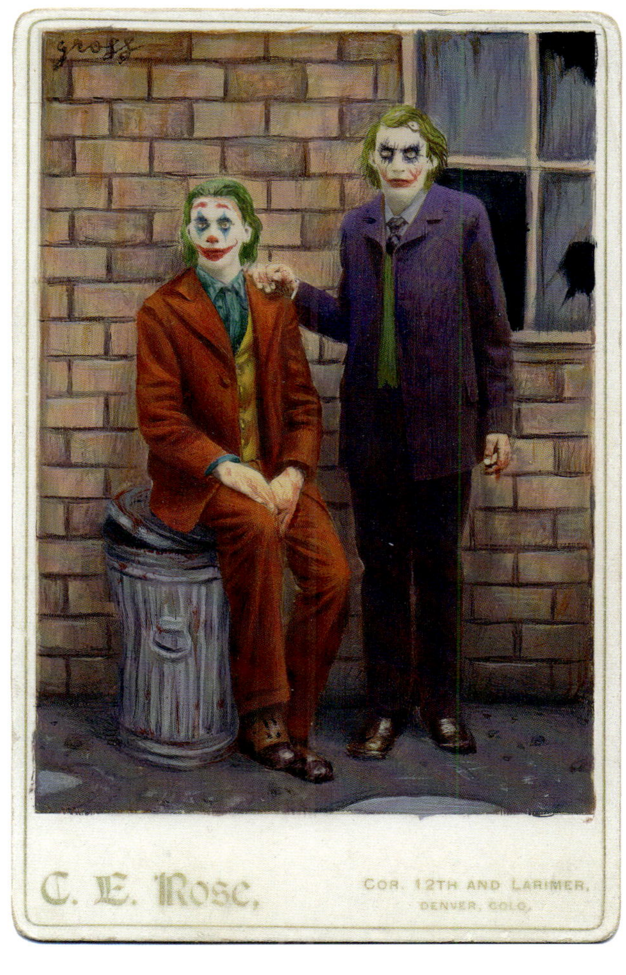

gross
C. E. Rose,
COR. 12TH AND LARIMER,
DENVER, COLO.

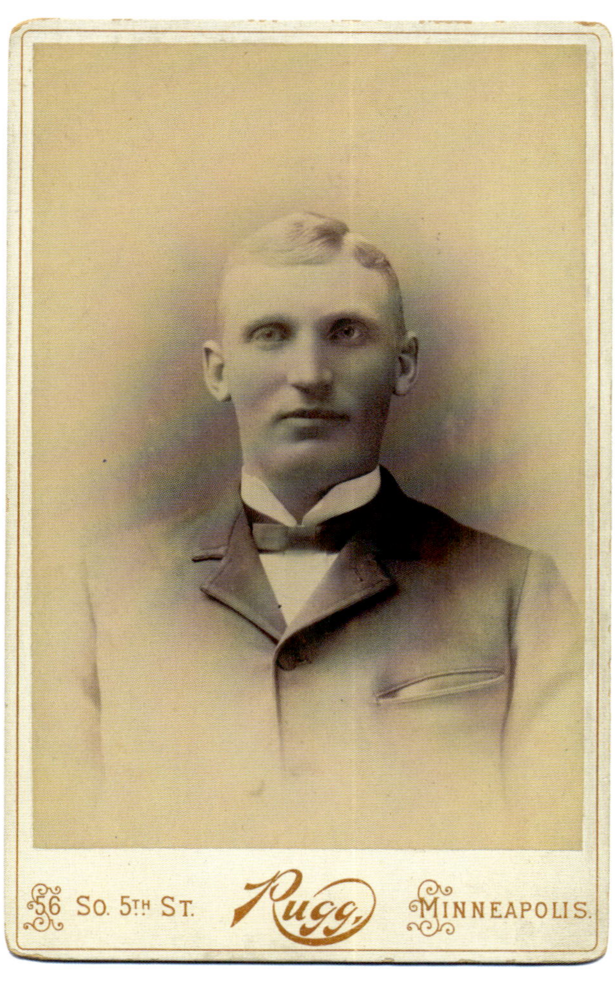
56 So. 5th St. Rugg MINNEAPOLIS.

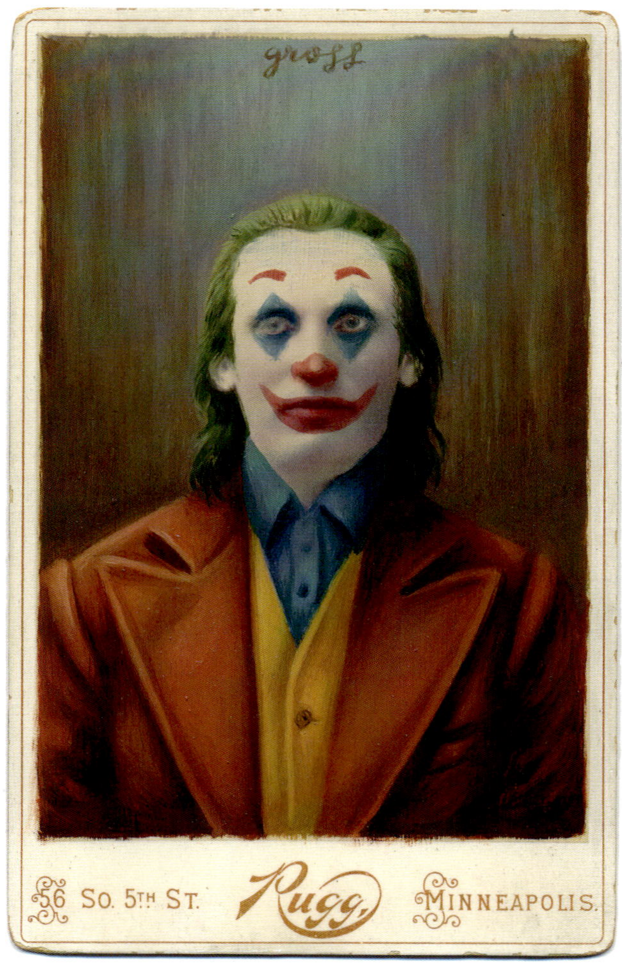
56 So. 5th St. Rugg MINNEAPOLIS.

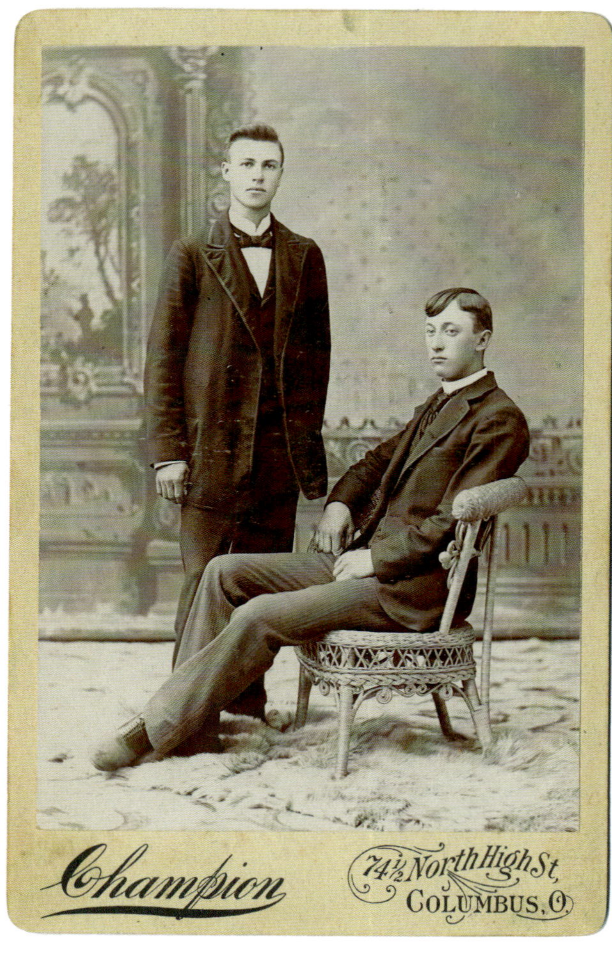
Champion 74½ North High St. COLUMBUS, O.

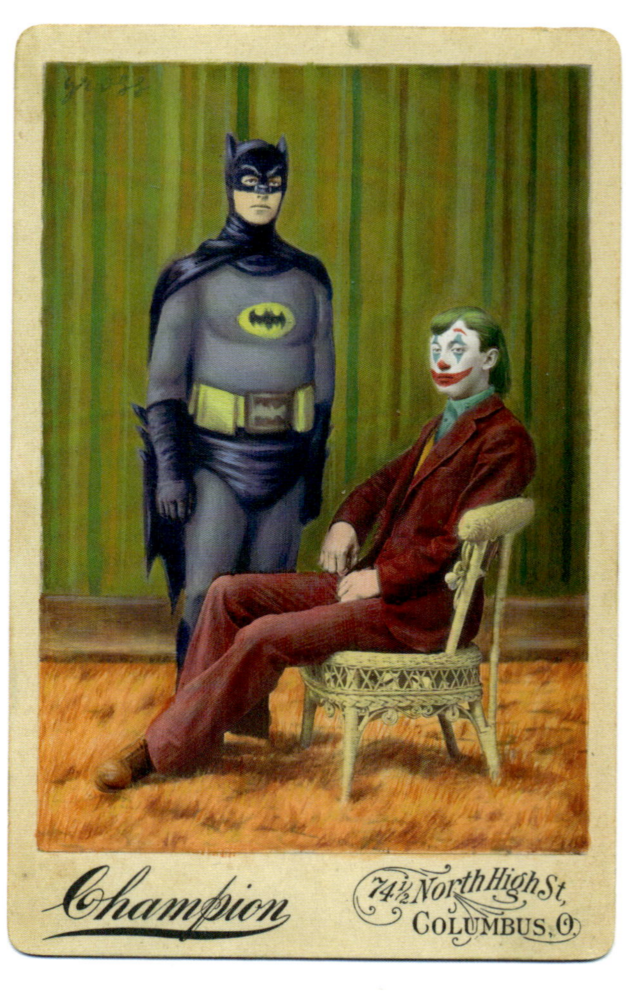
Champion 74½ North High St. COLUMBUS, O.

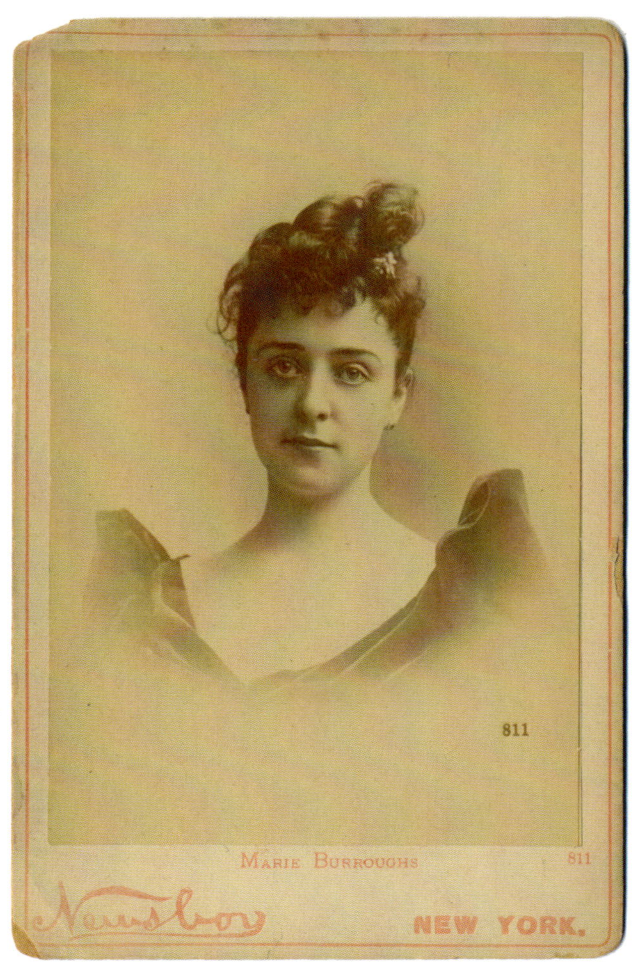
811
MARIE BURROUGHS 811
Newsboy NEW YORK.

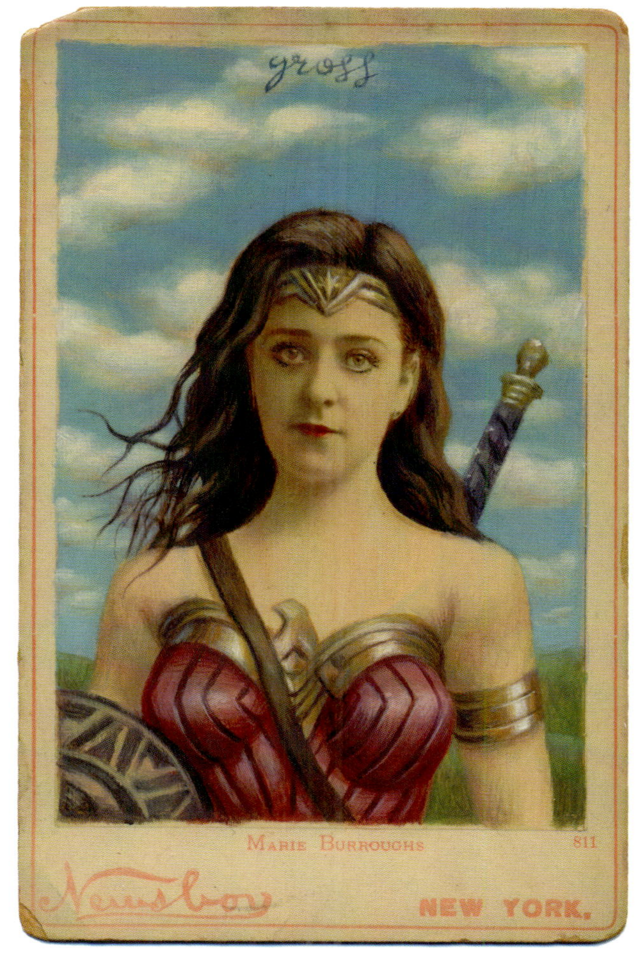
MARIE BURROUGHS 811
Newsboy NEW YORK.

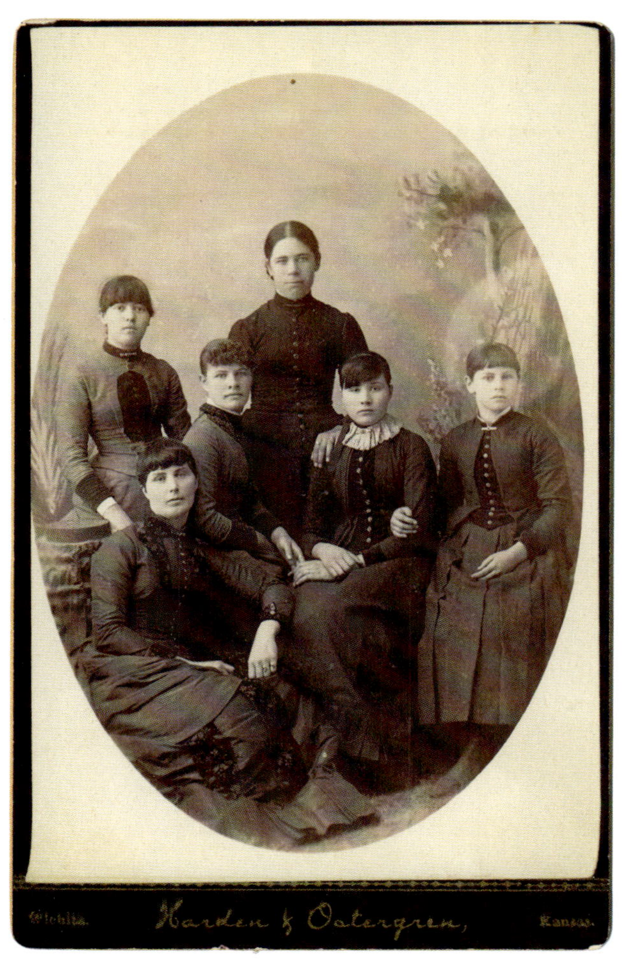
Harden & Ostergren, Kansas.

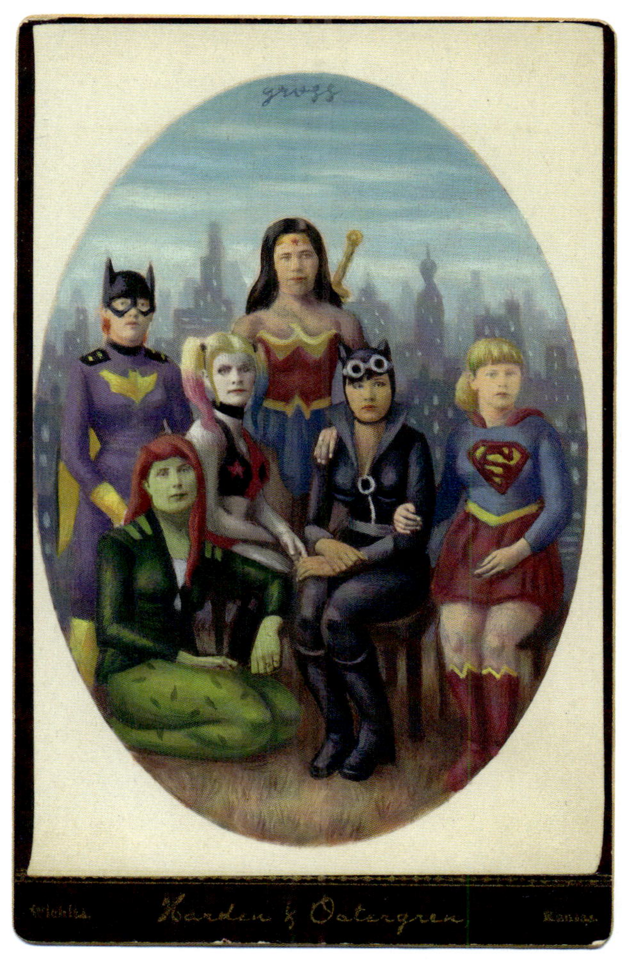
Harden & Ostergren Kansas.

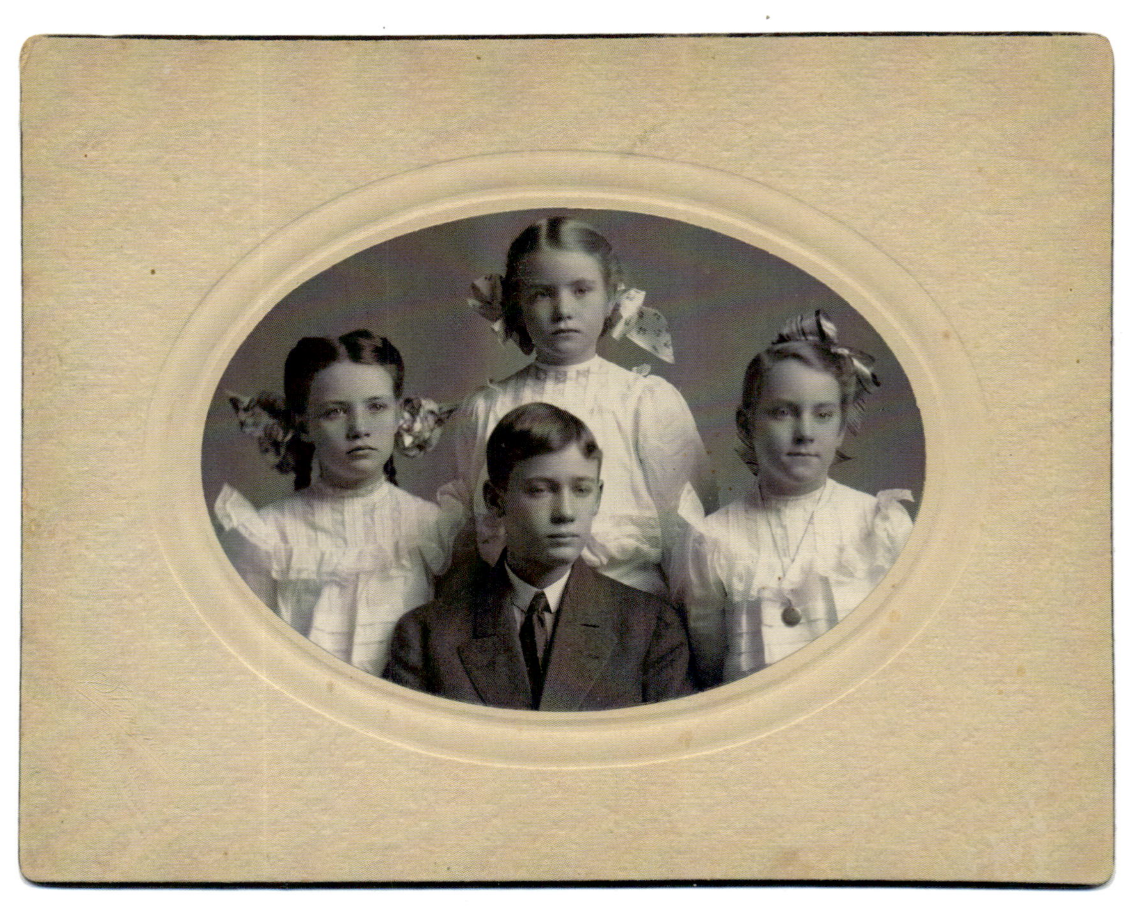

gross

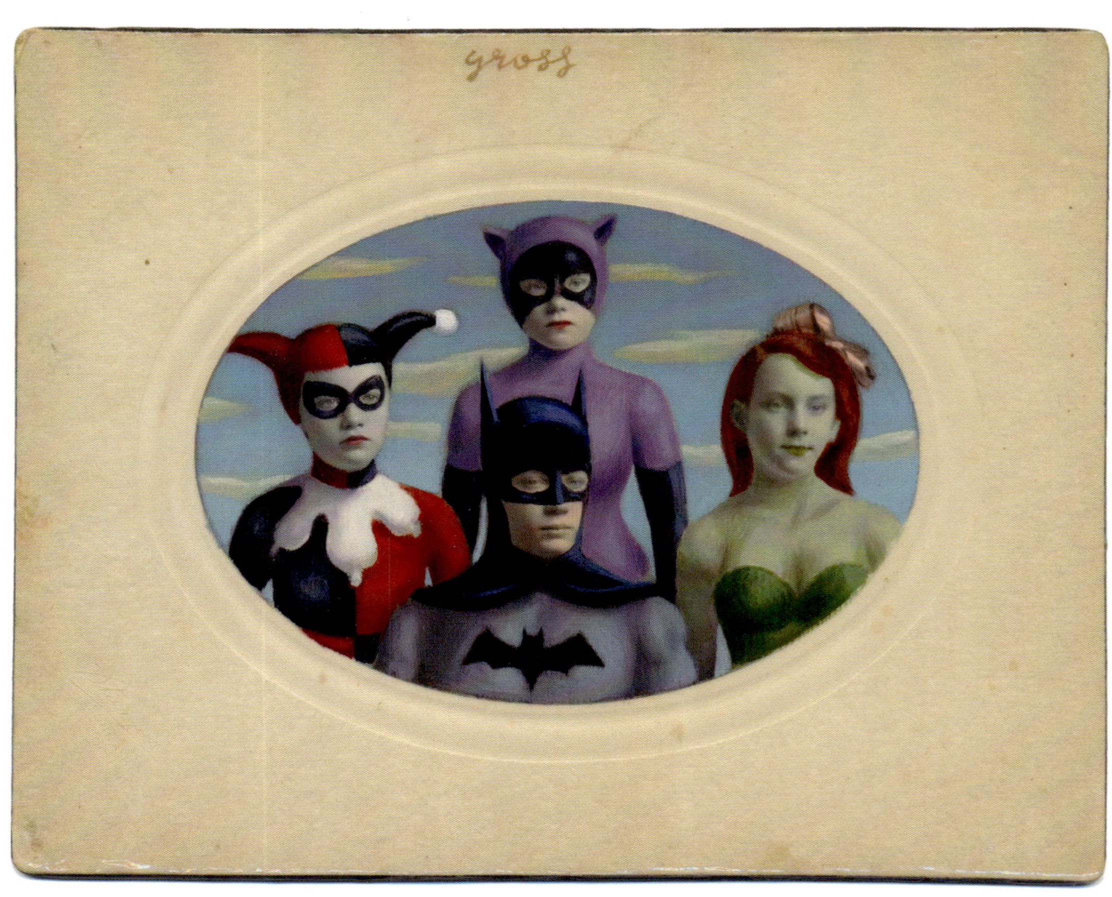

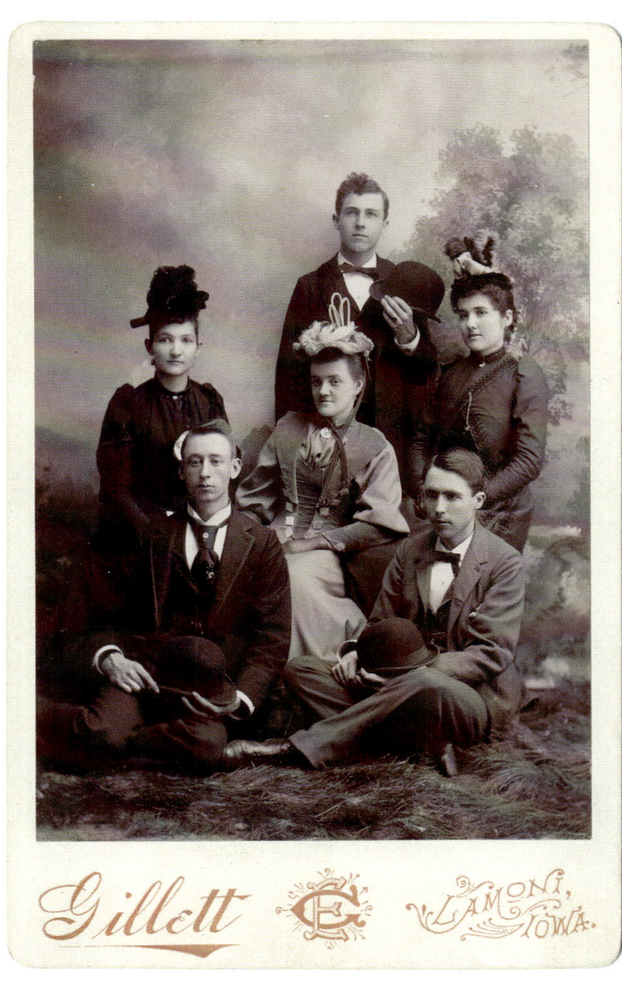

Gillett
LAMONI, IOWA.

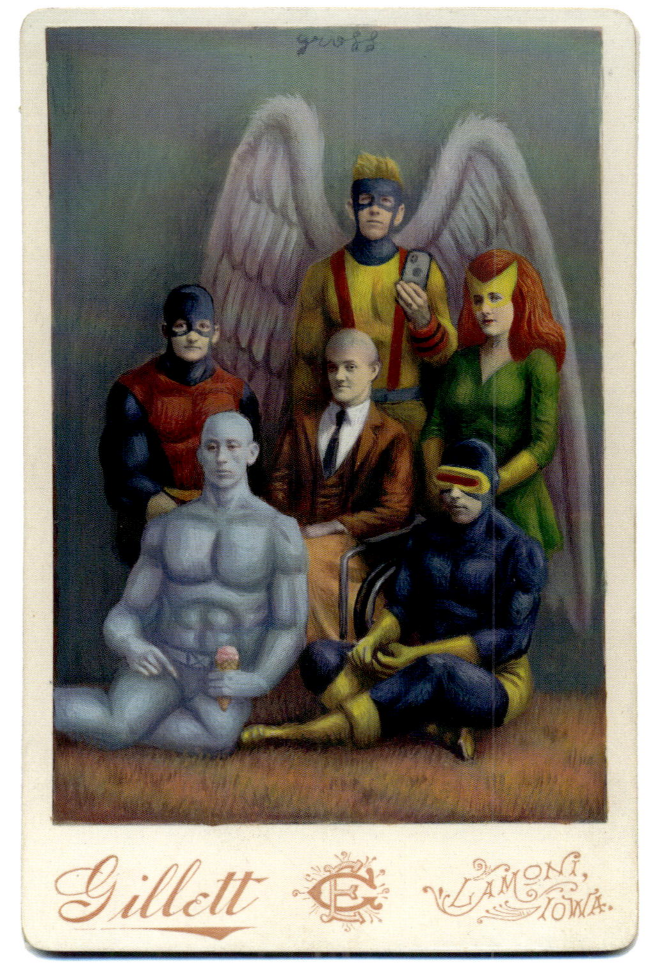

Gillett
LAMONI, IOWA.

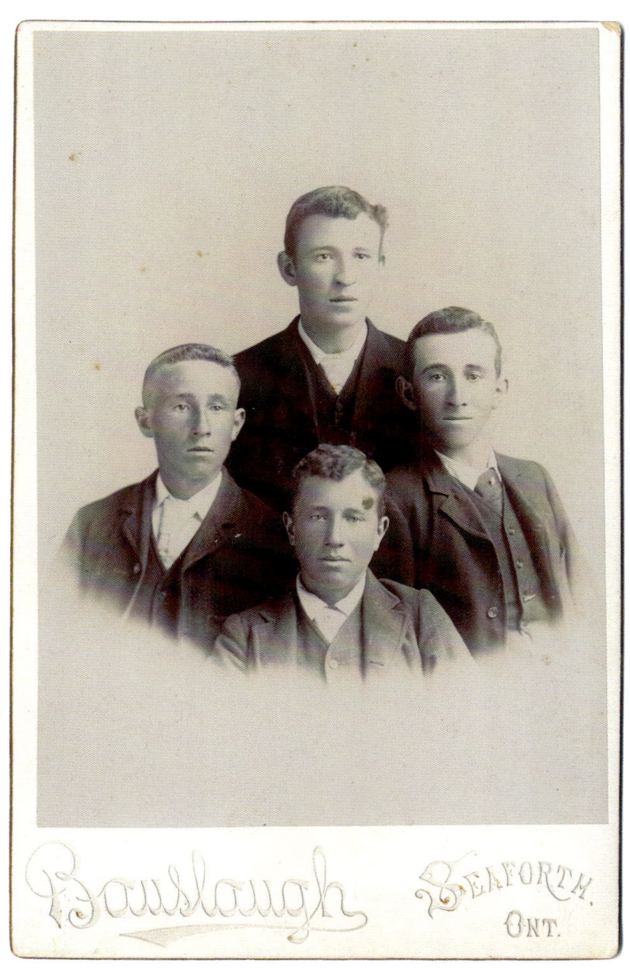

Baustaugh
SEAFORTH.
ONT.

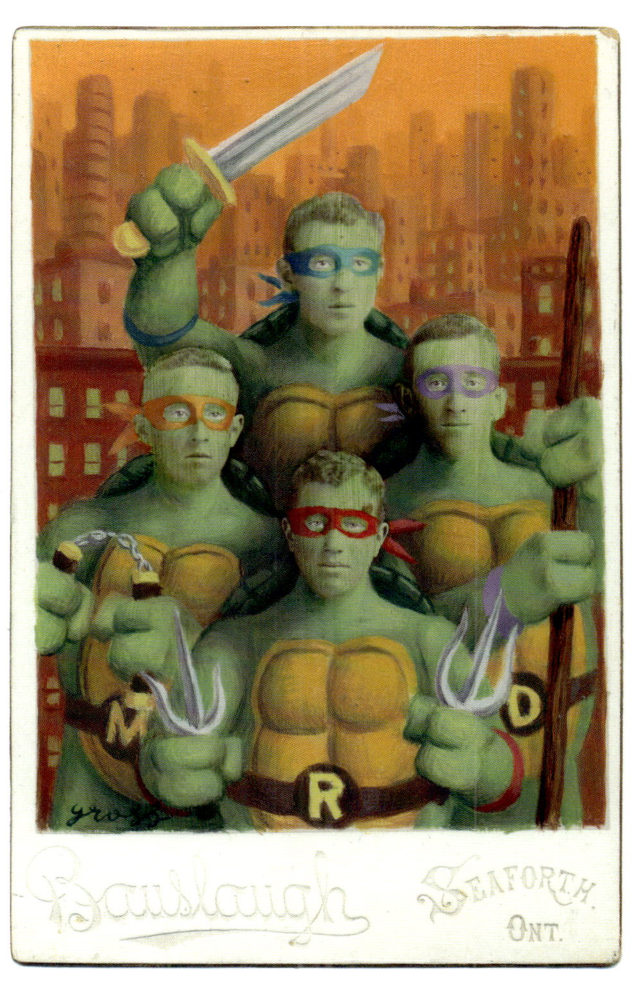

M   R   D
Baustaugh
SEAFORTH.
ONT.

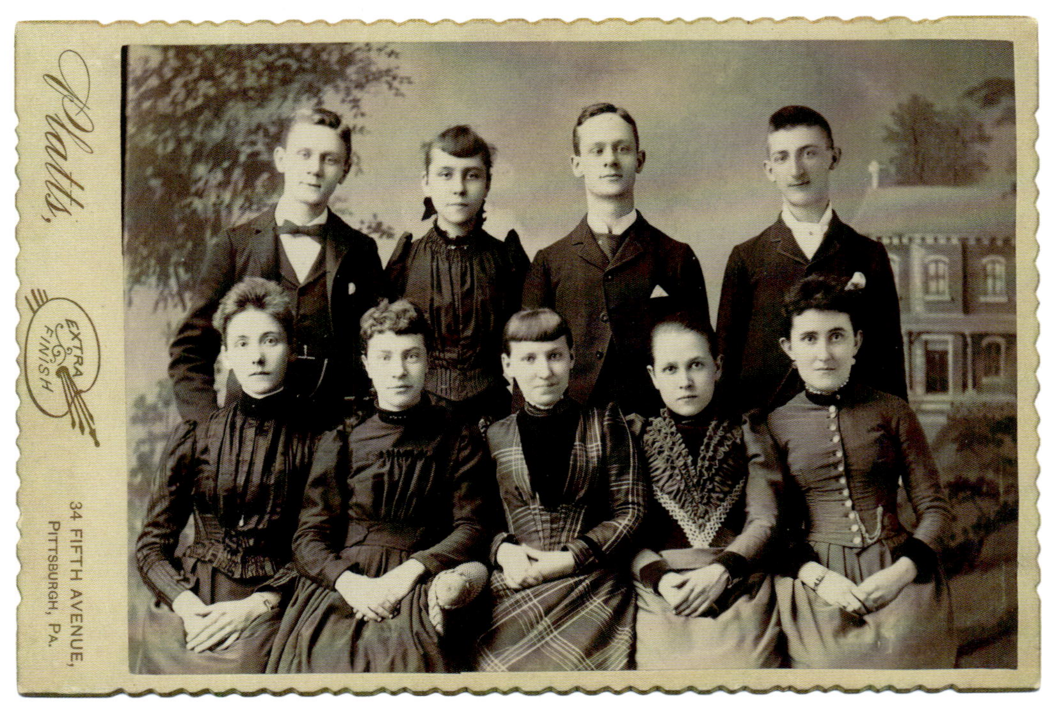
Platts,
EXTRA FINISH
34 FIFTH AVENUE,
PITTSBURGH, PA.

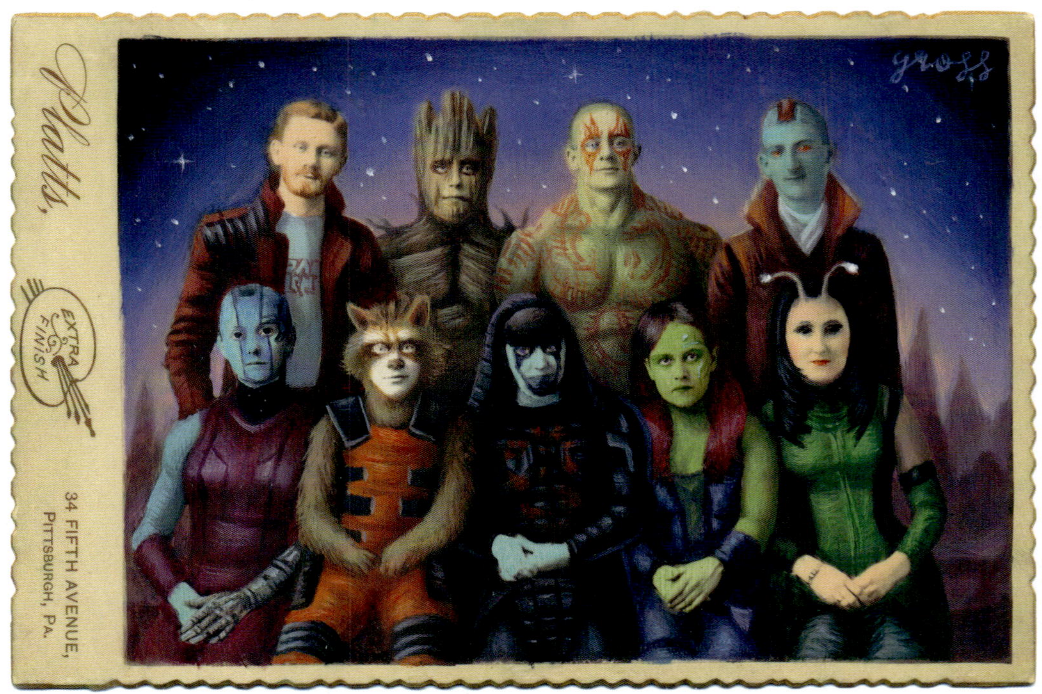
Platts,
EXTRA FINISH
34 FIFTH AVENUE,
PITTSBURGH, PA.

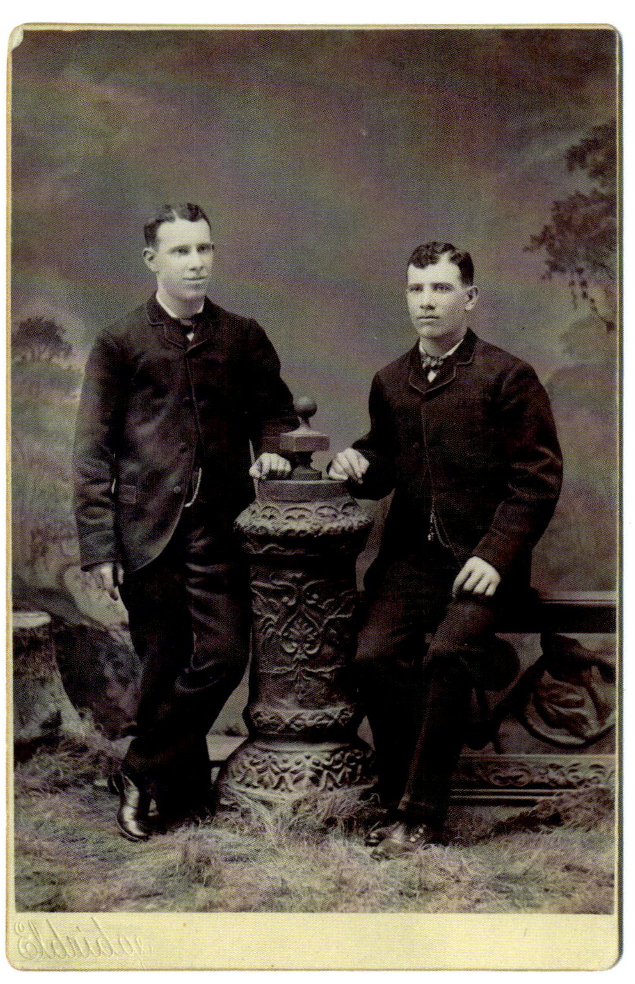
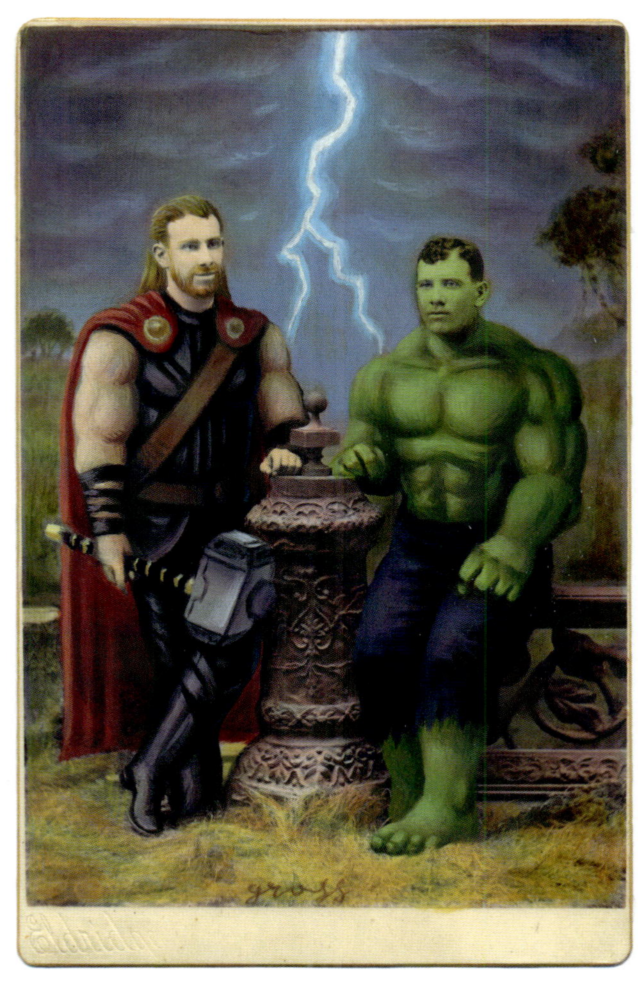

gross

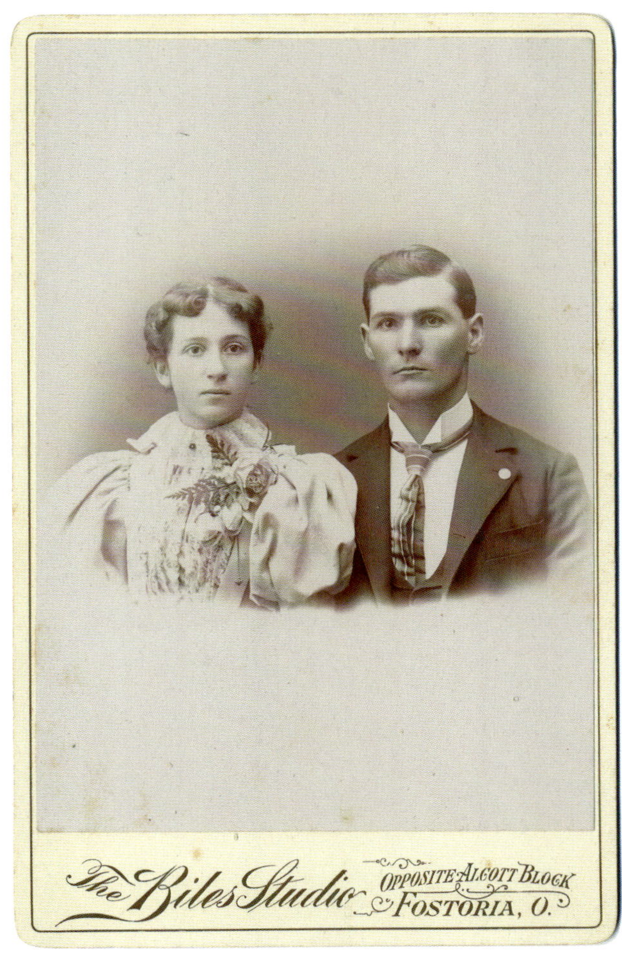

The Biles Studio
OPPOSITE ALCOTT BLOCK
FOSTORIA, O.

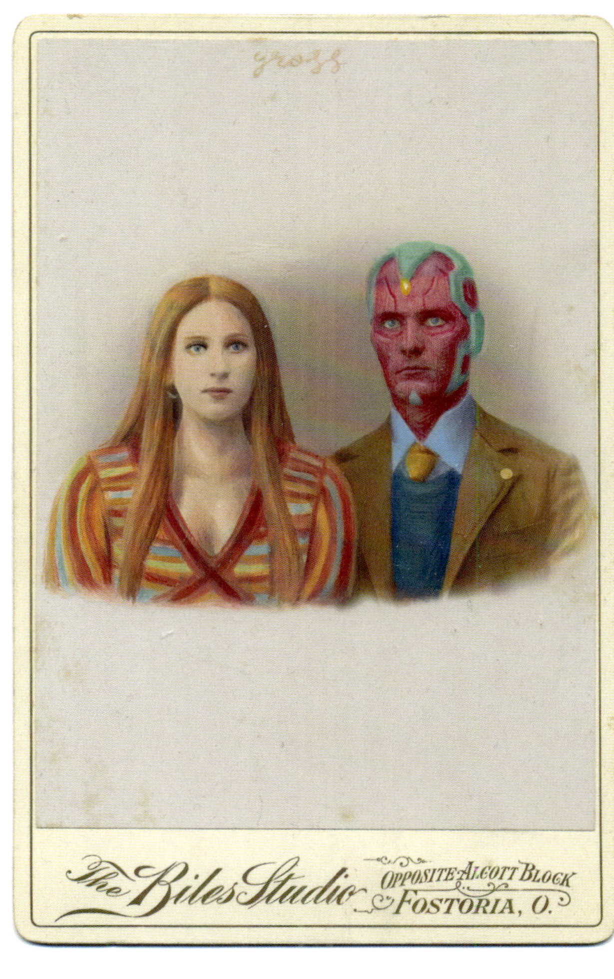

gross
The Biles Studio
OPPOSITE ALCOTT BLOCK
FOSTORIA, O.

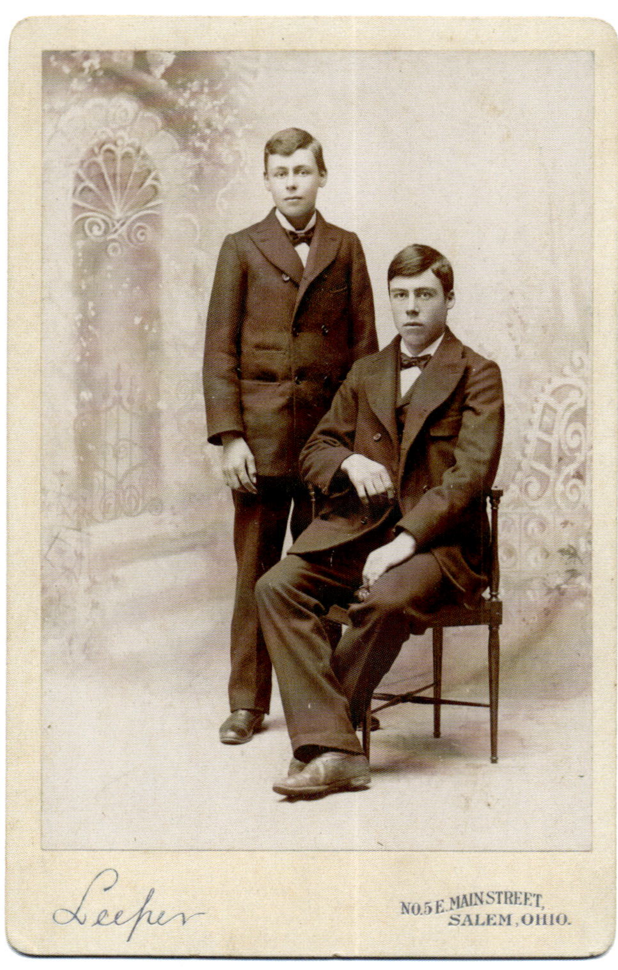

Leeper
NO.5 E. MAIN STREET,
SALEM, OHIO.

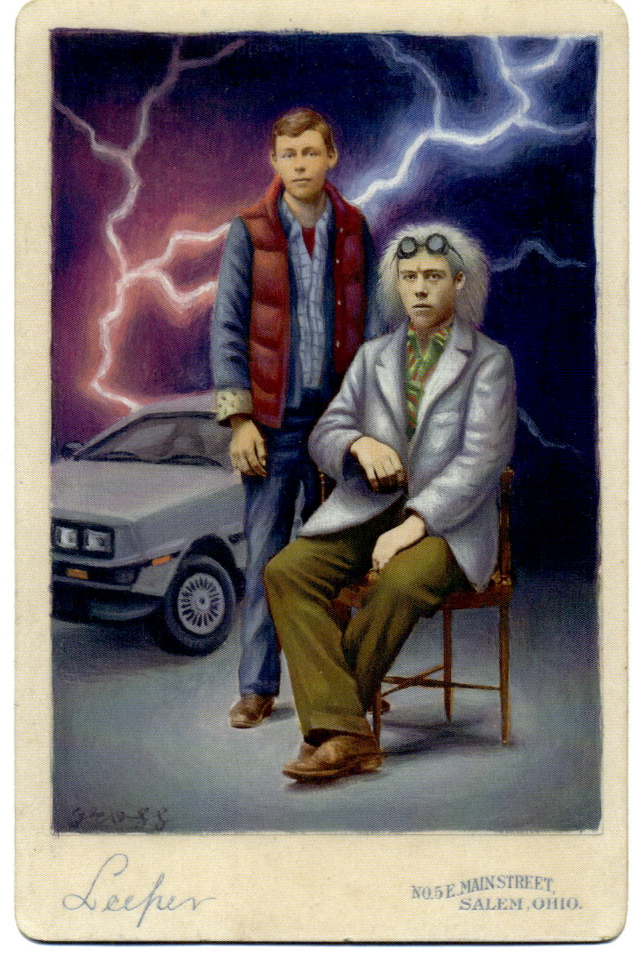

Leeper
NO.5 E. MAIN STREET,
SALEM, OHIO.

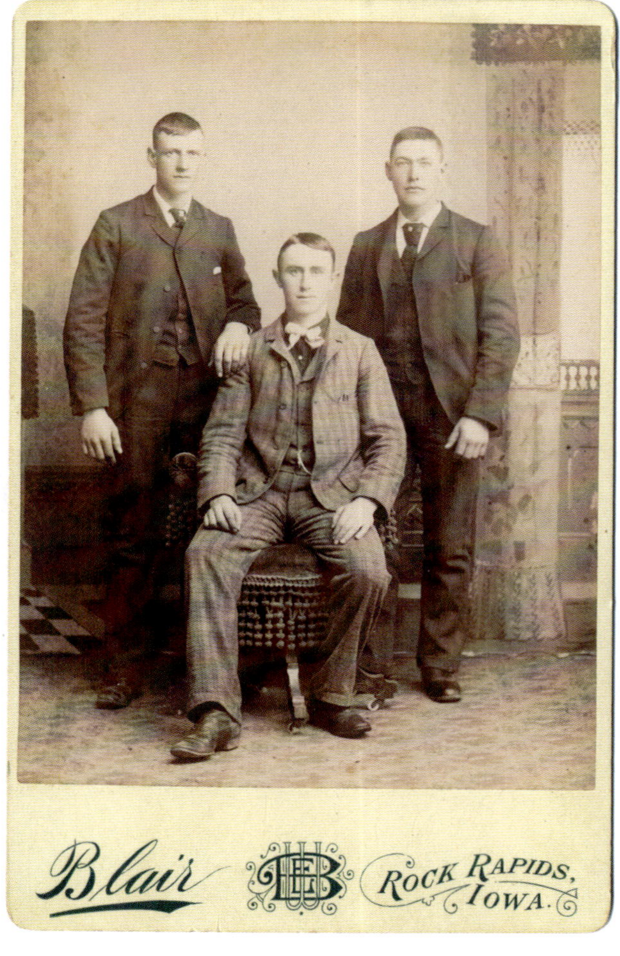

Blair
ROCK RAPIDS,
IOWA.

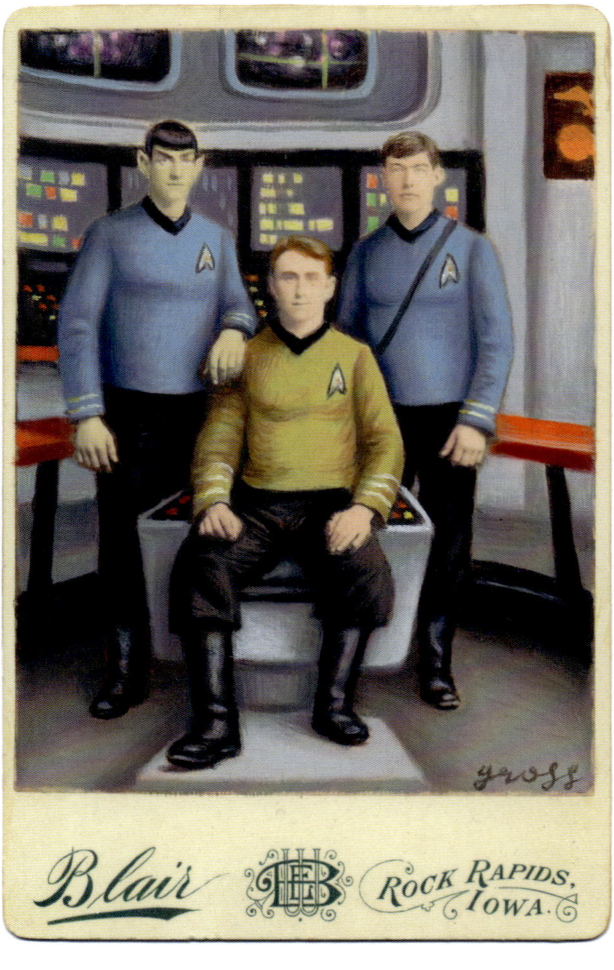

Blair
ROCK RAPIDS,
IOWA.

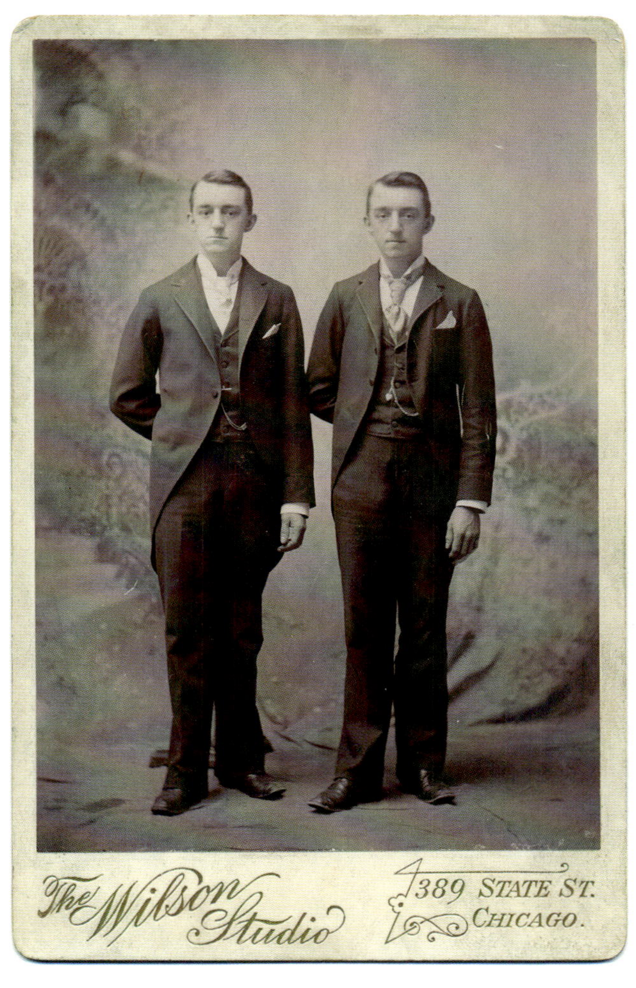

The Wilson Studio
389 STATE ST.
CHICAGO.

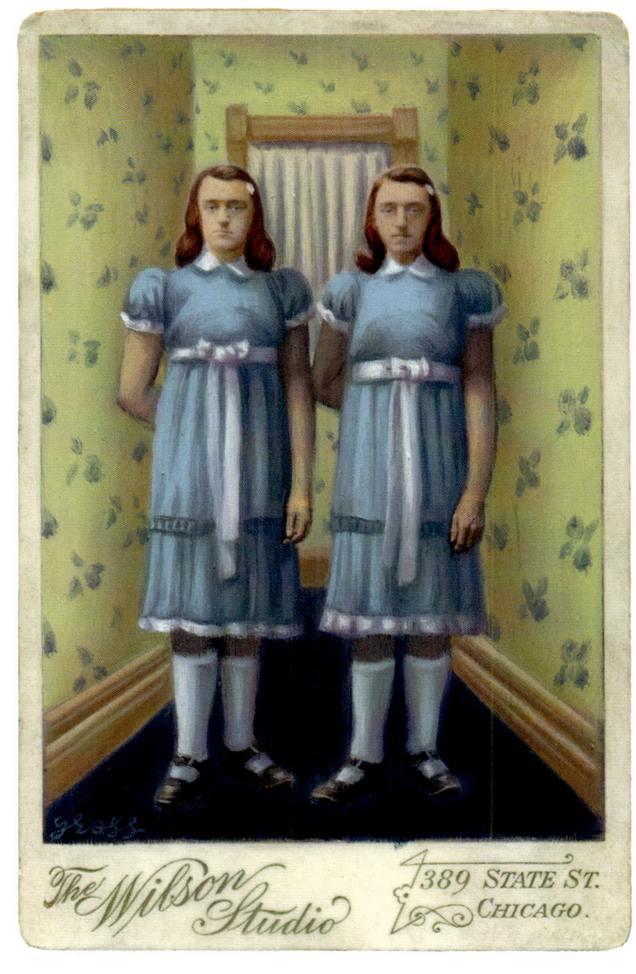

The Wilson Studio
389 STATE ST.
CHICAGO.

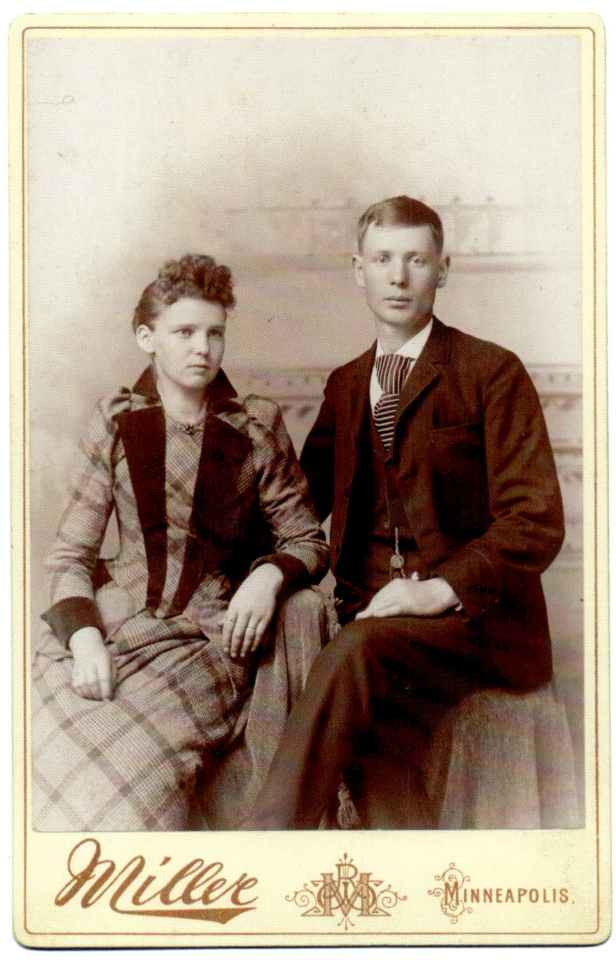

Miller
MINNEAPOLIS.

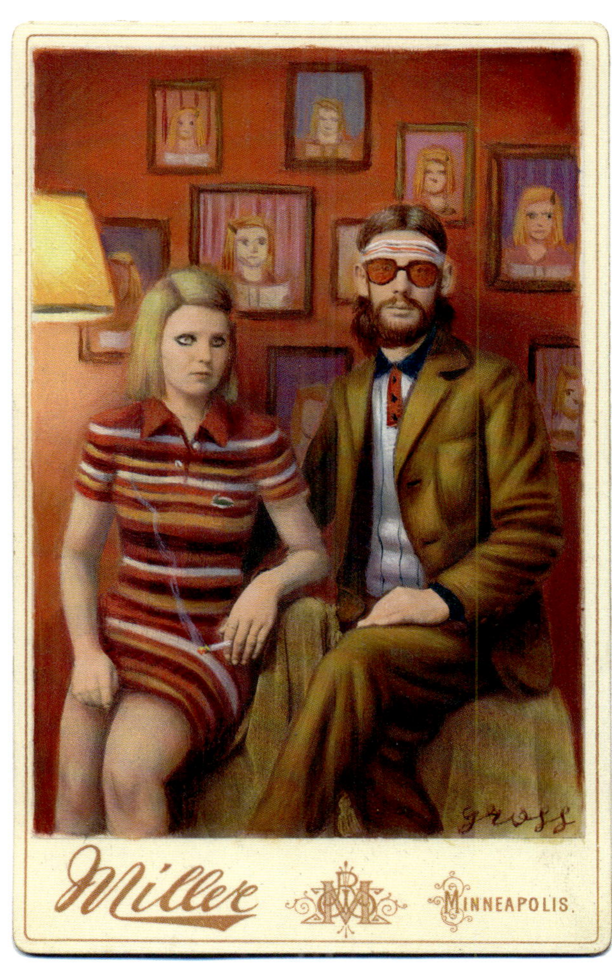

Miller
MINNEAPOLIS.

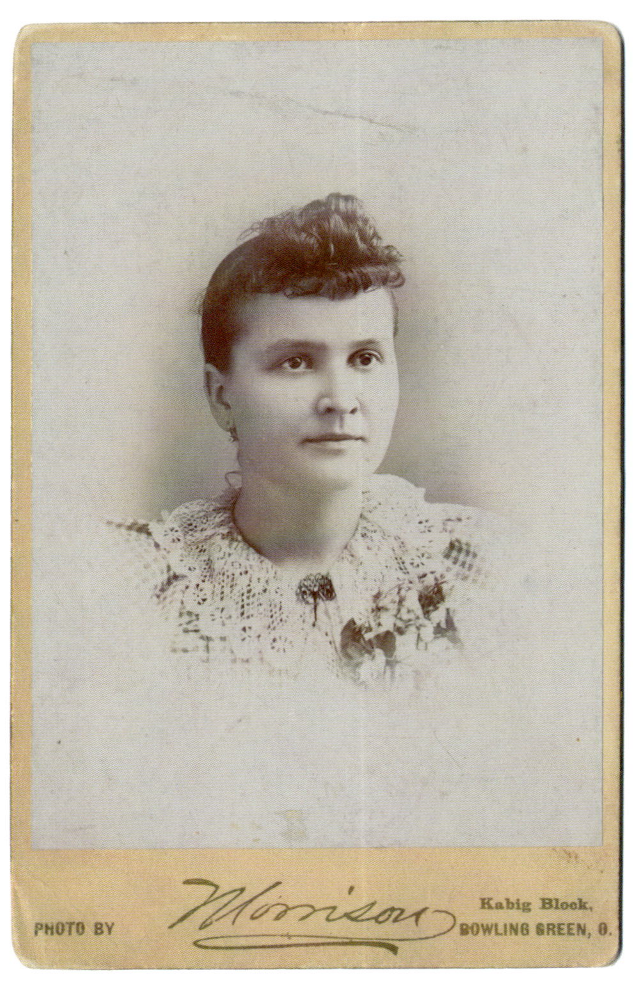

PHOTO BY
Morrison
Kabig Block,
BOWLING GREEN, O.

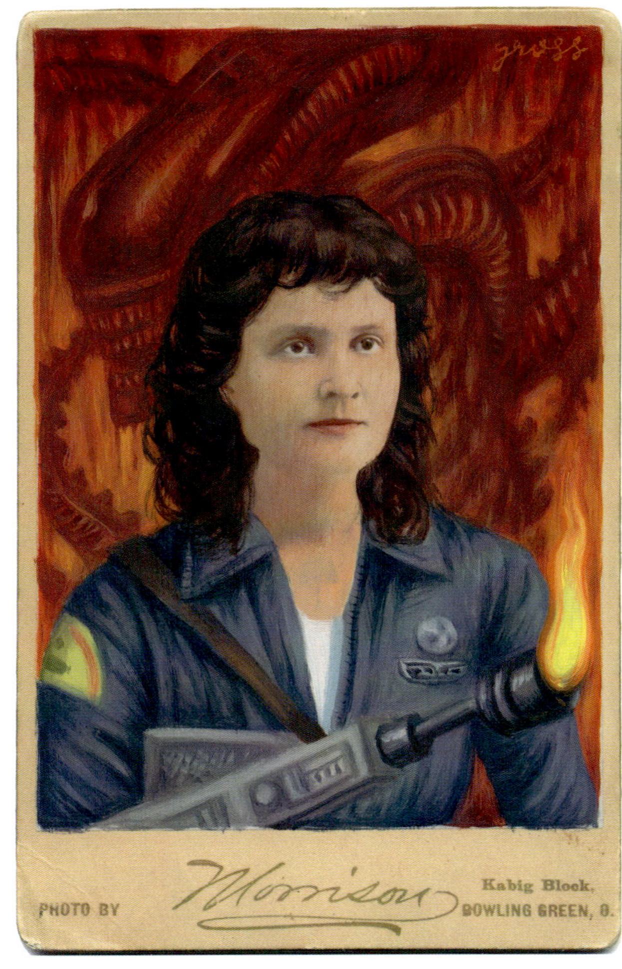

gross
PHOTO BY
Morrison
Kabig Block,
BOWLING GREEN, O.

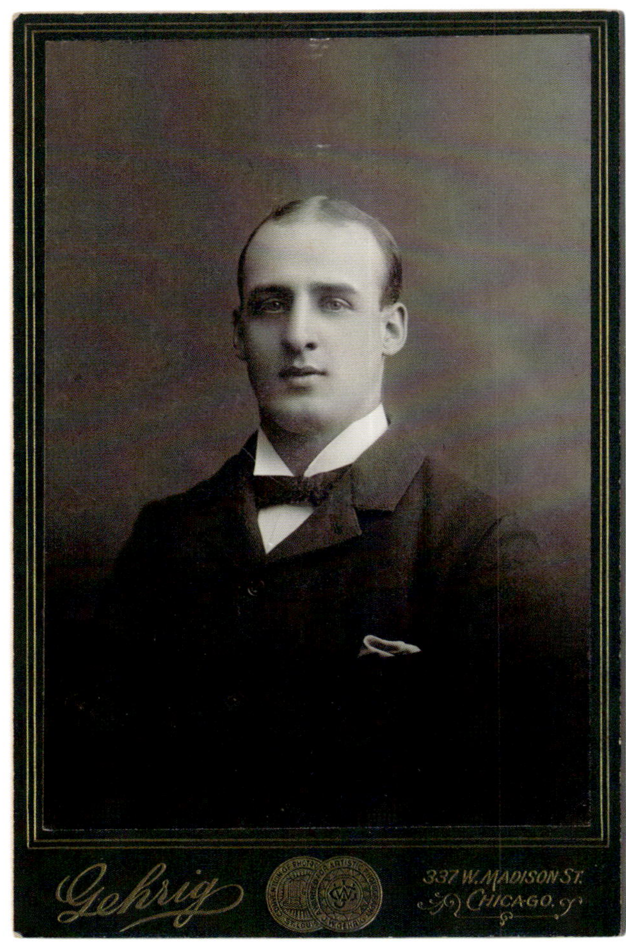

Gehrig
337 W. MADISON ST.
CHICAGO

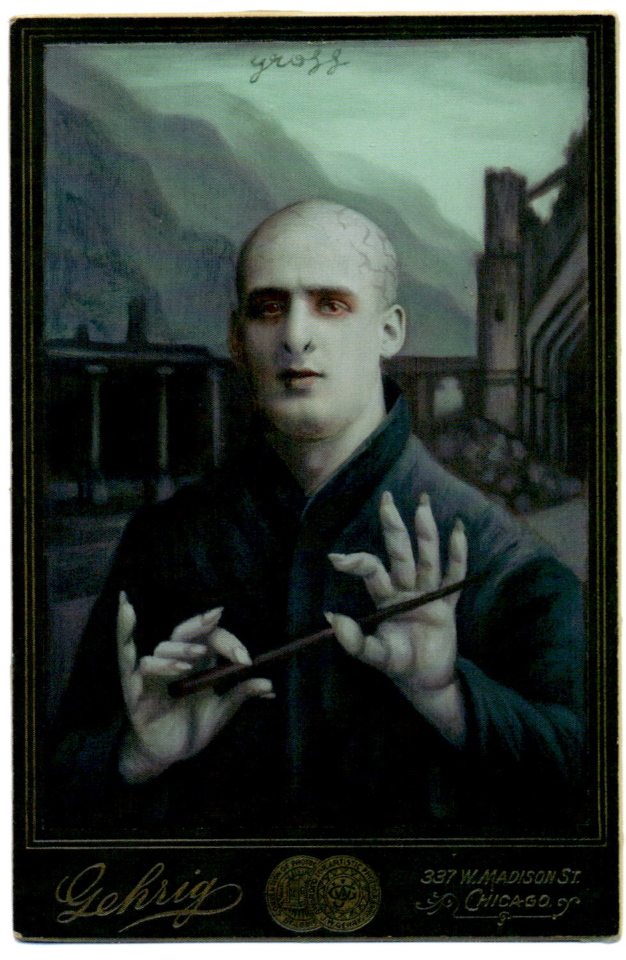

gross
Gehrig
337 W. MADISON ST.
CHICAGO

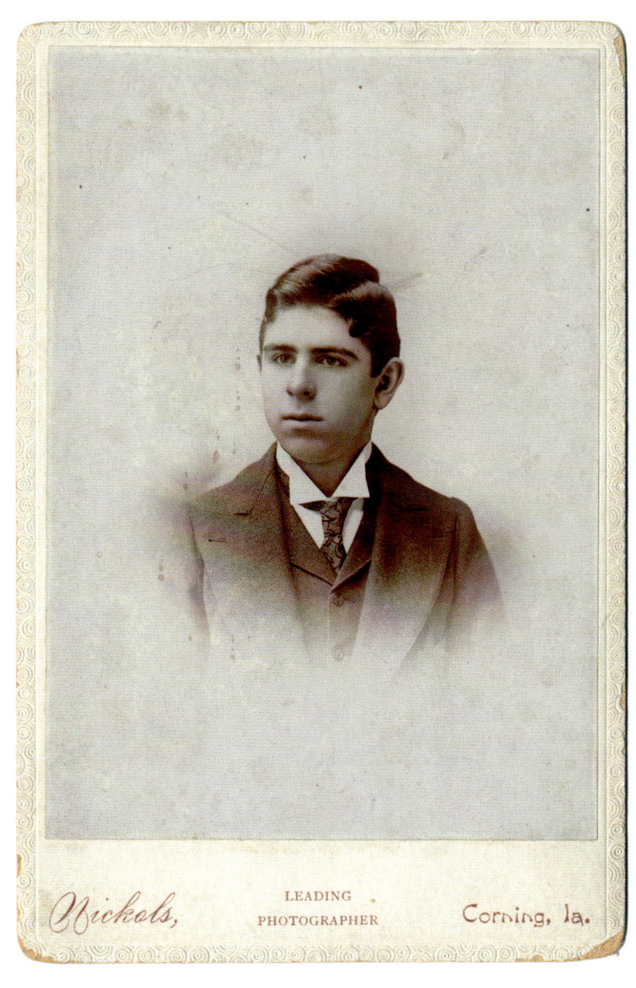
Nickols,
LEADING
PHOTOGRAPHER
Corning, Ia.

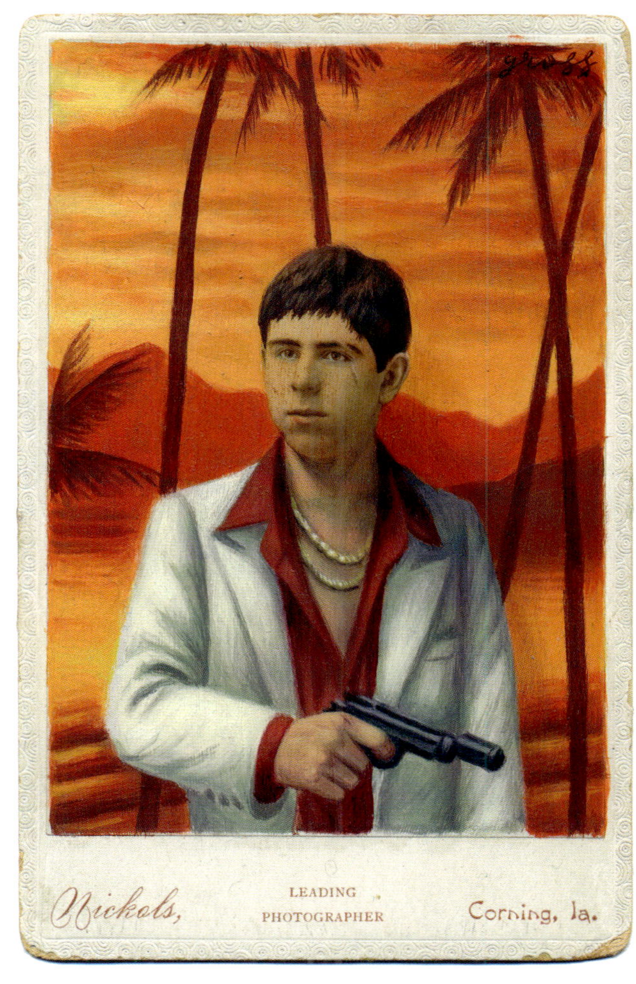
gross
Nickols,
LEADING
PHOTOGRAPHER
Corning, Ia.

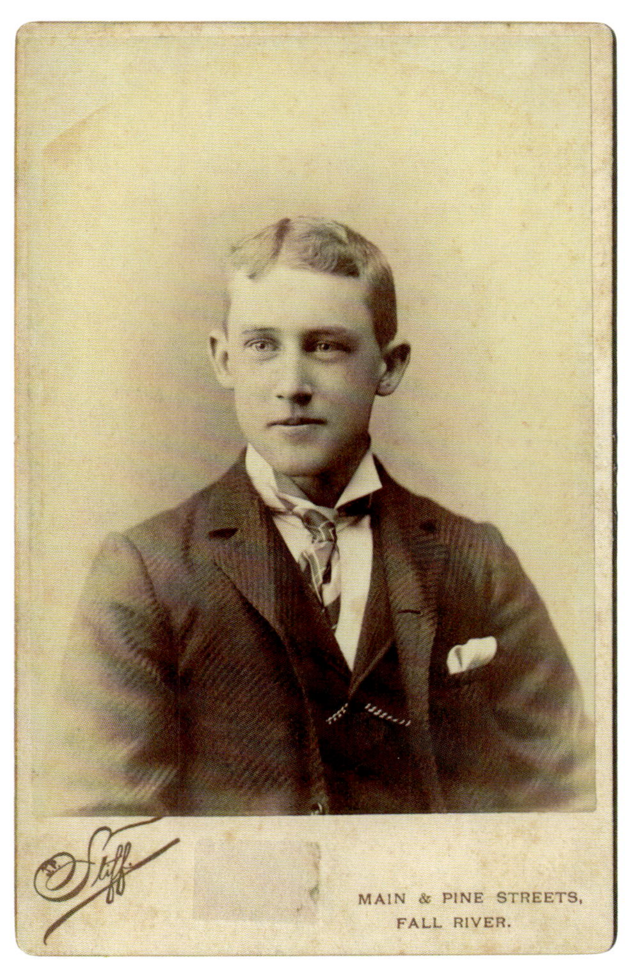
MAIN & PINE STREETS,
FALL RIVER.

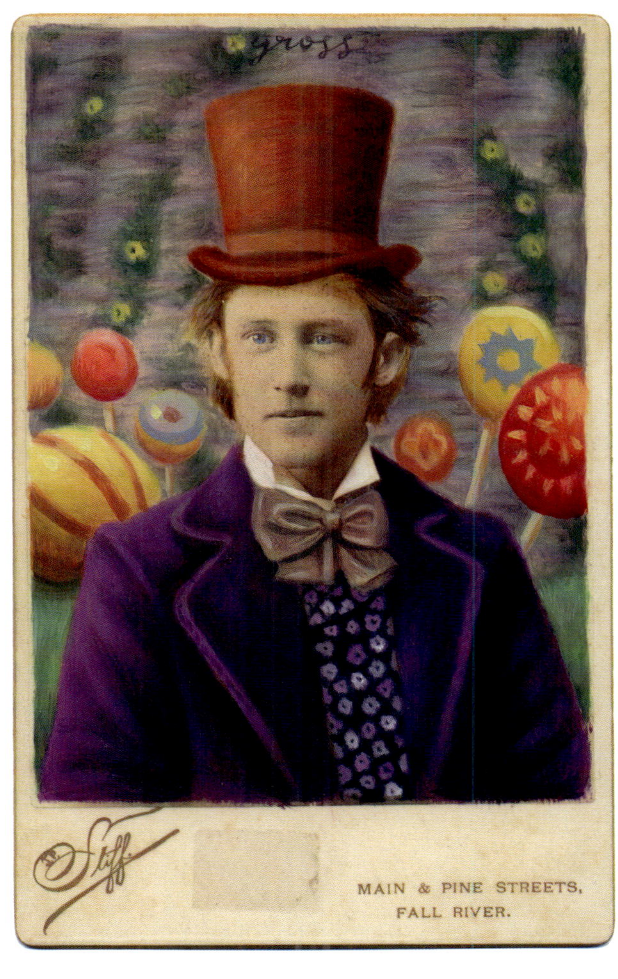
gross
MAIN & PINE STREETS,
FALL RIVER.

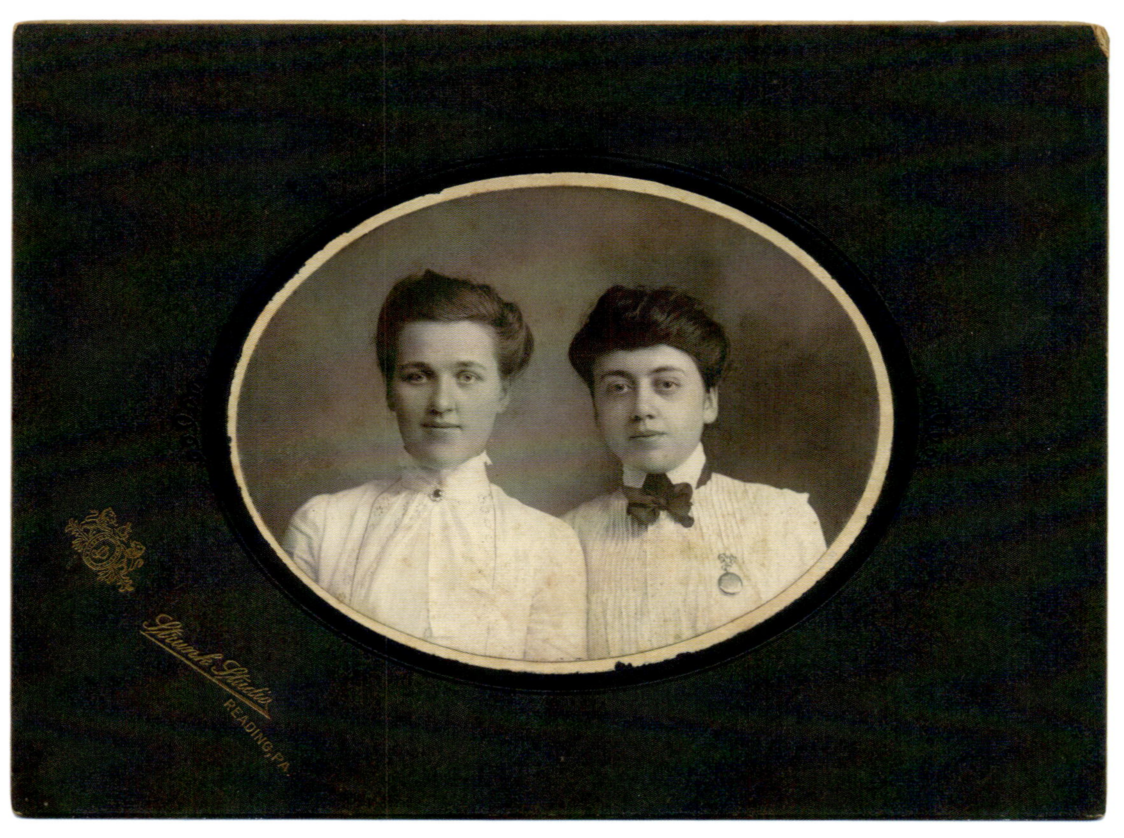

Strunk Studio
READING, PA.

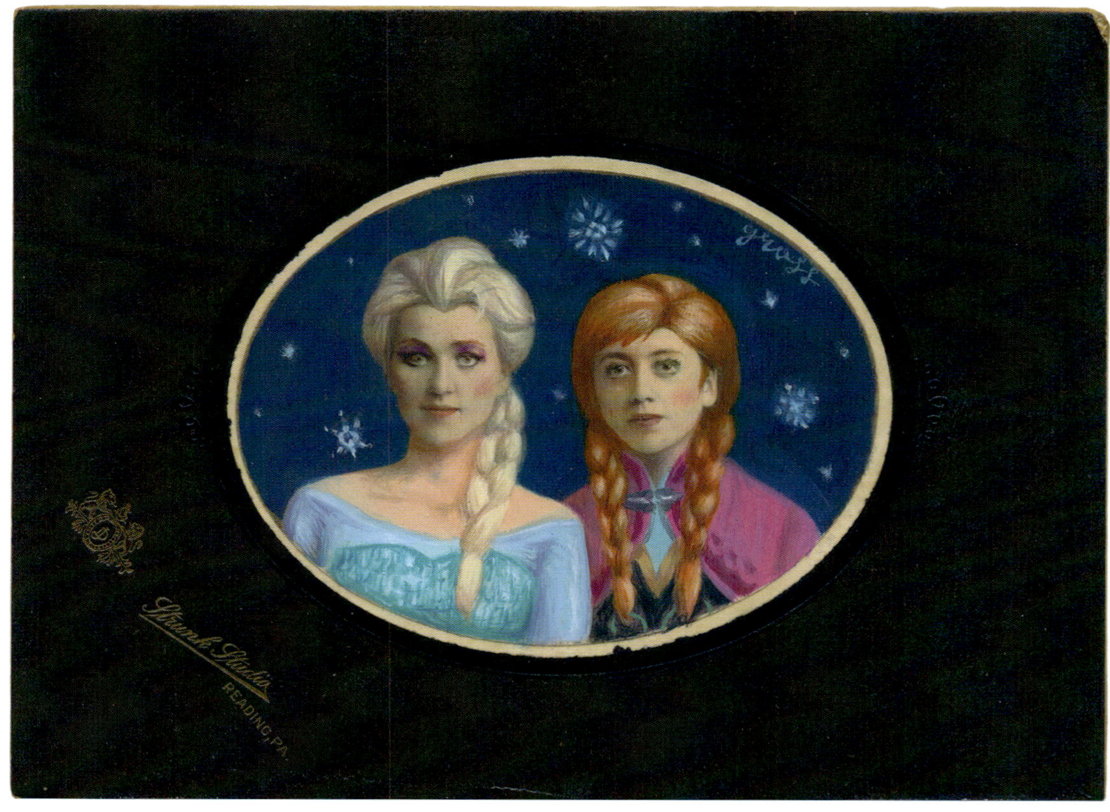

Strunk Studio
READING, PA.

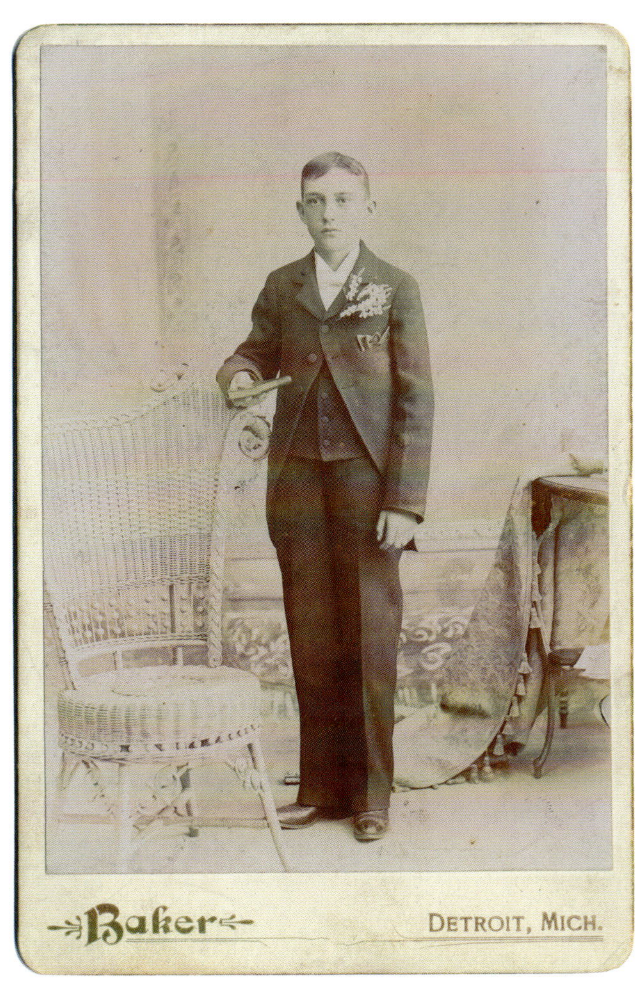

Baker
DETROIT, MICH.

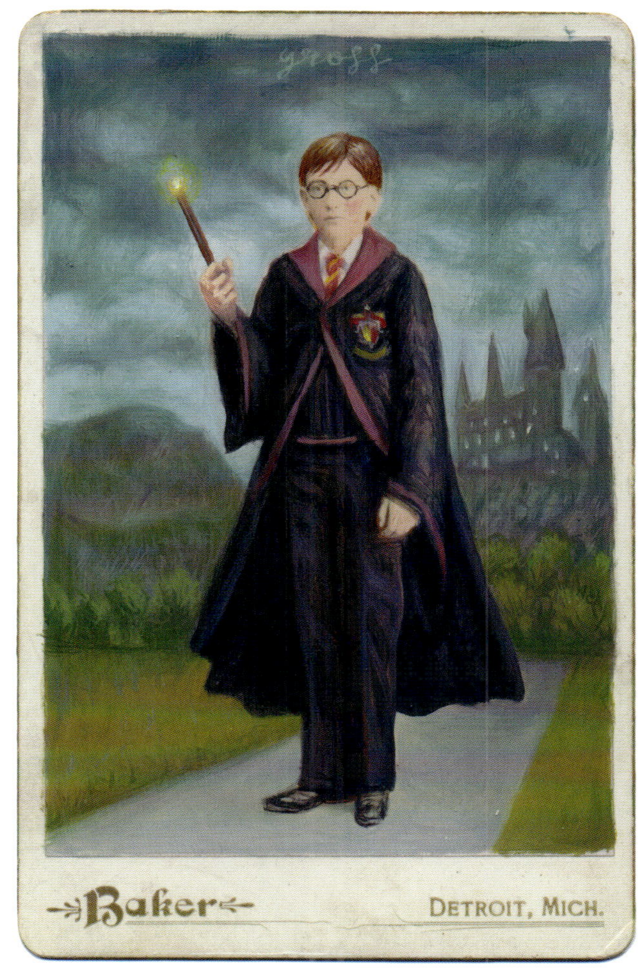

Baker
DETROIT, MICH.

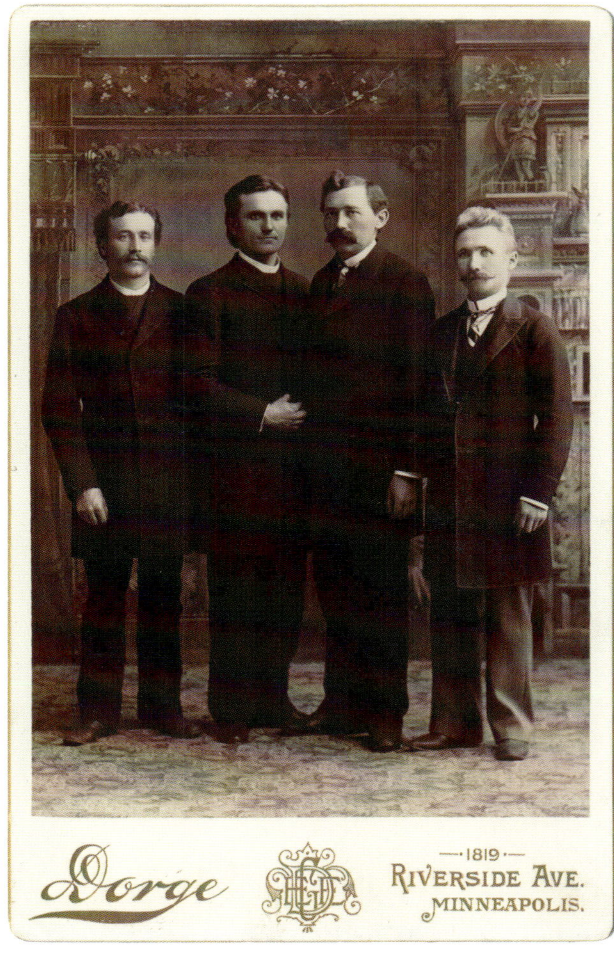

Dorge
1819
RIVERSIDE AVE.
MINNEAPOLIS.

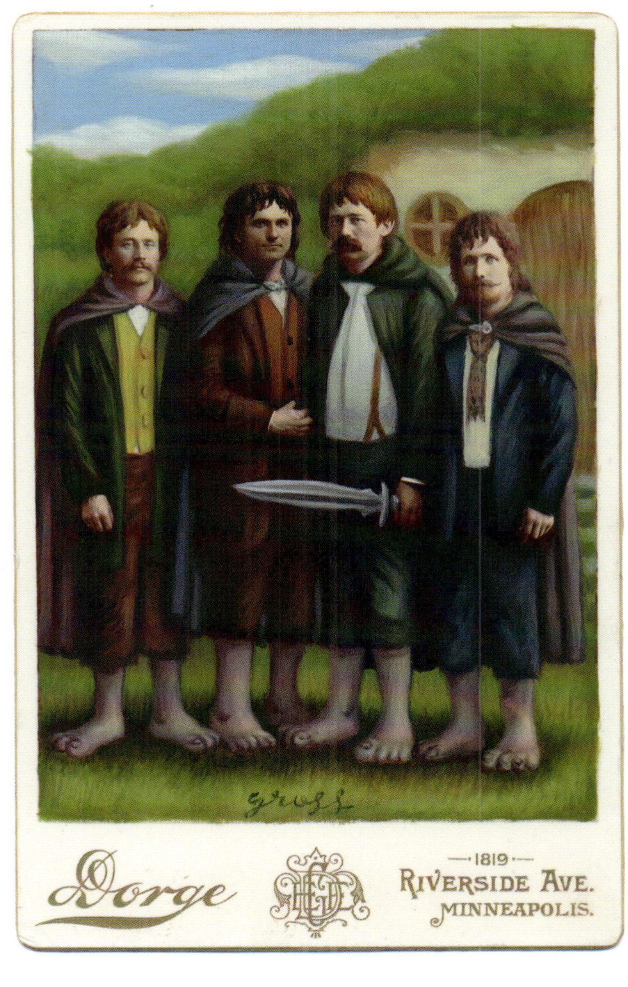

Dorge
1819
RIVERSIDE AVE.
MINNEAPOLIS.

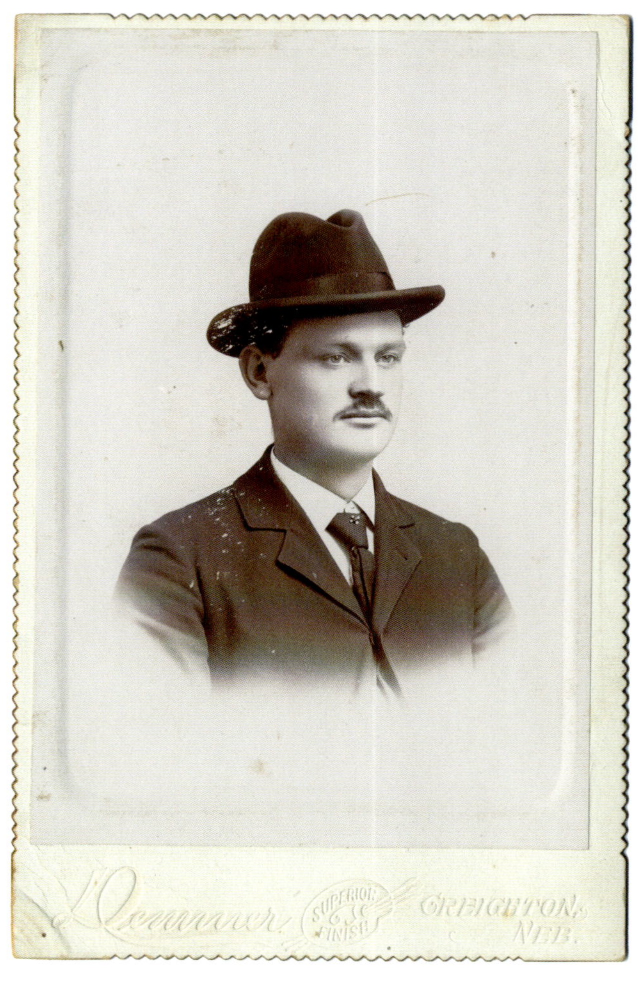

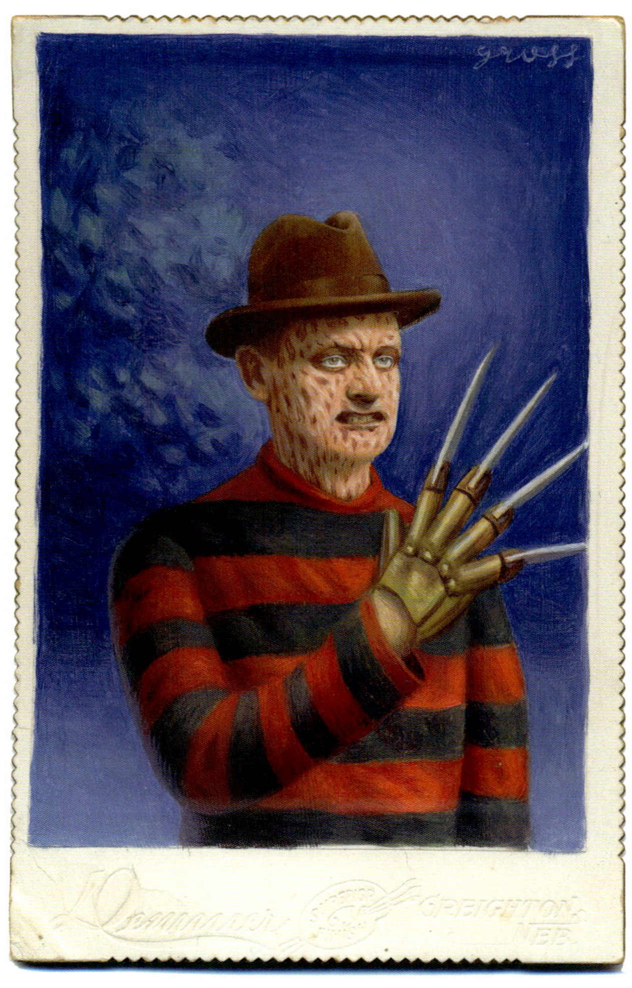

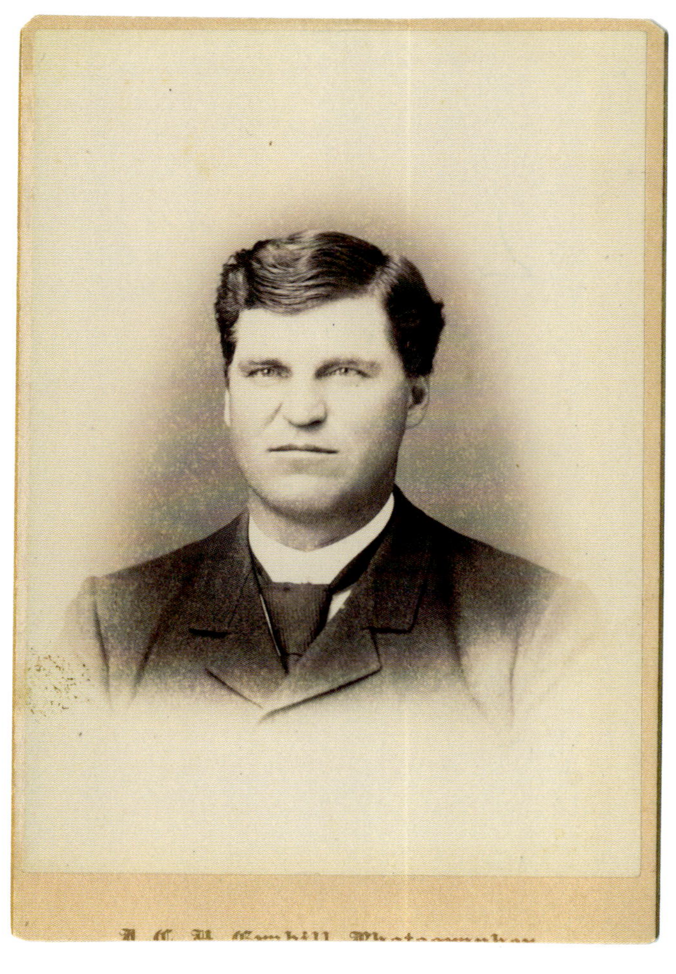

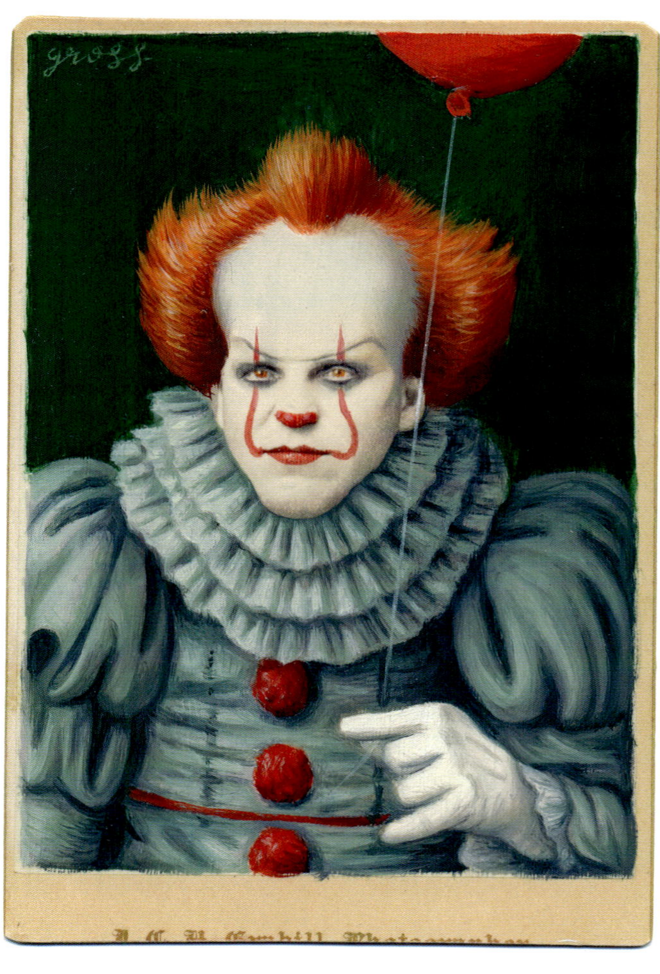

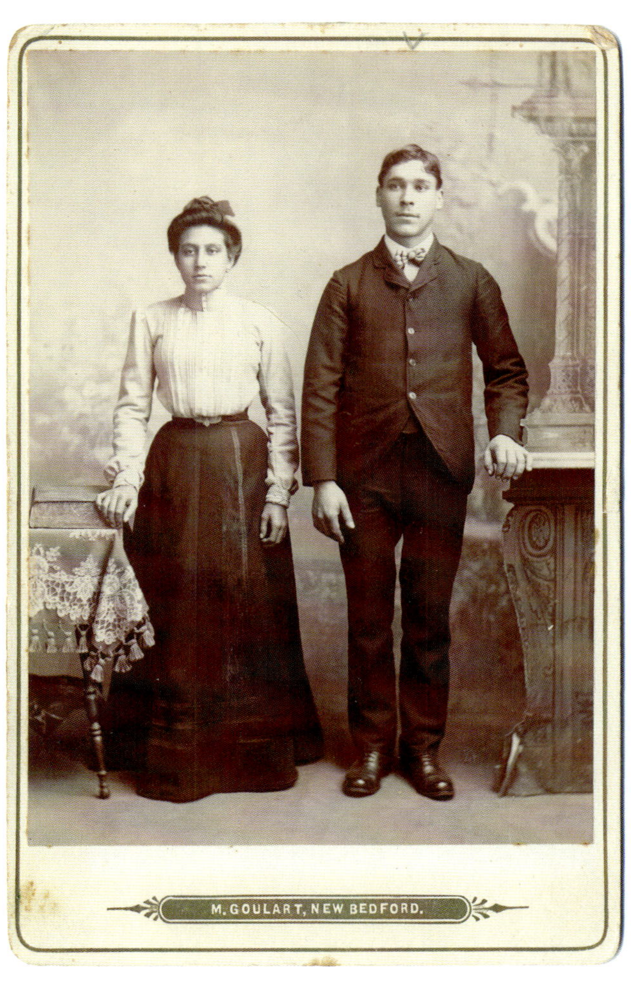

M. GOULART, NEW BEDFORD.

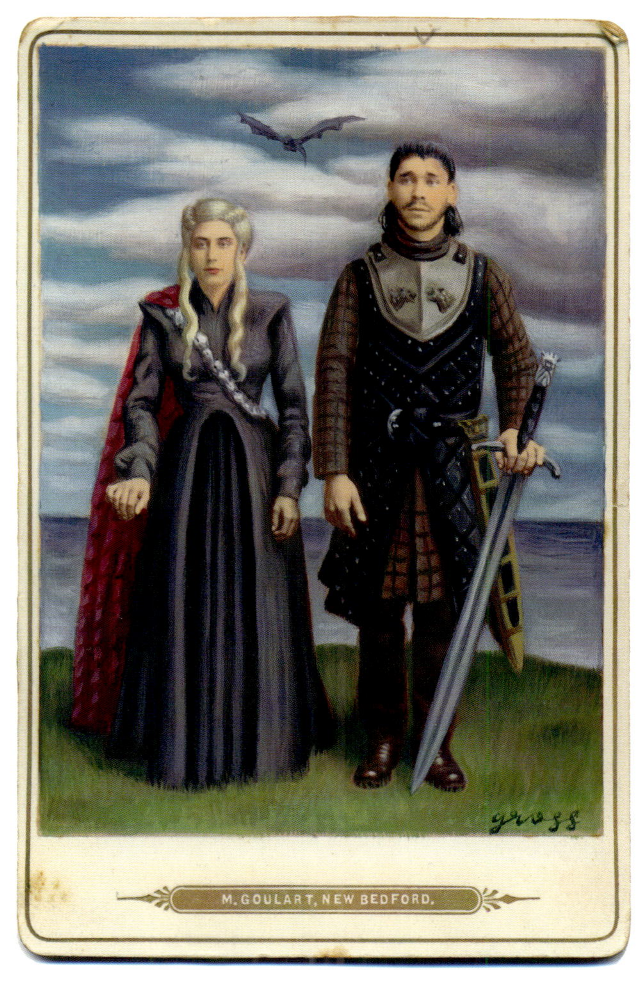

gross
M. GOULART, NEW BEDFORD.

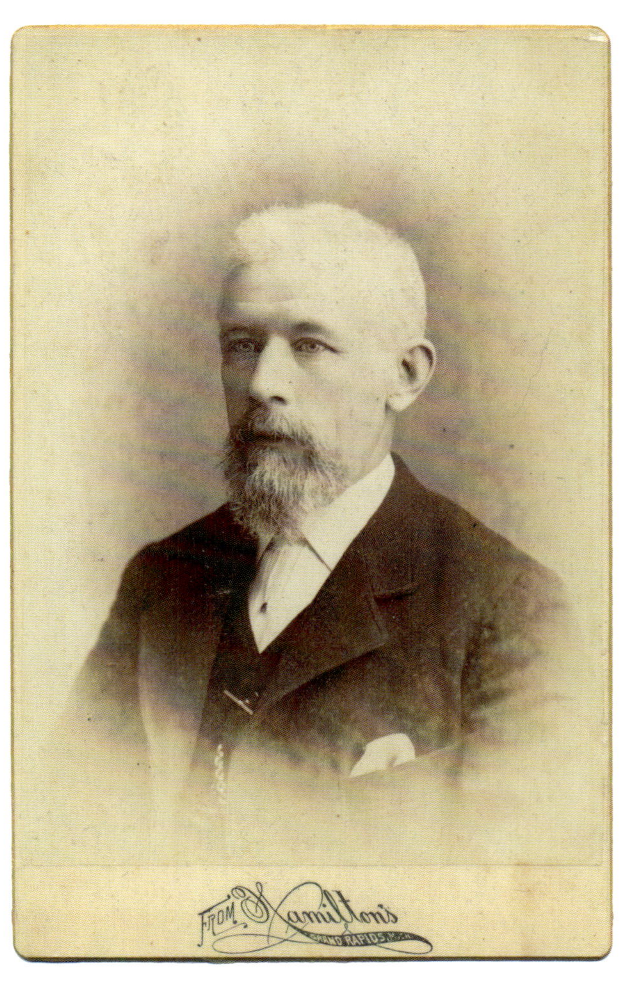

FROM Hamilton's

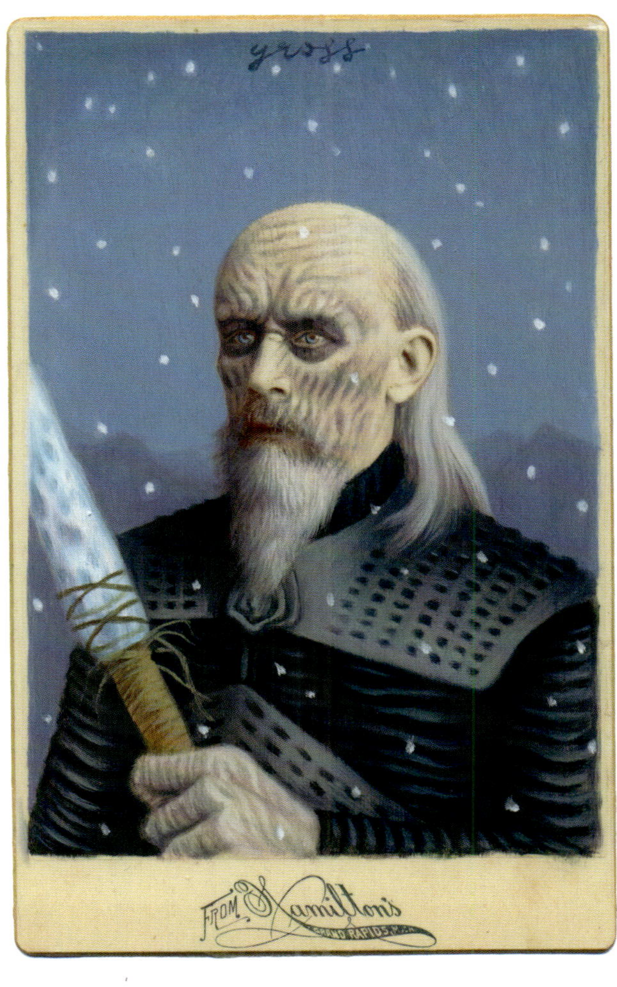

gross
FROM Hamilton's

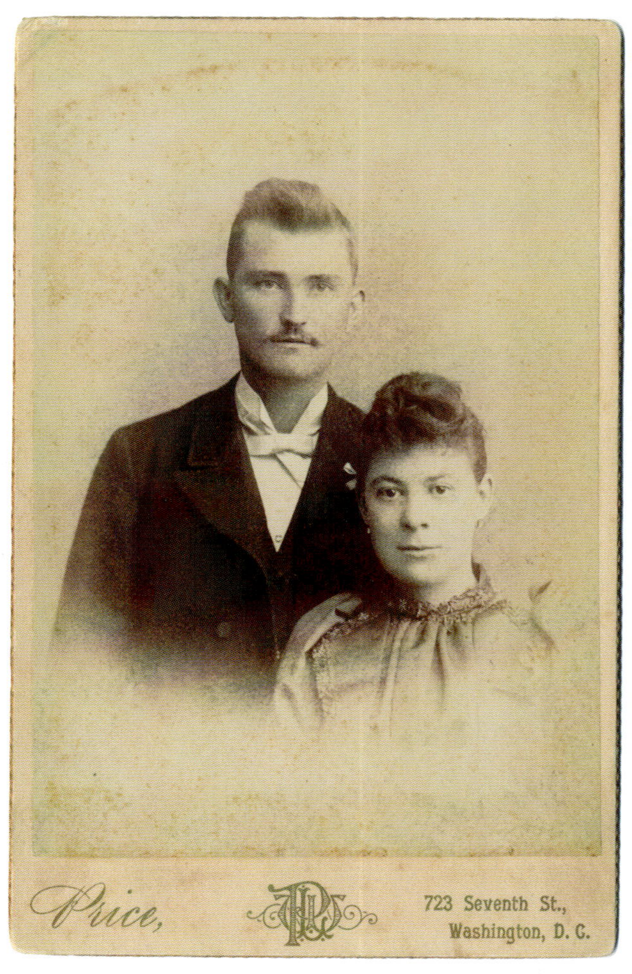

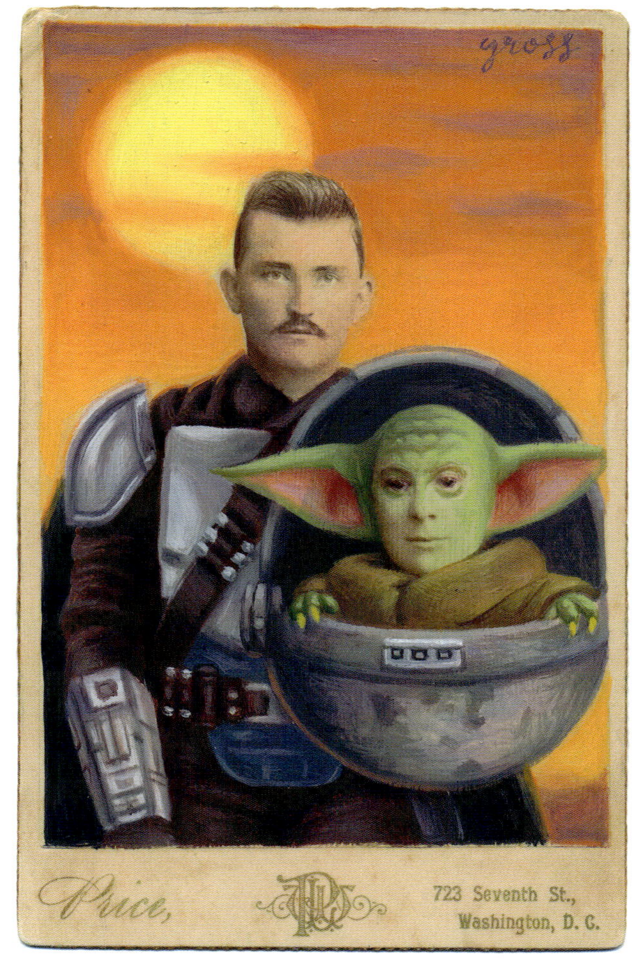
gross
Price,
723 Seventh St.,
Washington, D. C.

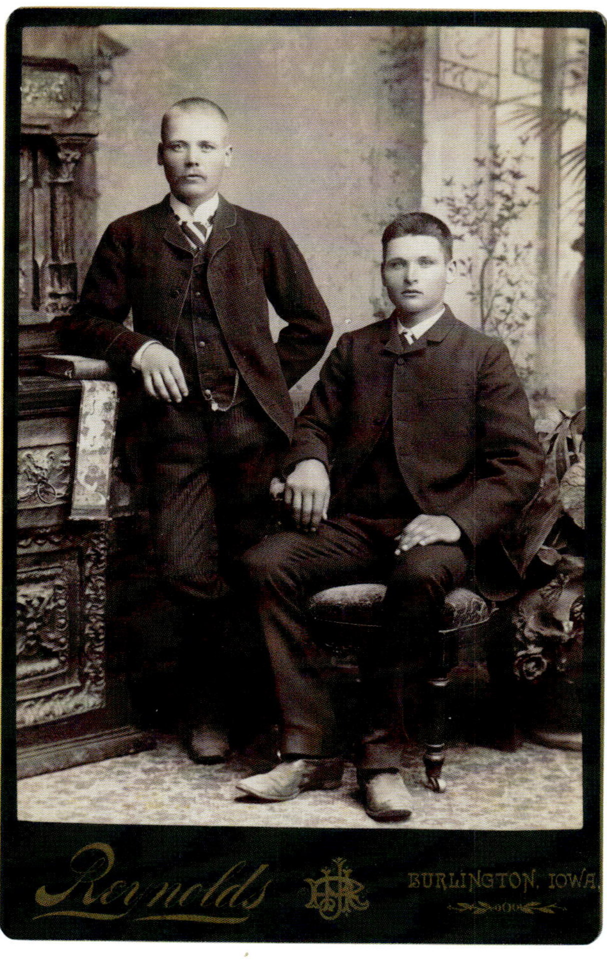
Reynolds
BURLINGTON. IOWA.

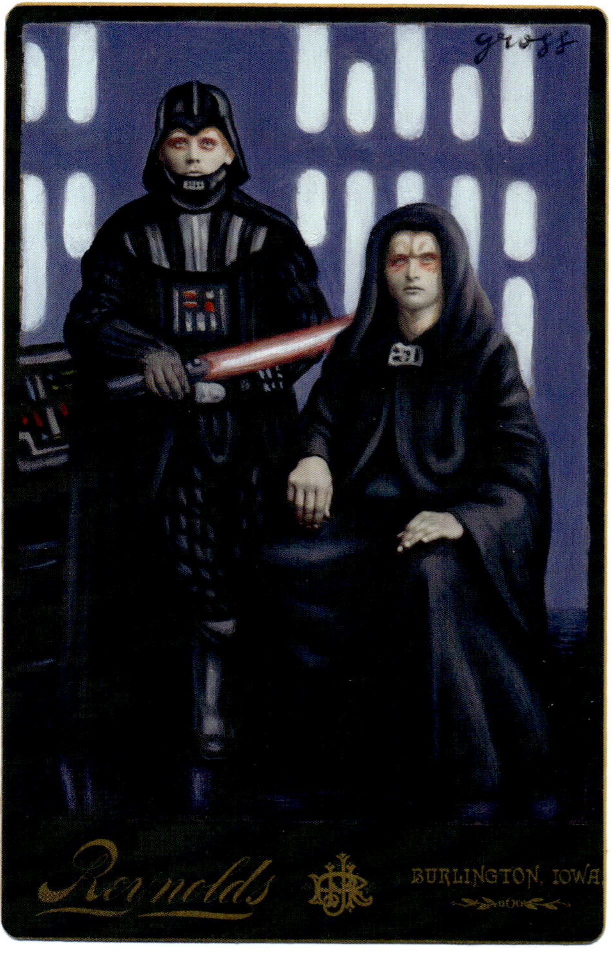
gross
Reynolds
BURLINGTON. IOWA.

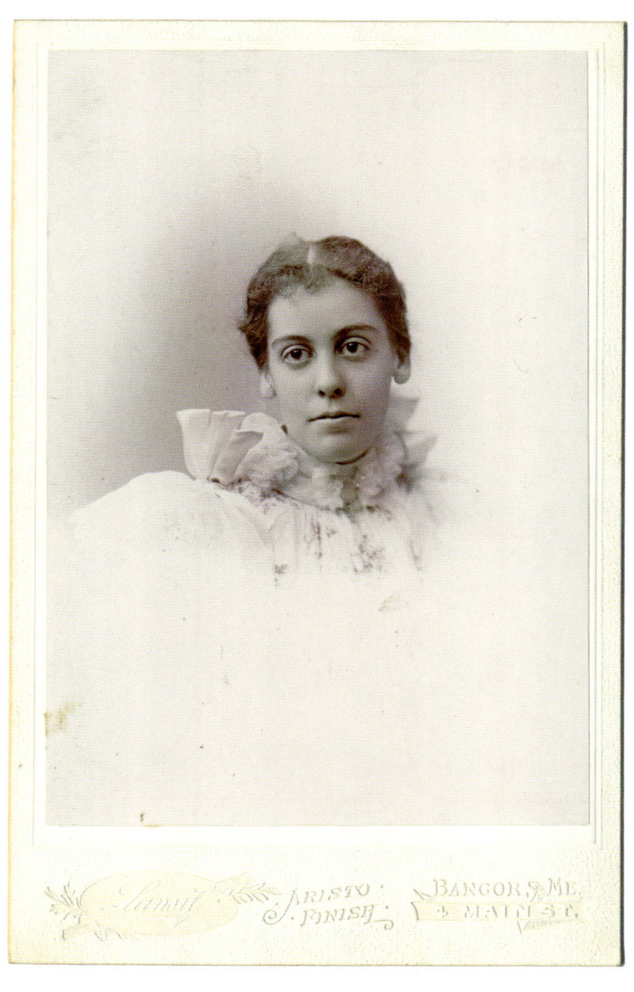
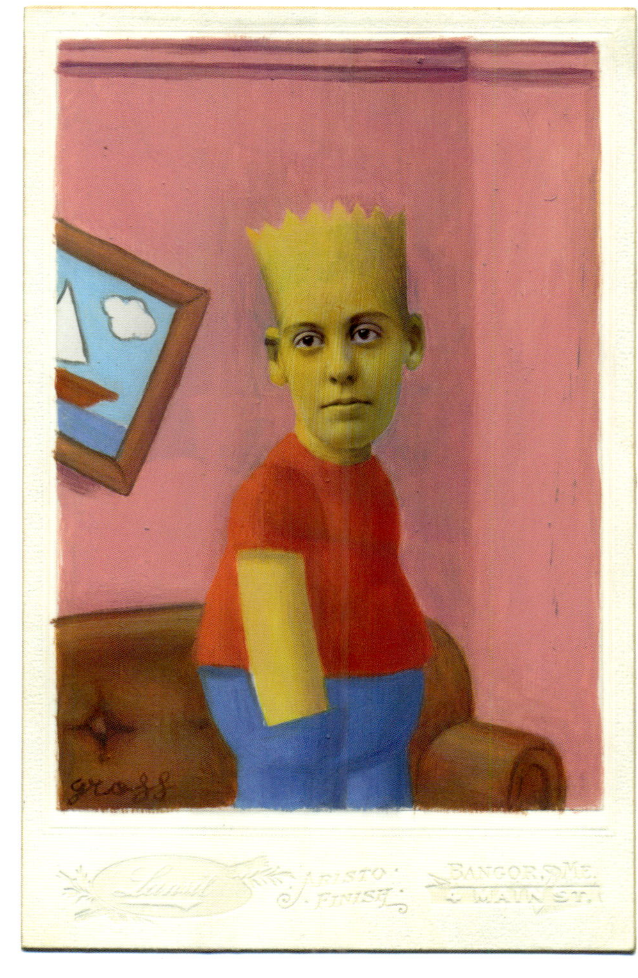

gross

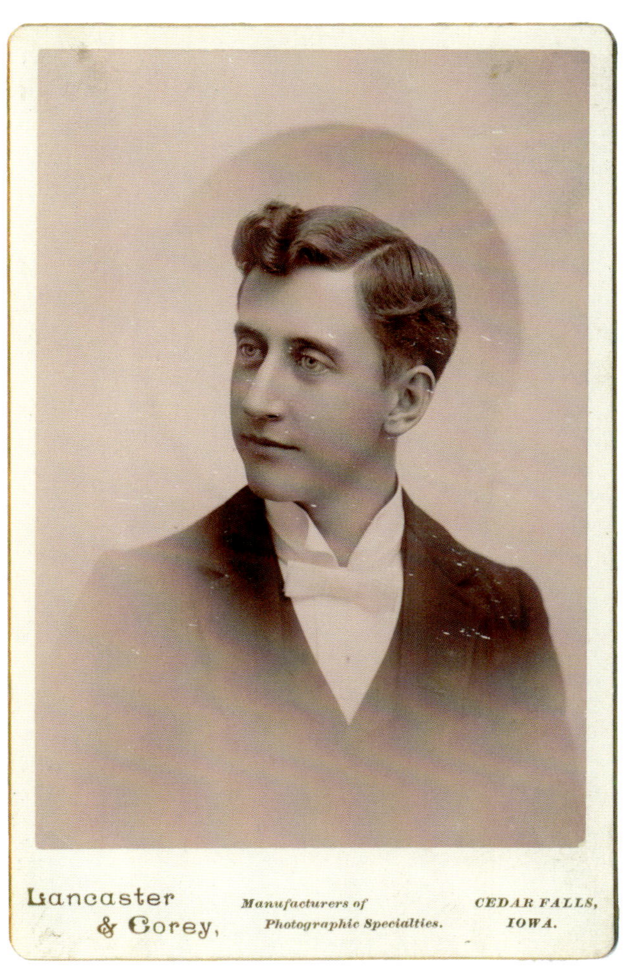

Lancaster
& Corey,
Manufacturers of
Photographic Specialties.
CEDAR FALLS,
IOWA.

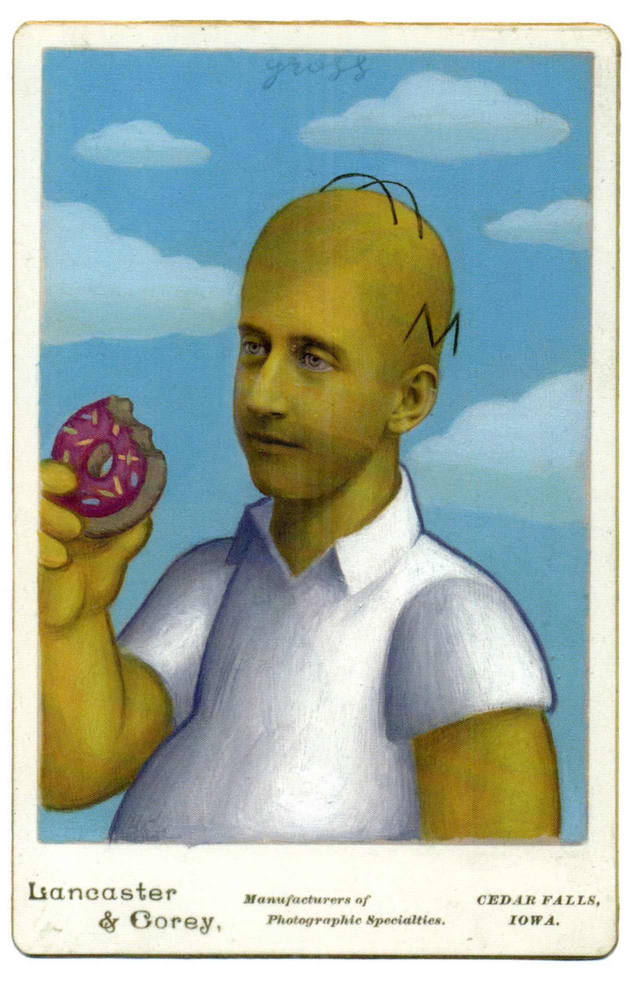

gross
Lancaster
& Corey,
Manufacturers of
Photographic Specialties.
CEDAR FALLS,
IOWA.

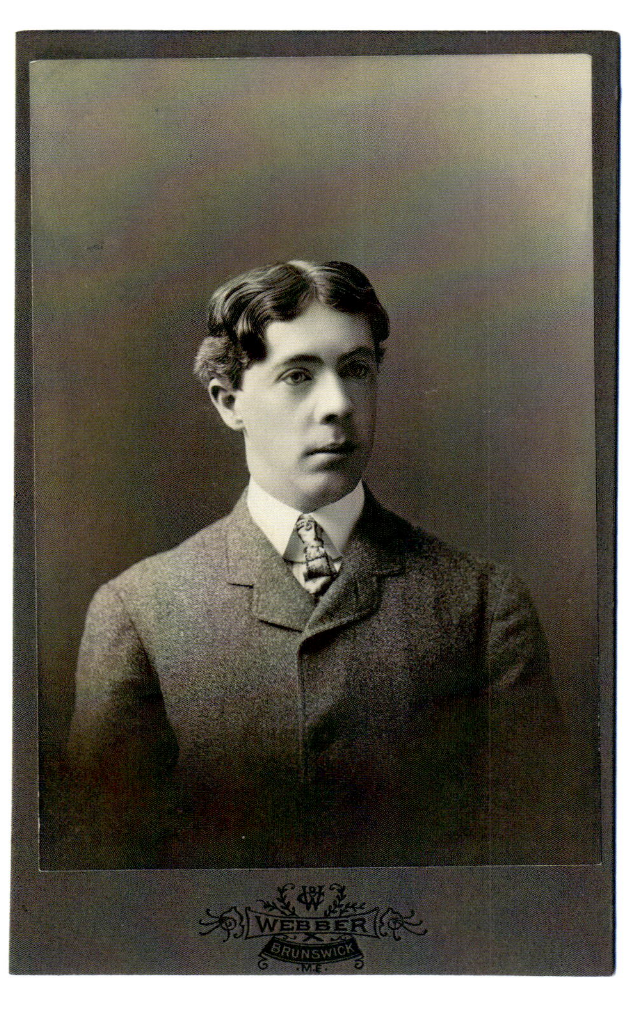
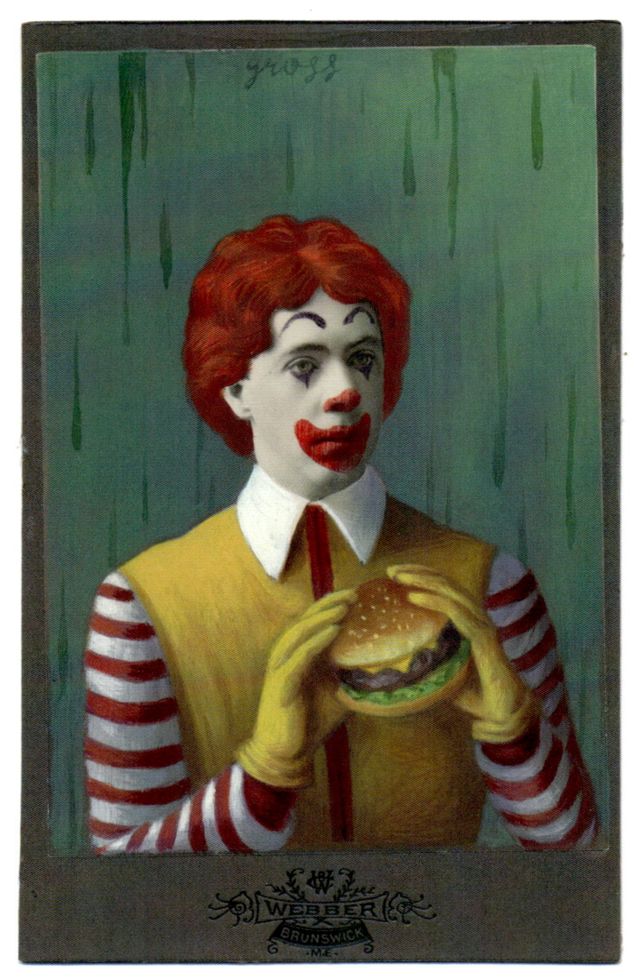
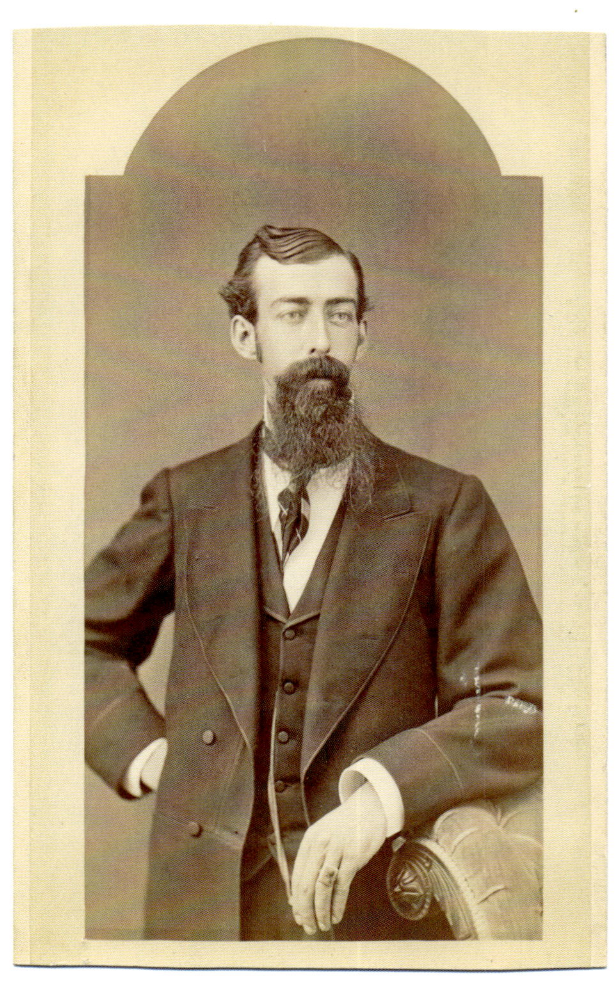
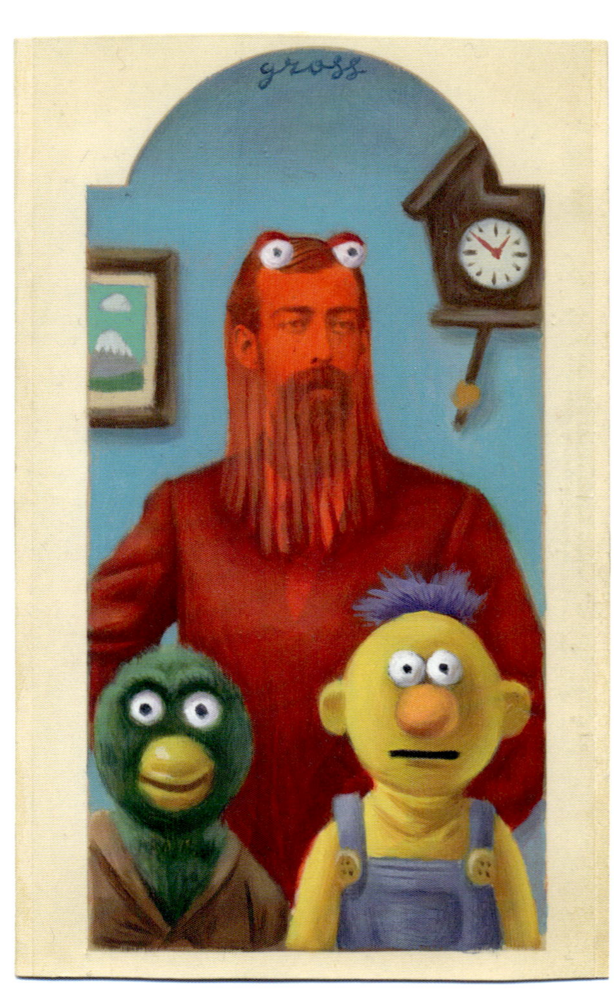

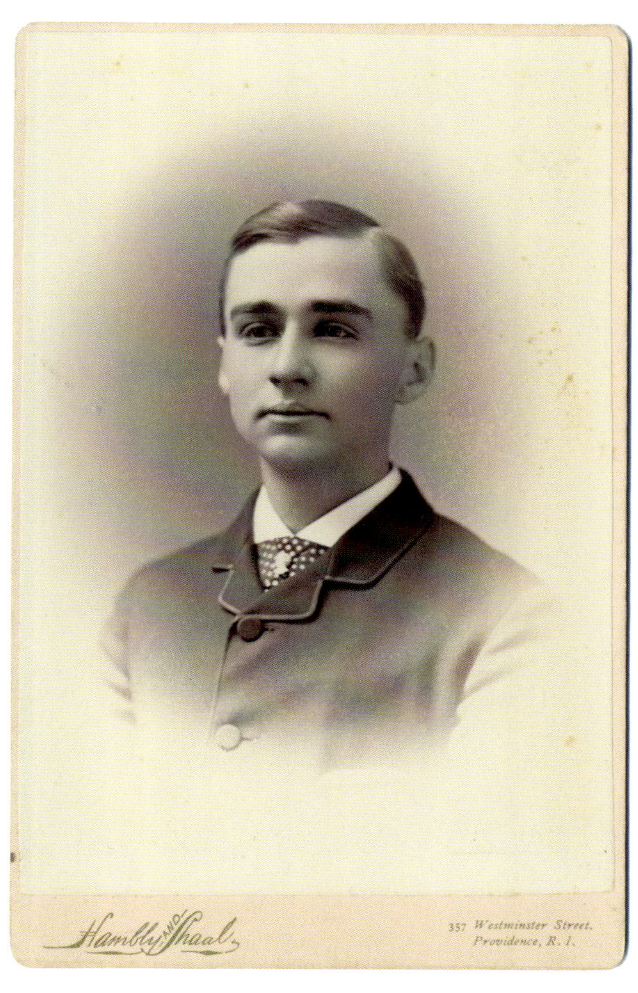
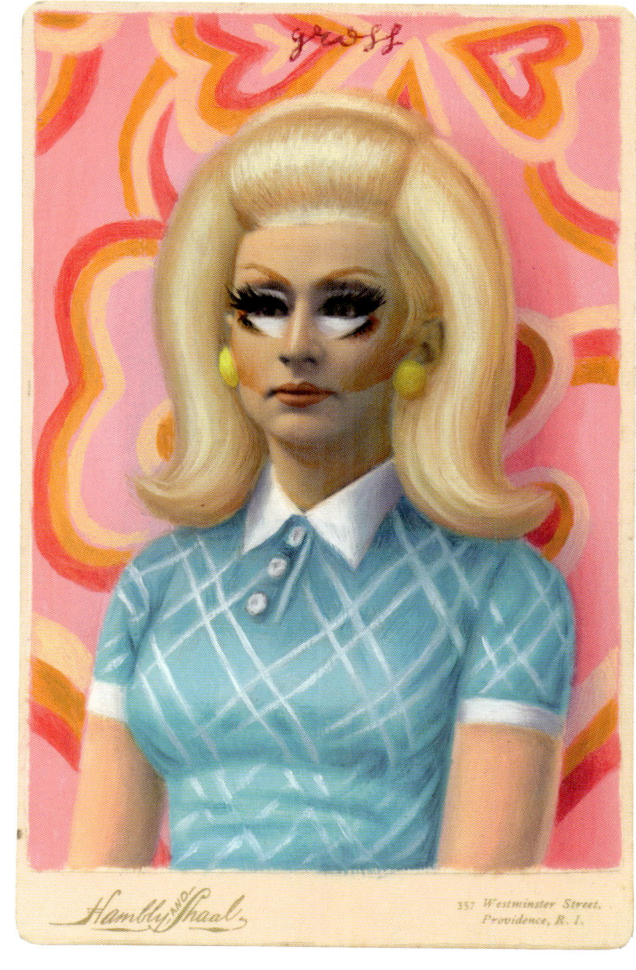

gross

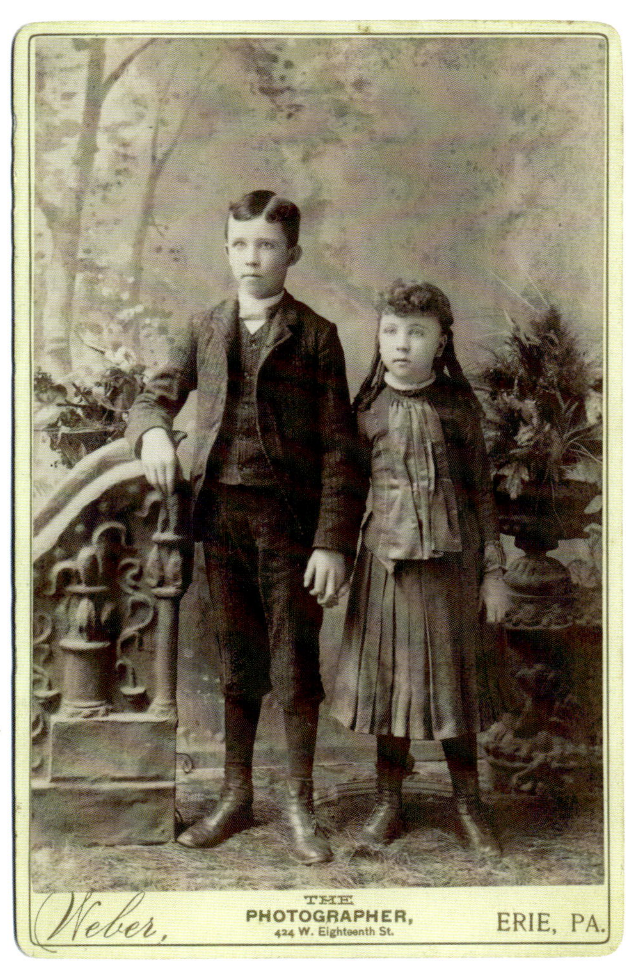
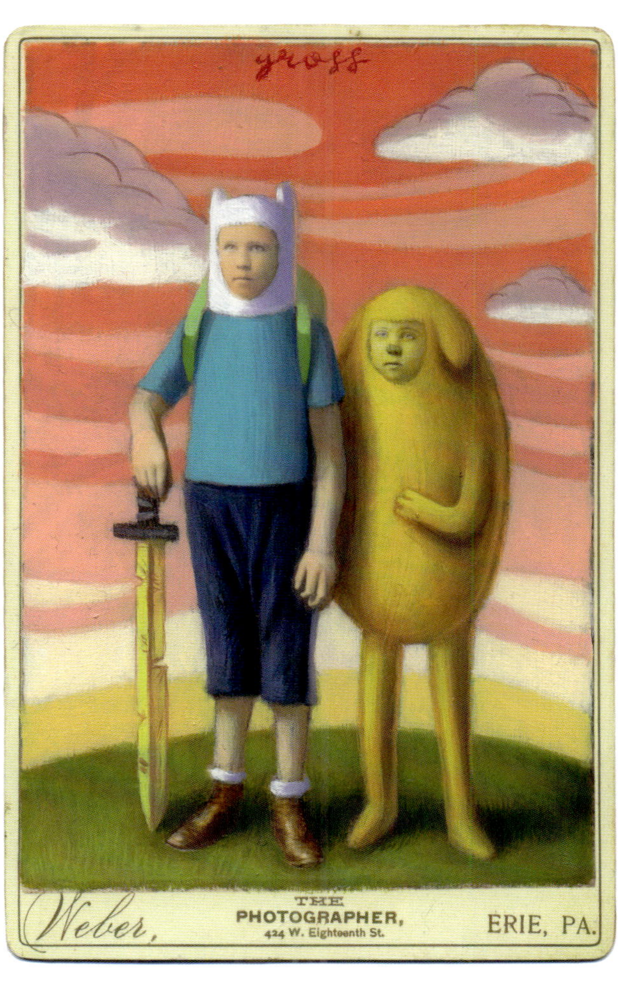

gross

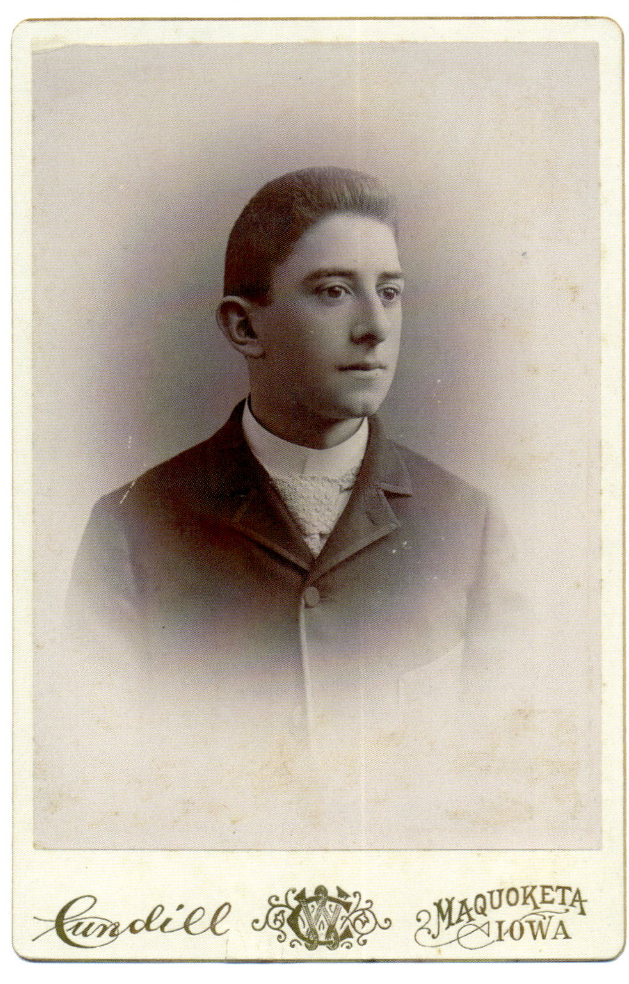
Cundill
MAQUOKETA
IOWA

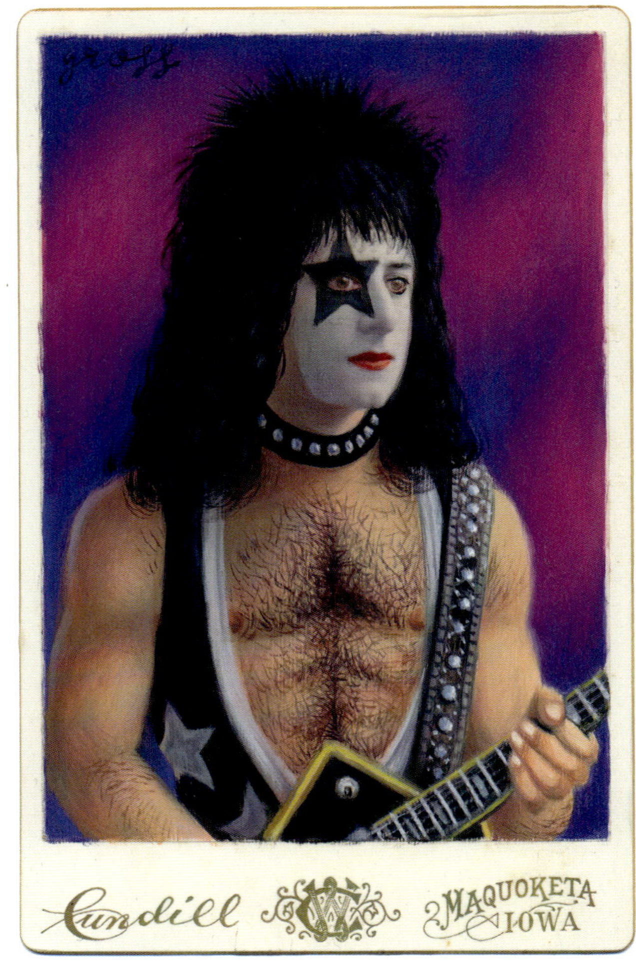
Cundill
MAQUOKETA
IOWA

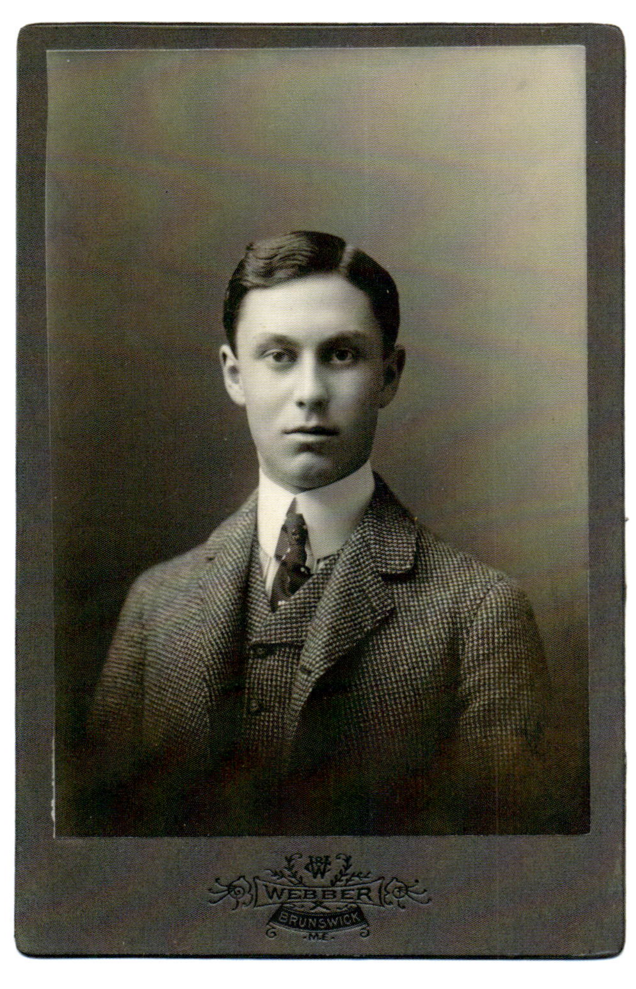
WEBBER
BRUNSWICK
ME.

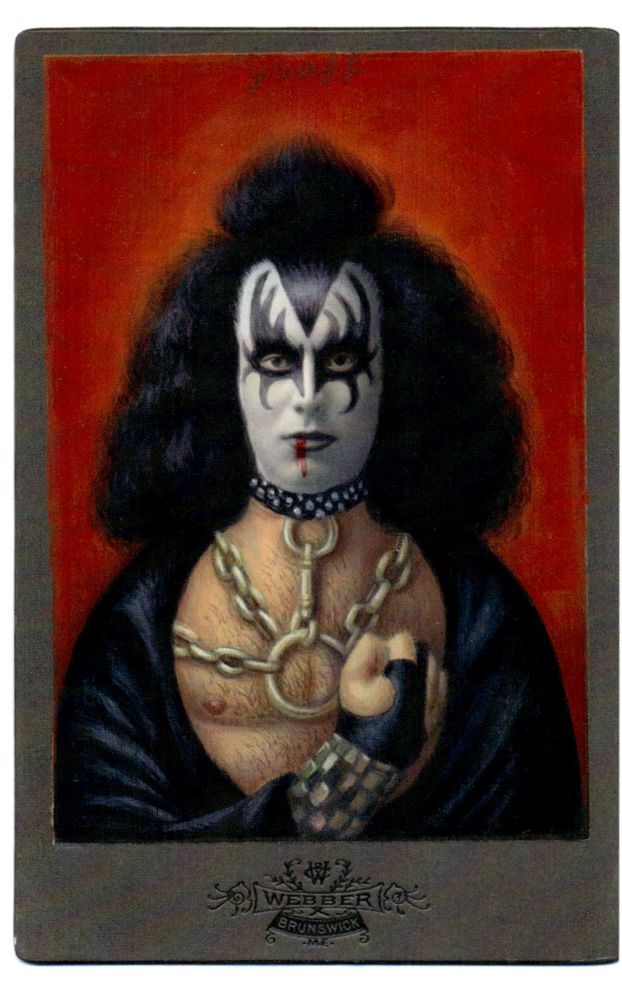
WEBBER
BRUNSWICK
ME.

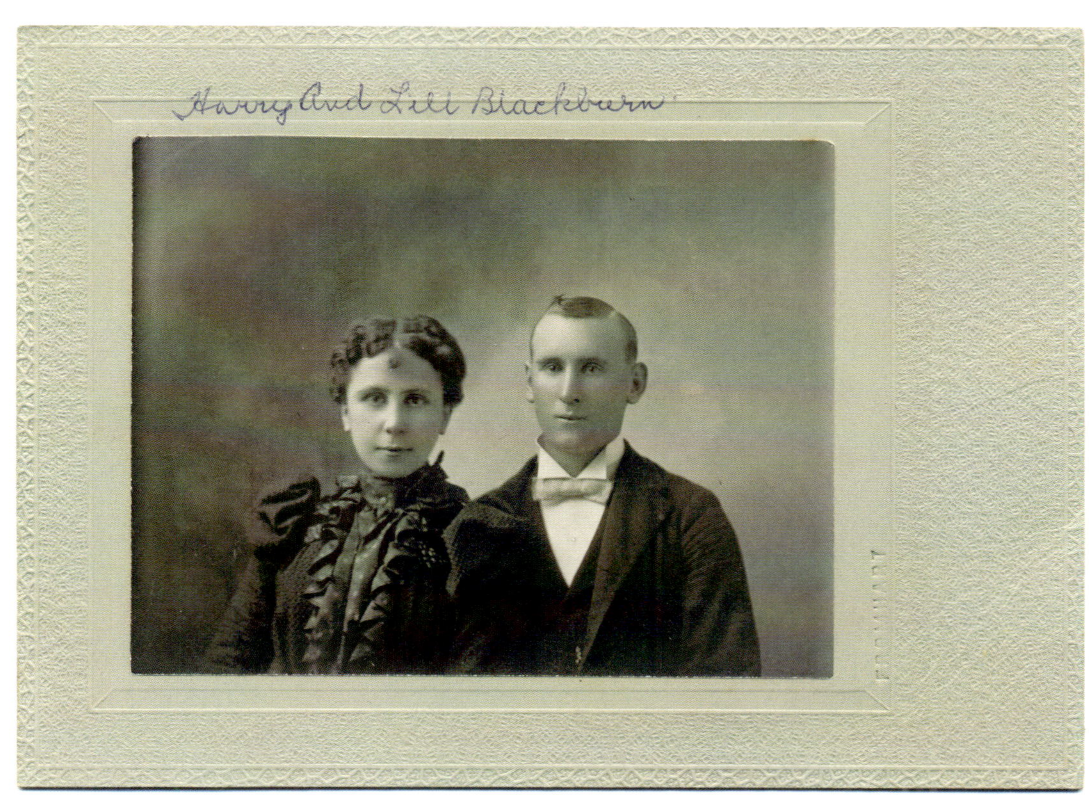

Harry And Lili Blackburn

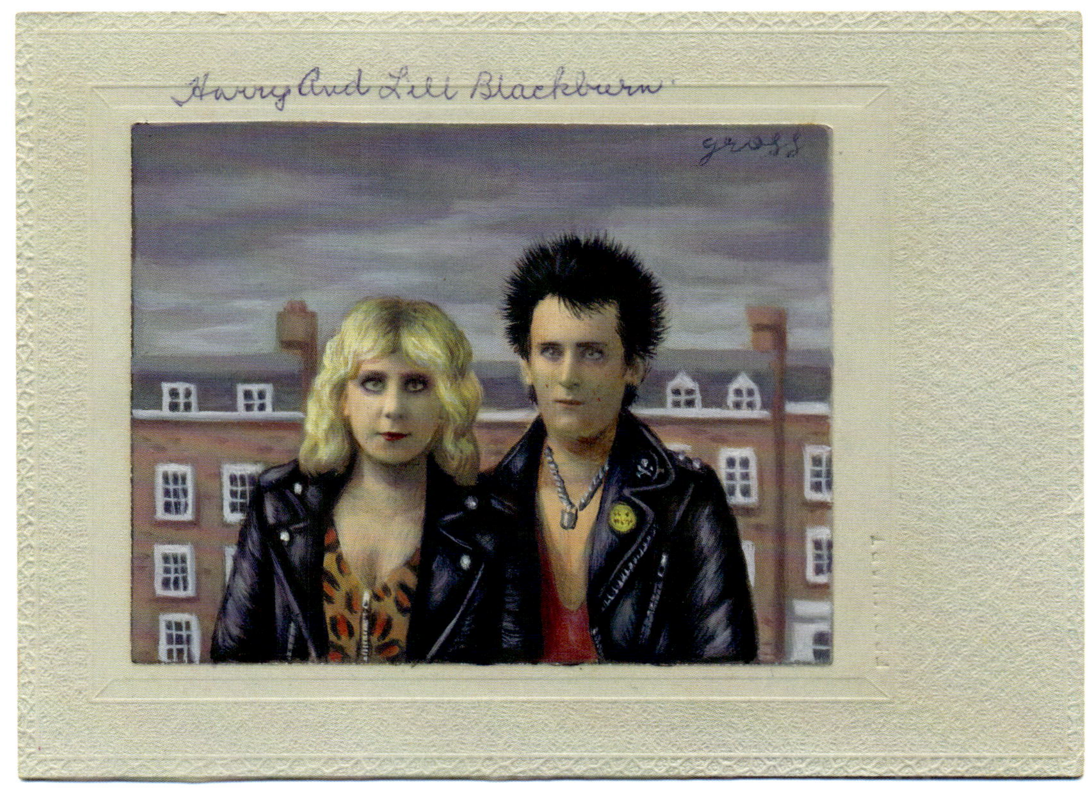

Harry And Lili Blackburn
grogg

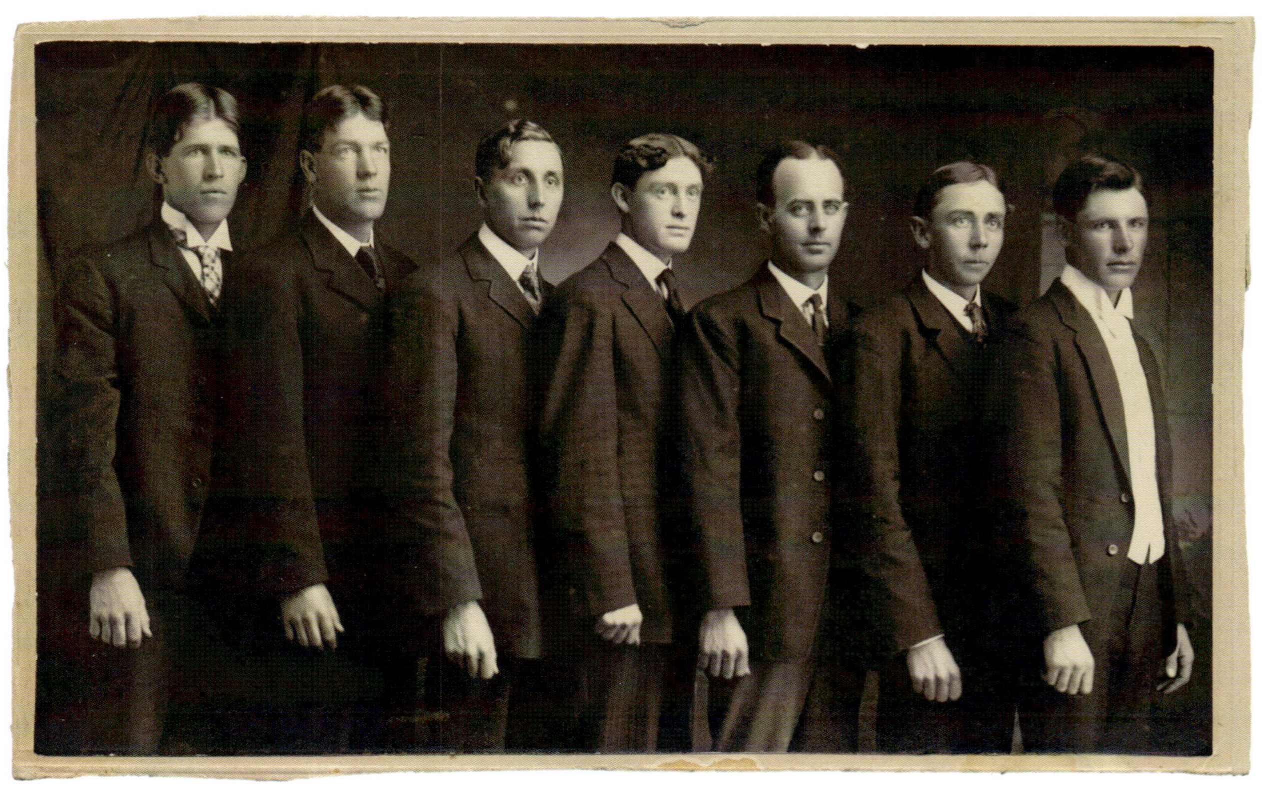

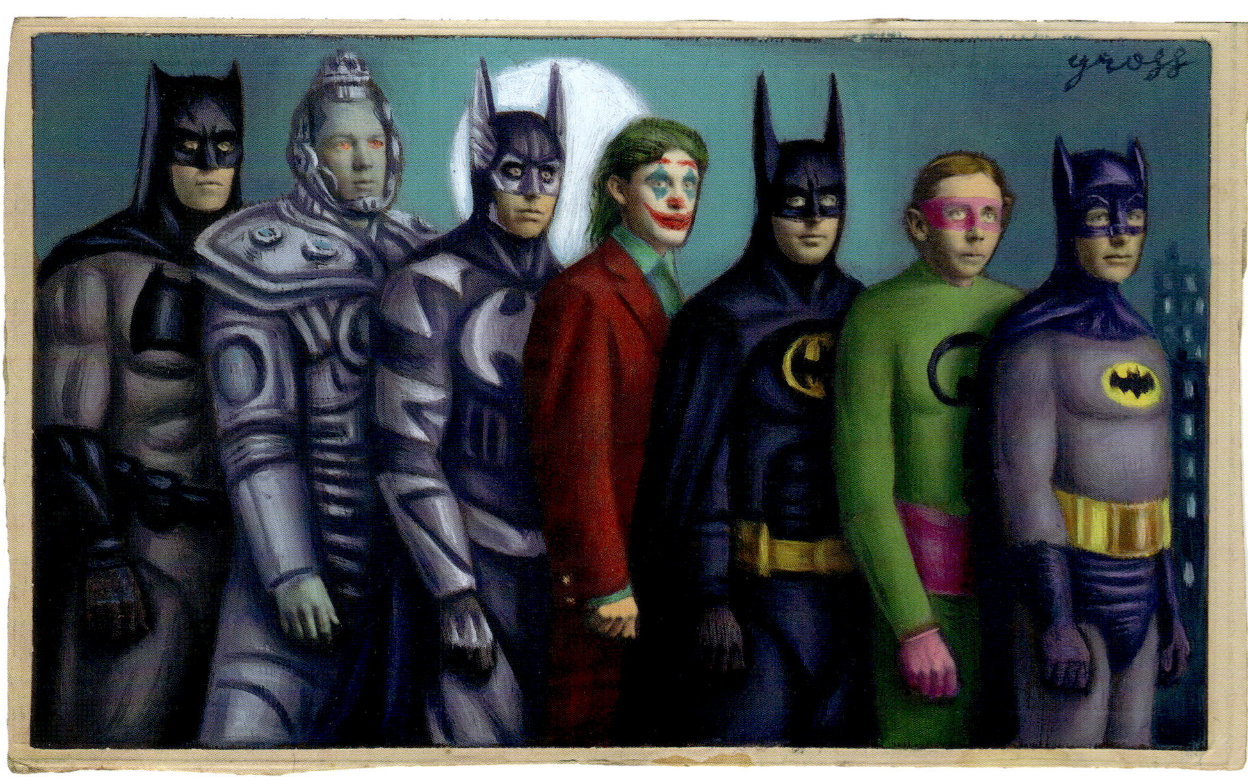
gross

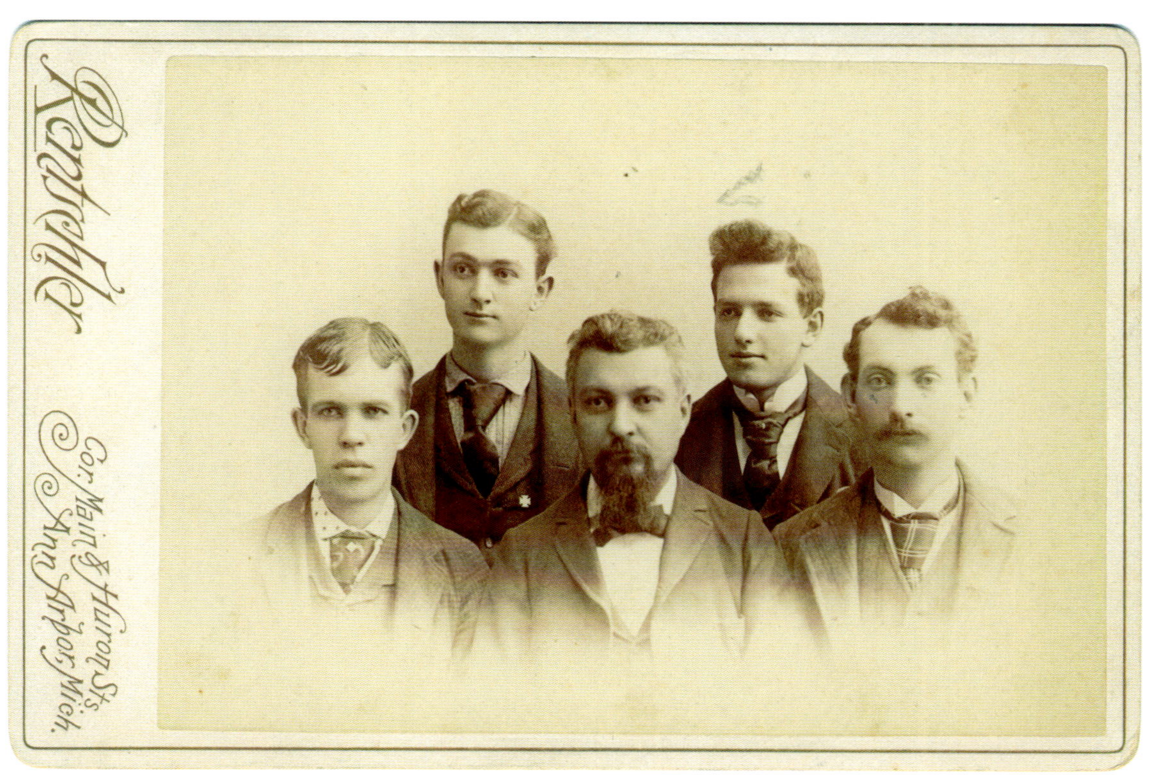

Rentschler
Cor. Main & Huron Sts.
Ann Arbor, Mich.

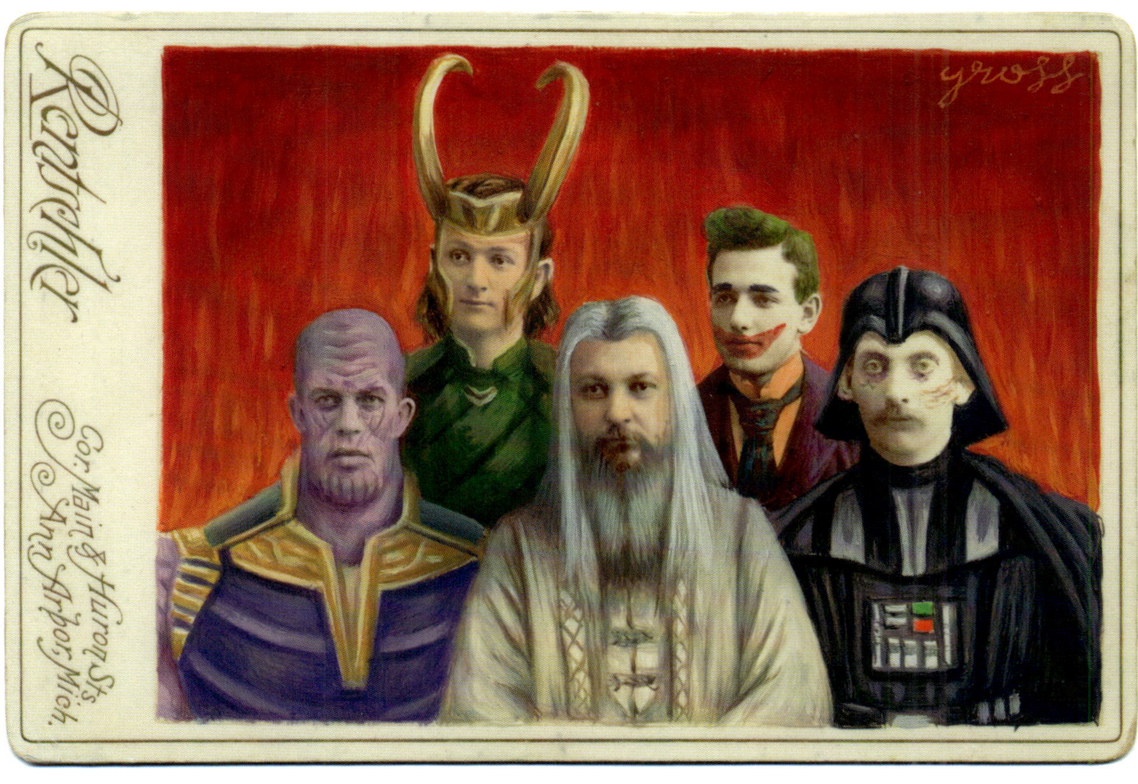

gross
Rentschler
Cor. Main & Huron Sts.
Ann Arbor, Mich.

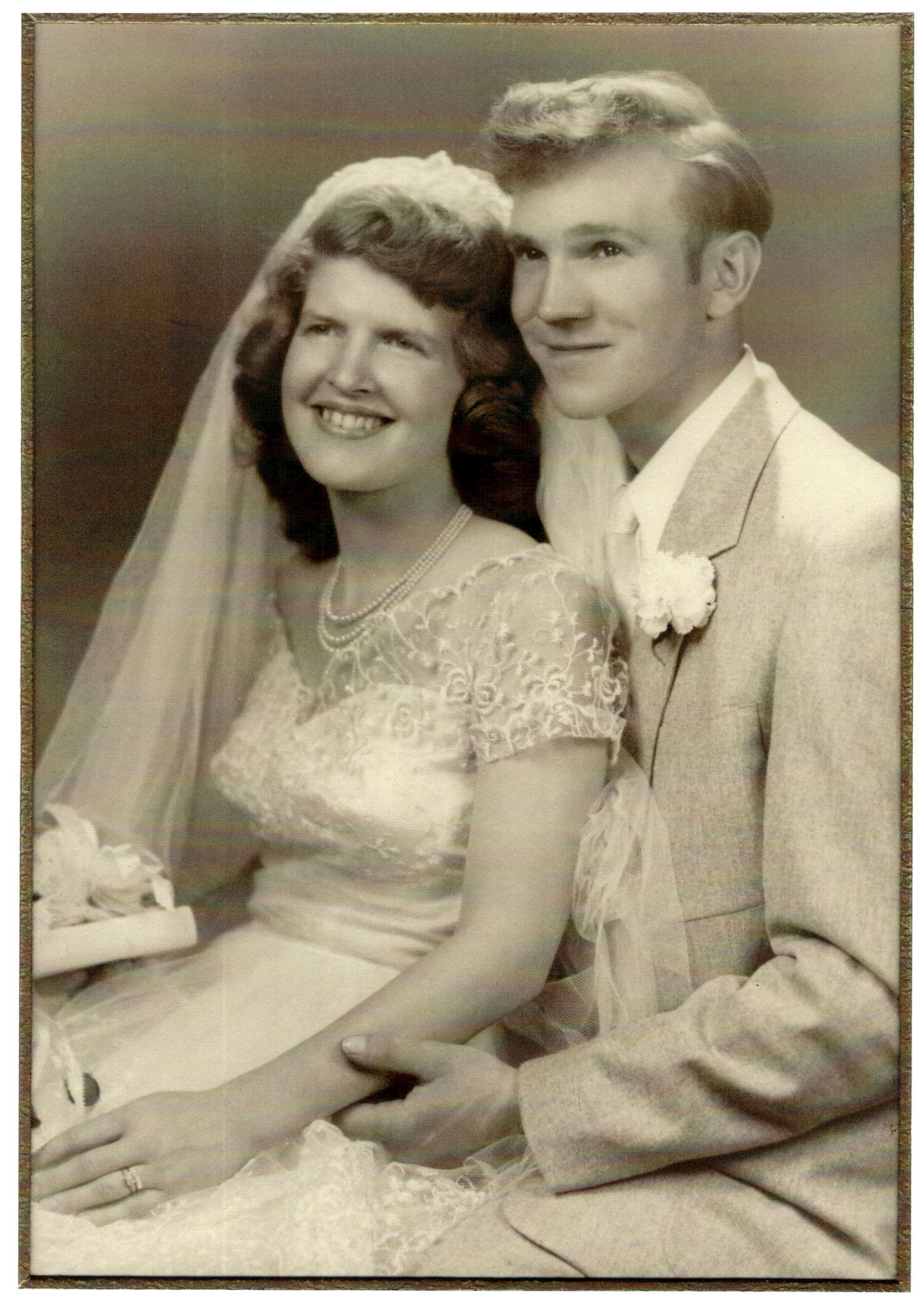

WEDDING JOKERS

Oil and Acrylic on Antique Vintage Photograph / 16.5" x 11.75" / 2021

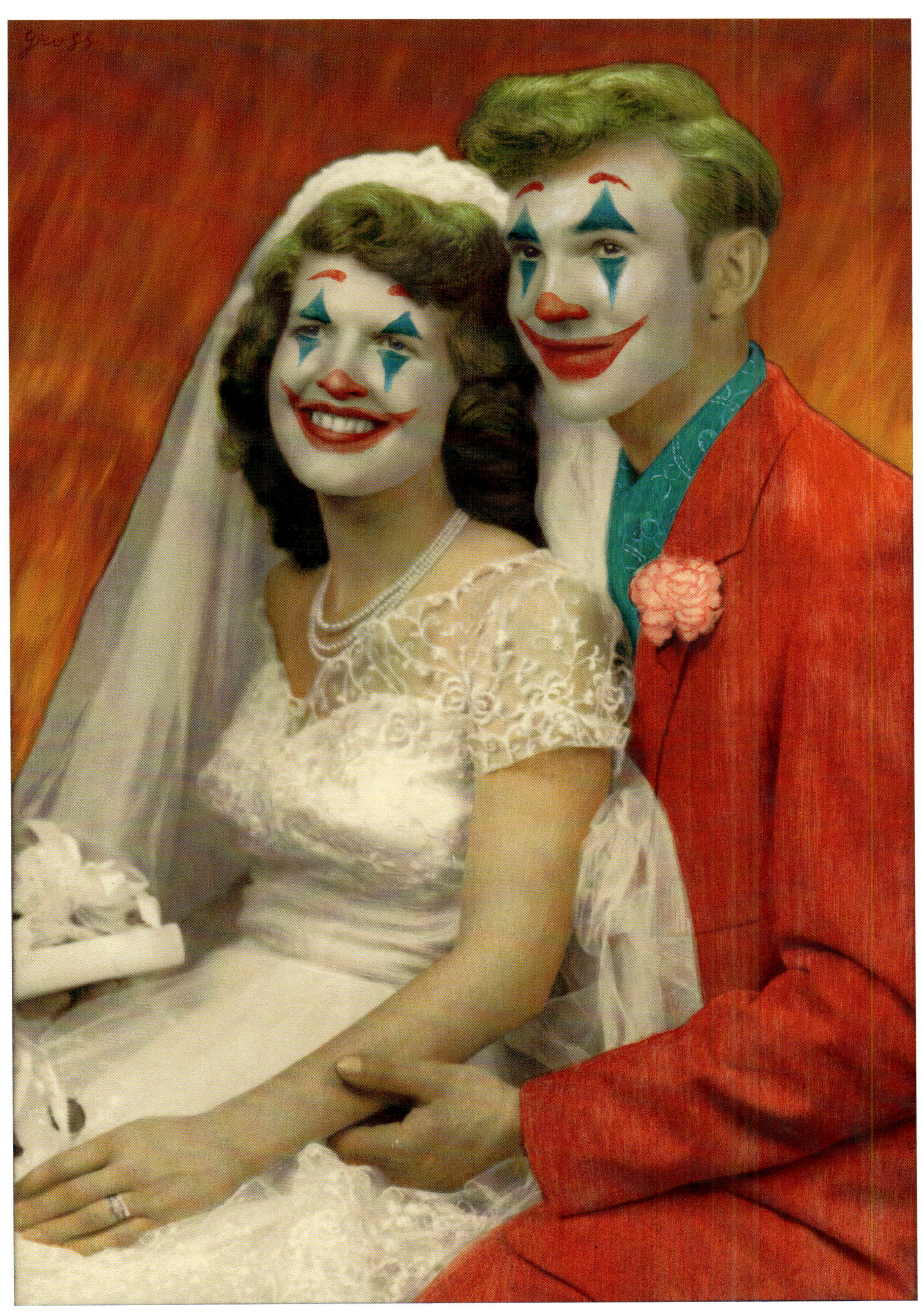

Gross

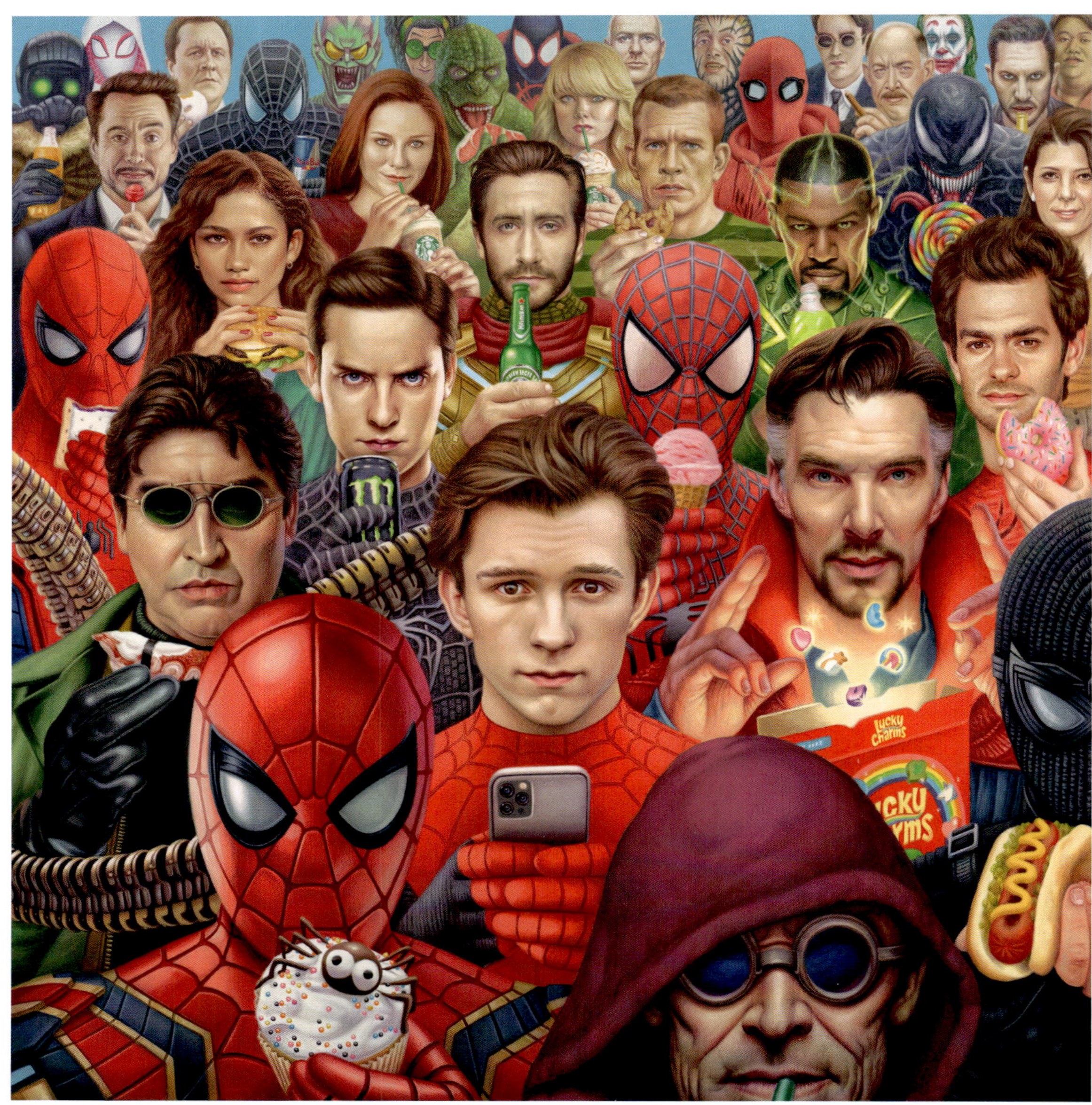

SPIDERVERSE

Oil on Canvas / 33" x 33" / 2022

TRASH

Oil on Canvas / 36" x 30" / 2019

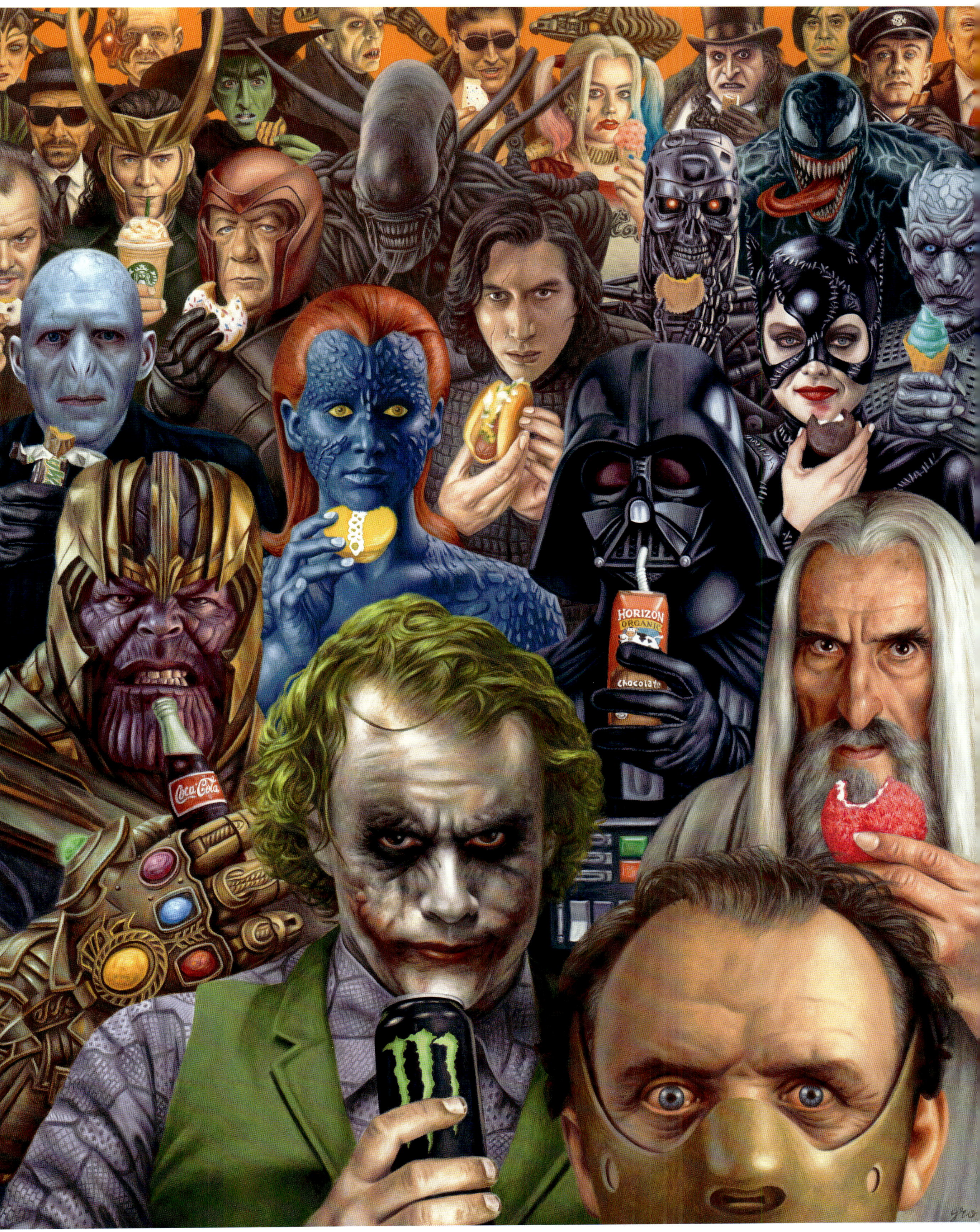

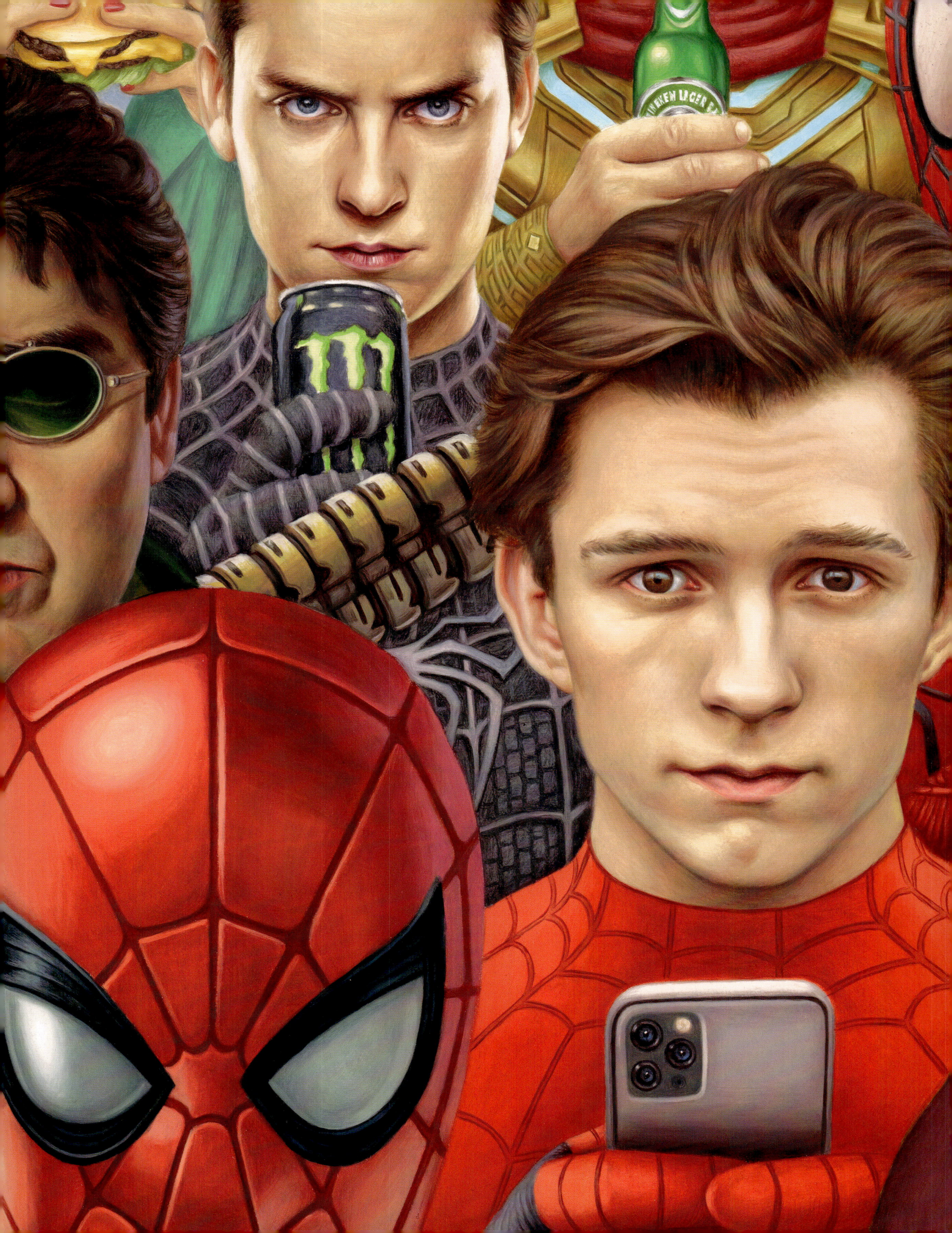

HEINEKEN LAGER

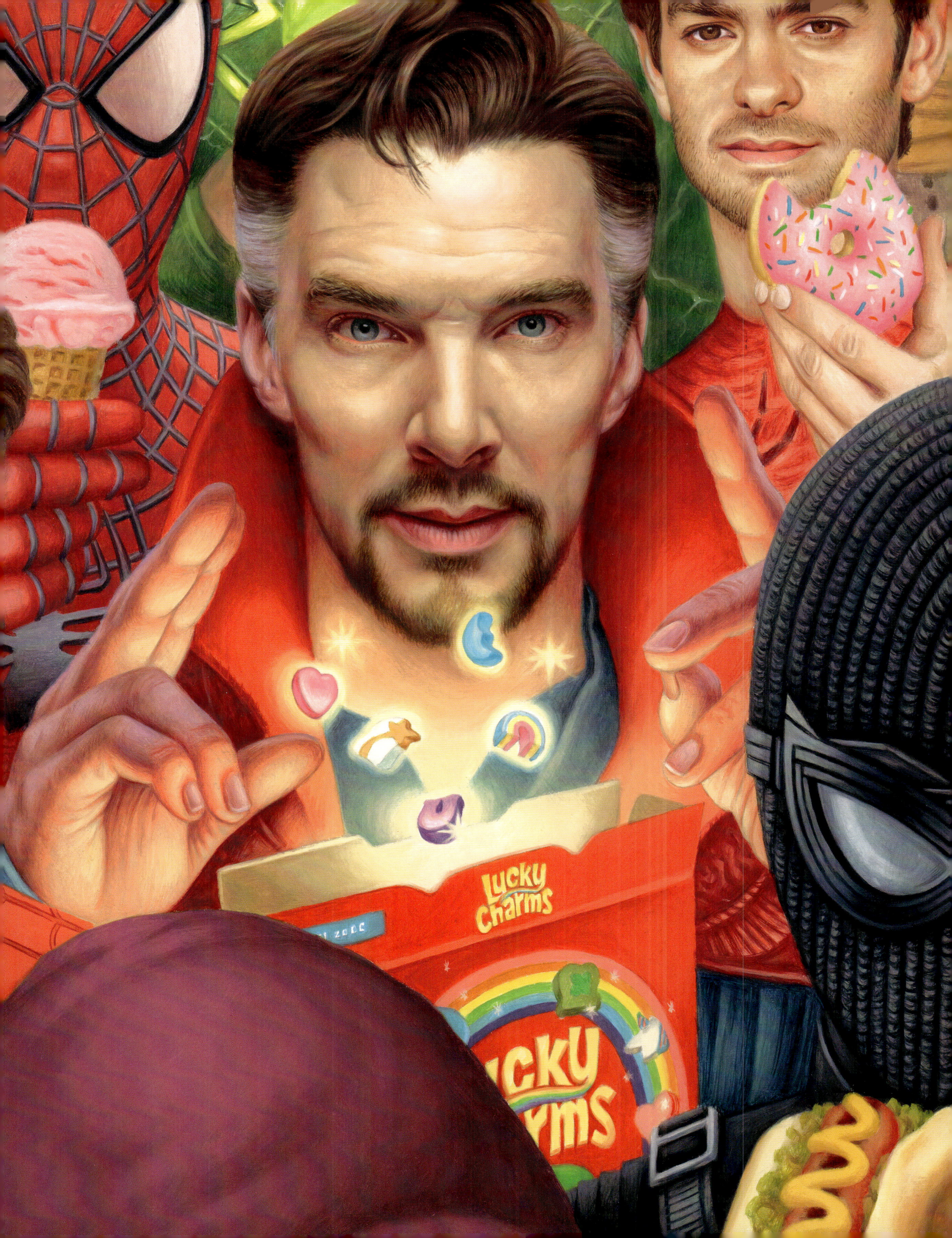

Lucky Charms
Lucky Charms

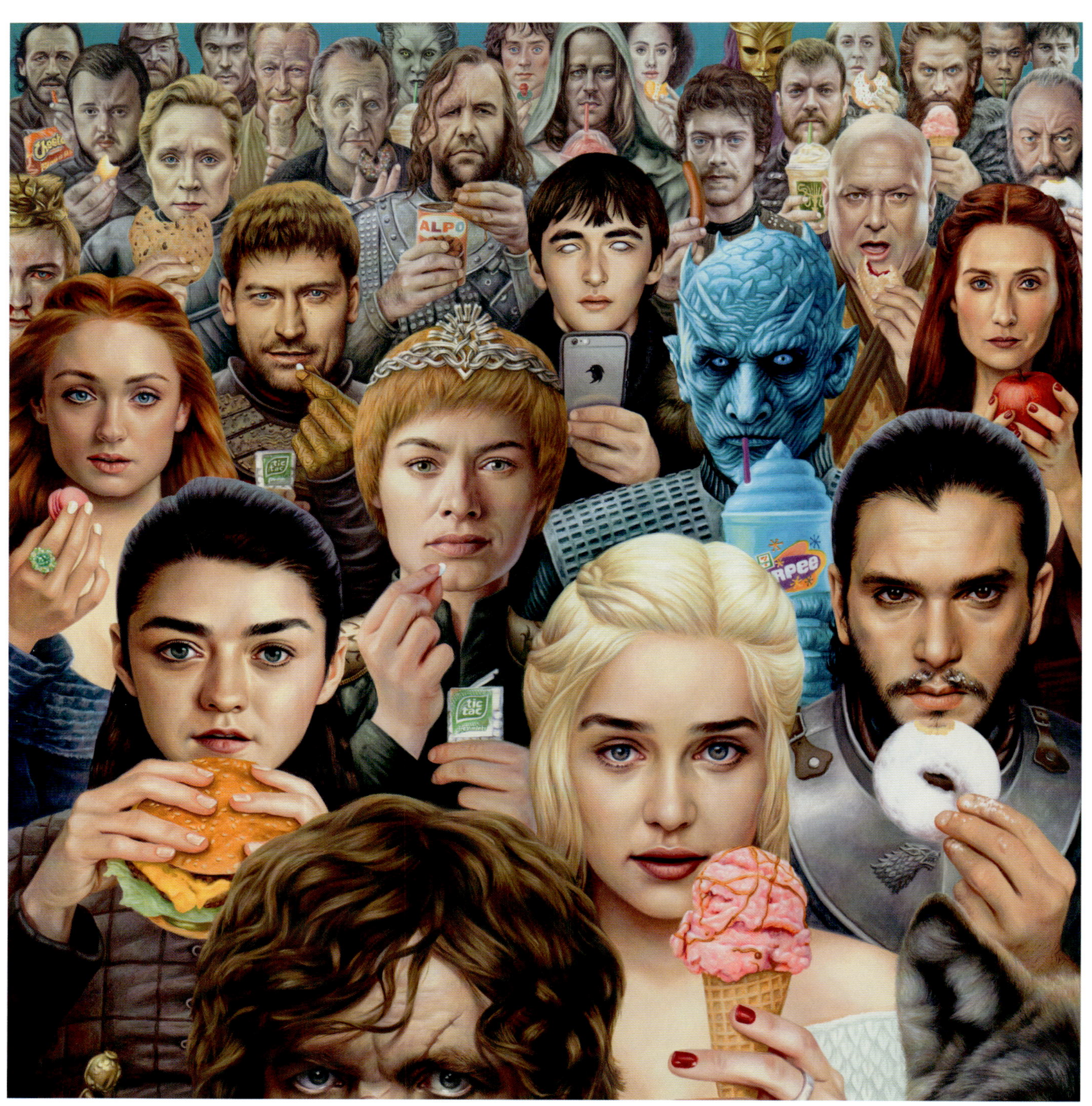

OBSESSION

Oil on Canvas / 42" x 42" / 2019

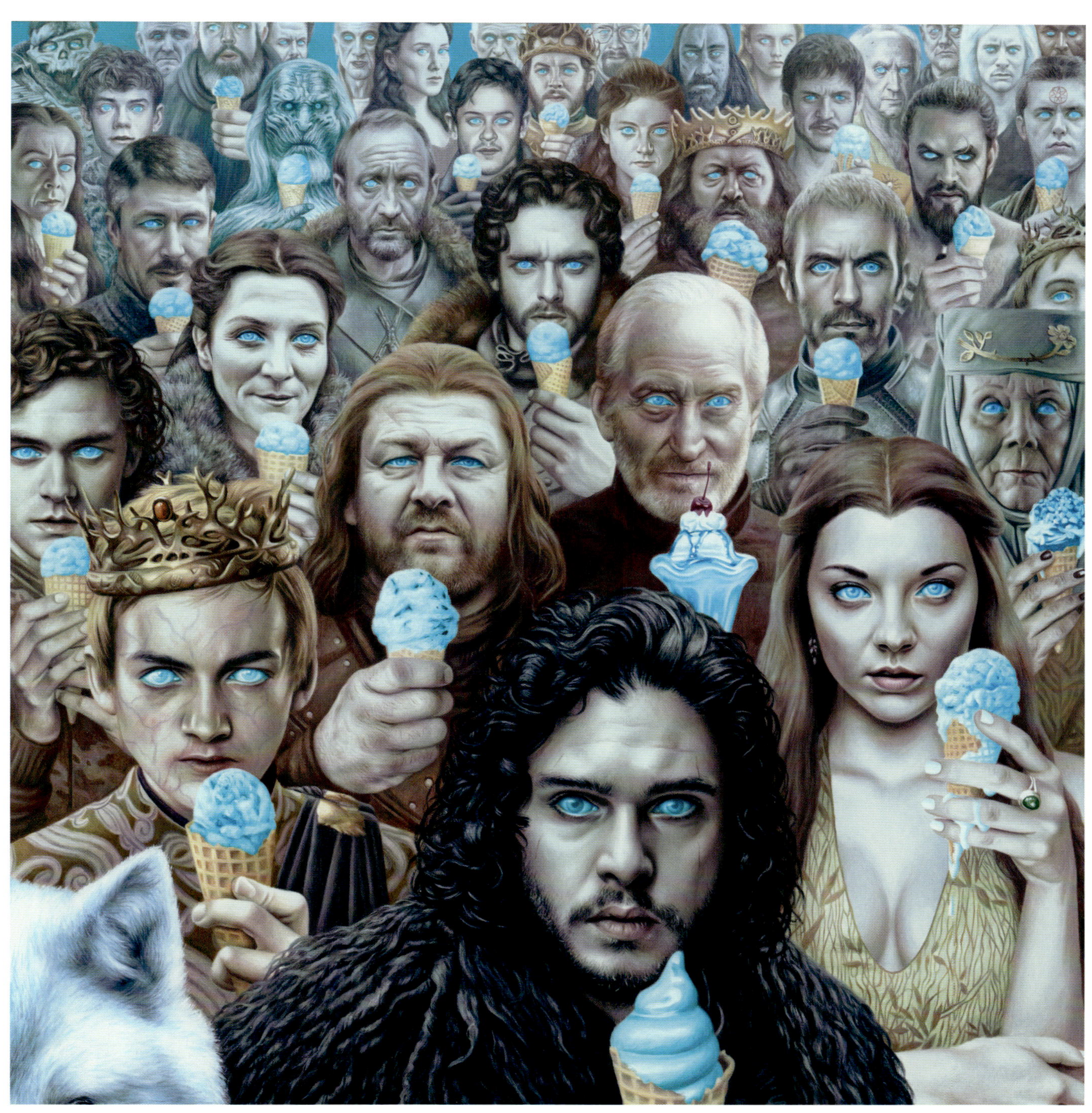

VALAR MORGHULIS

Oil on Canvas / 36" x 36" / 2019

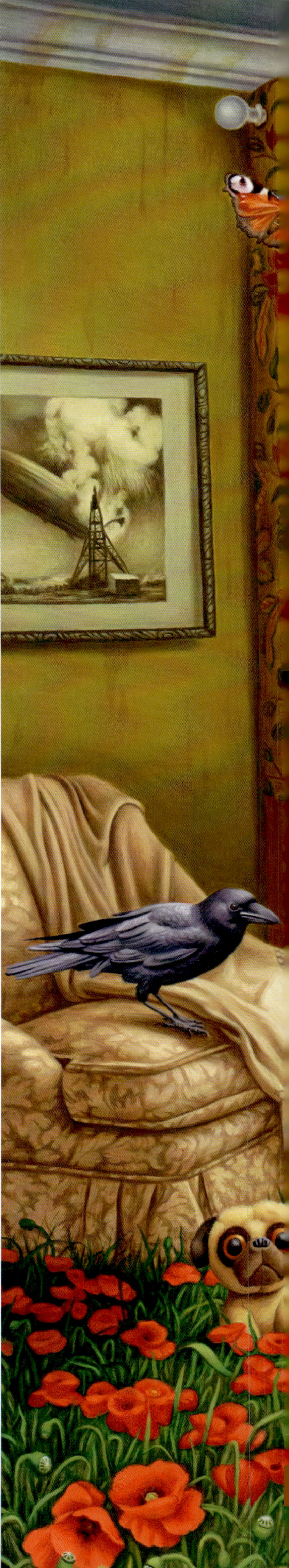

PRISON OF THE MIND II

Oil on Canvas / 36" x 36" / 2022

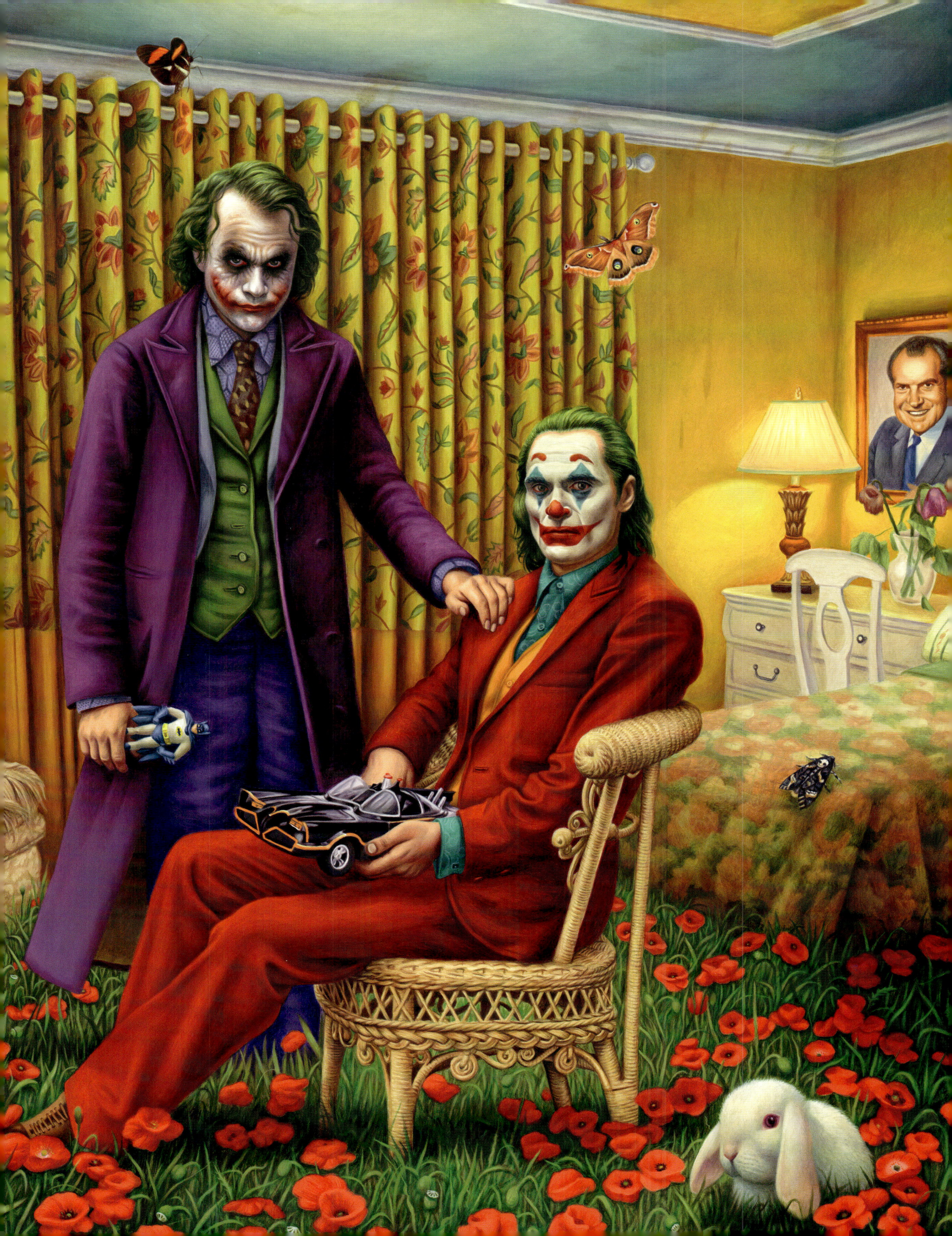

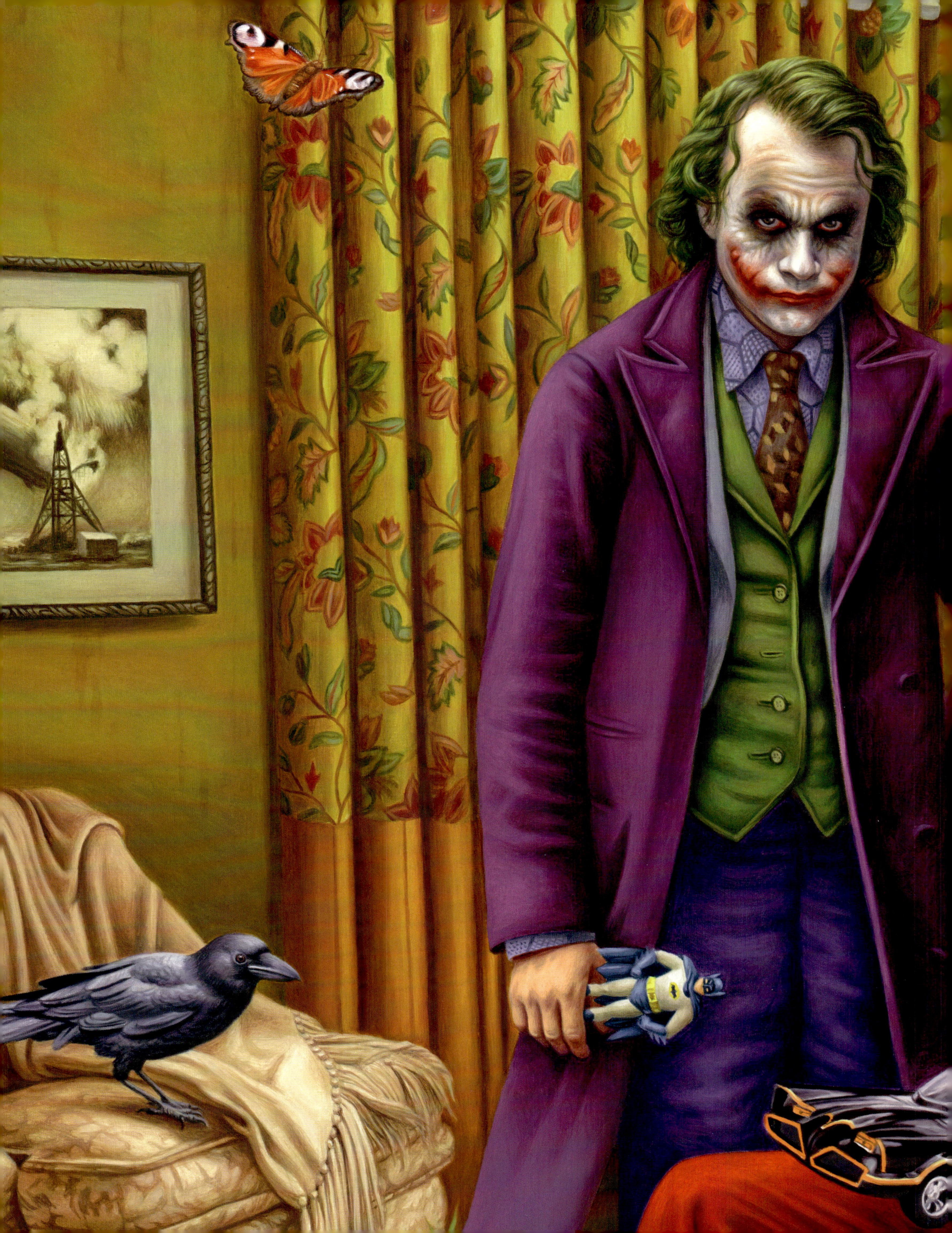

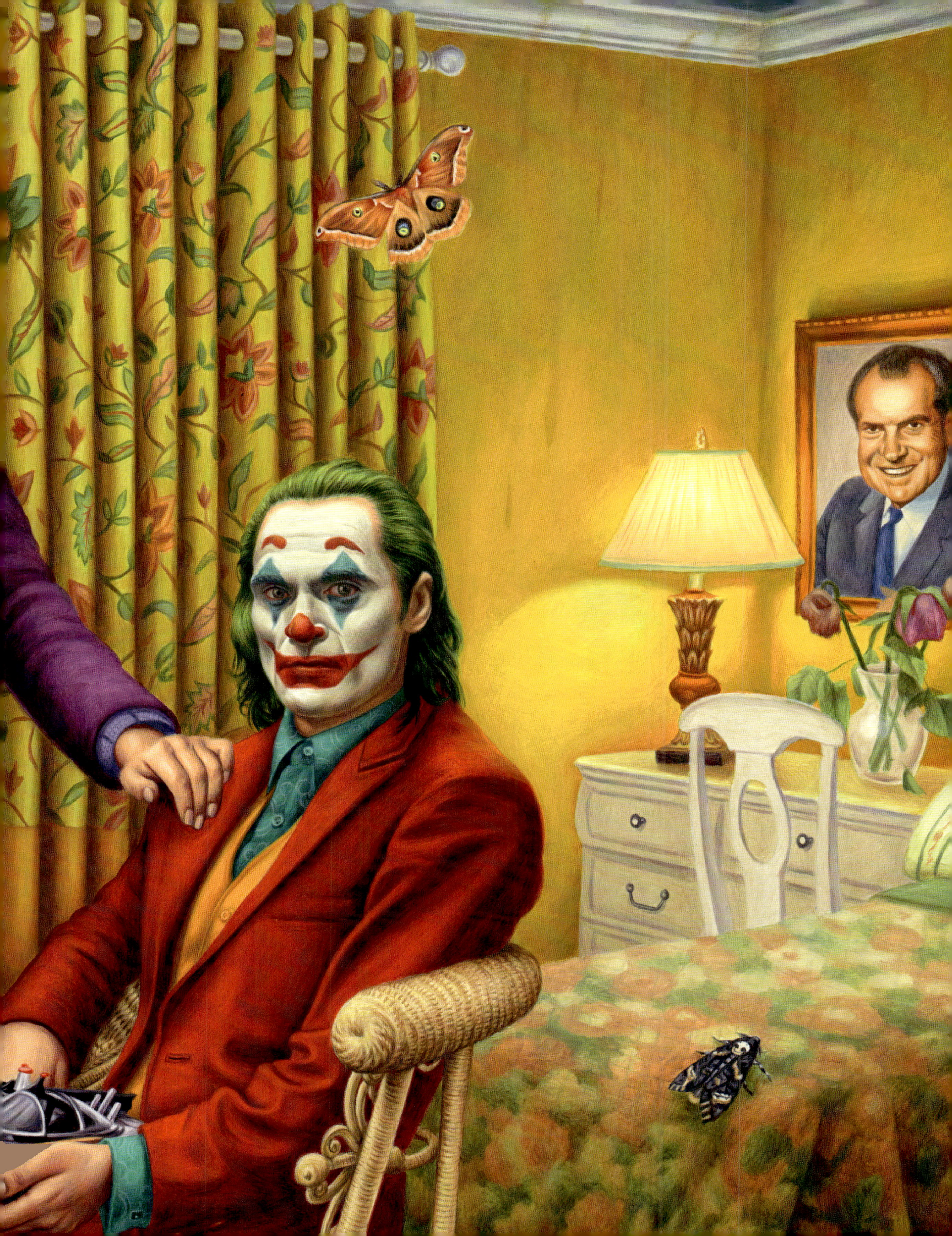

BATMANIA
Oil on Canvas / 36" x 36" / 2022

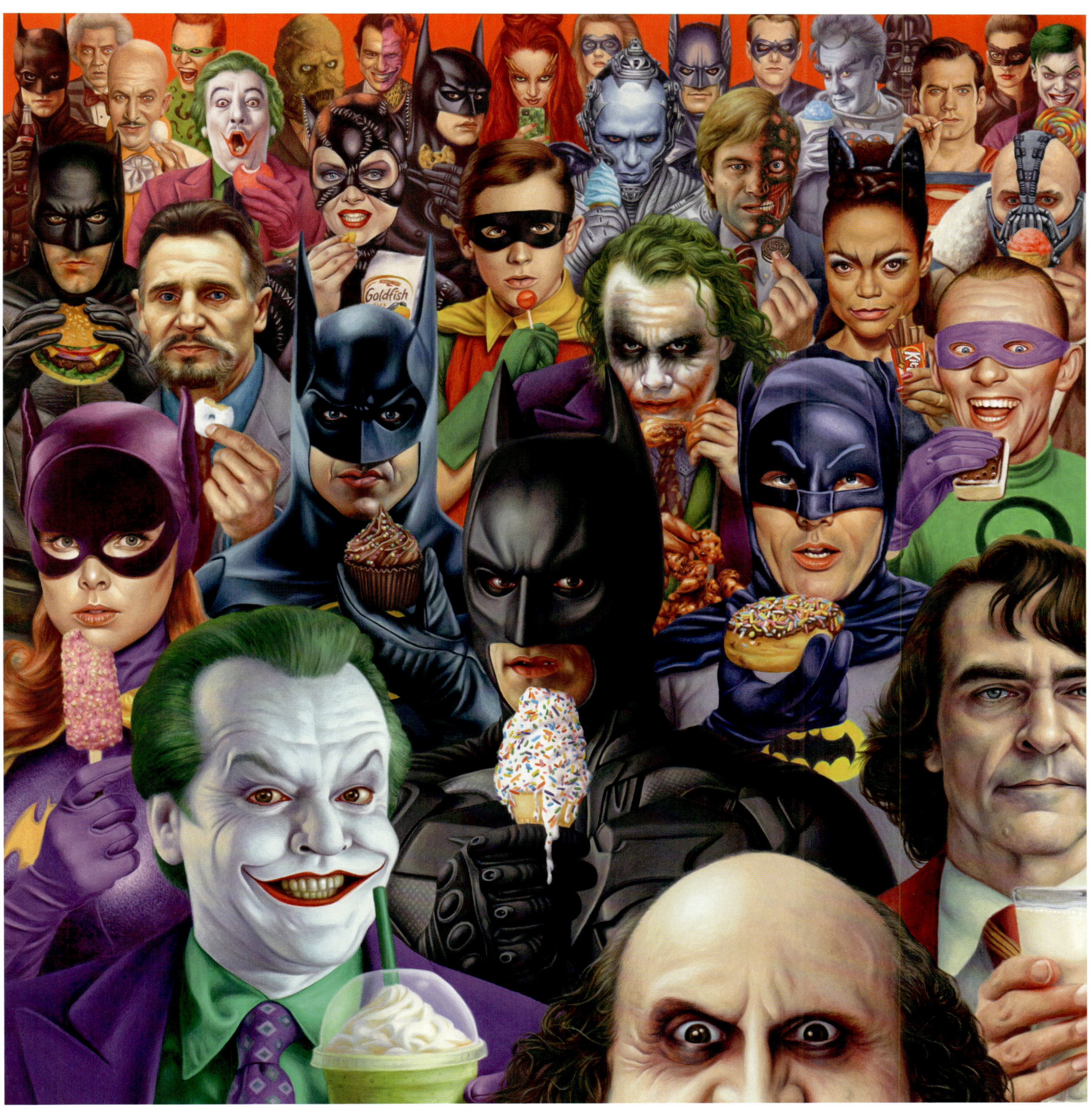

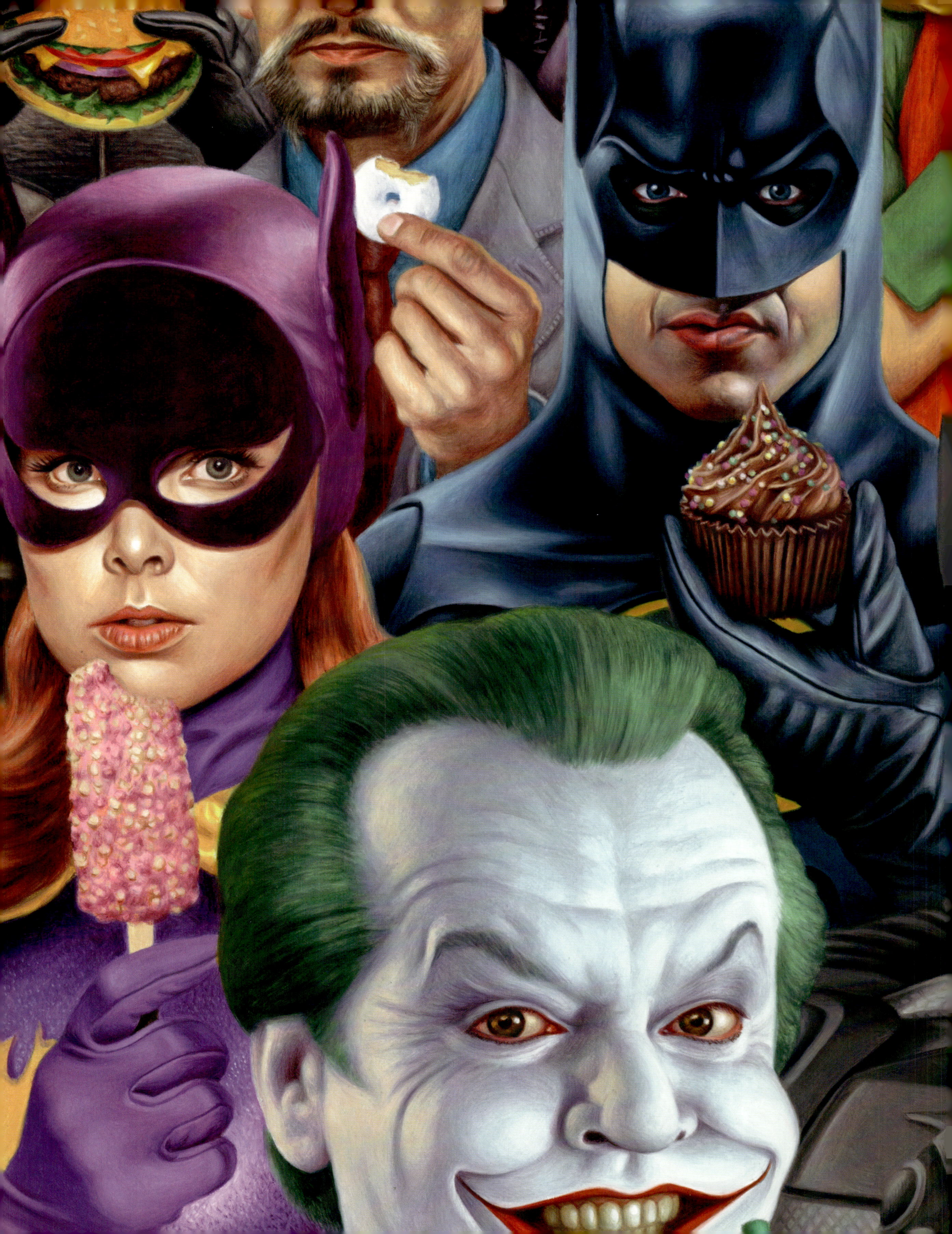

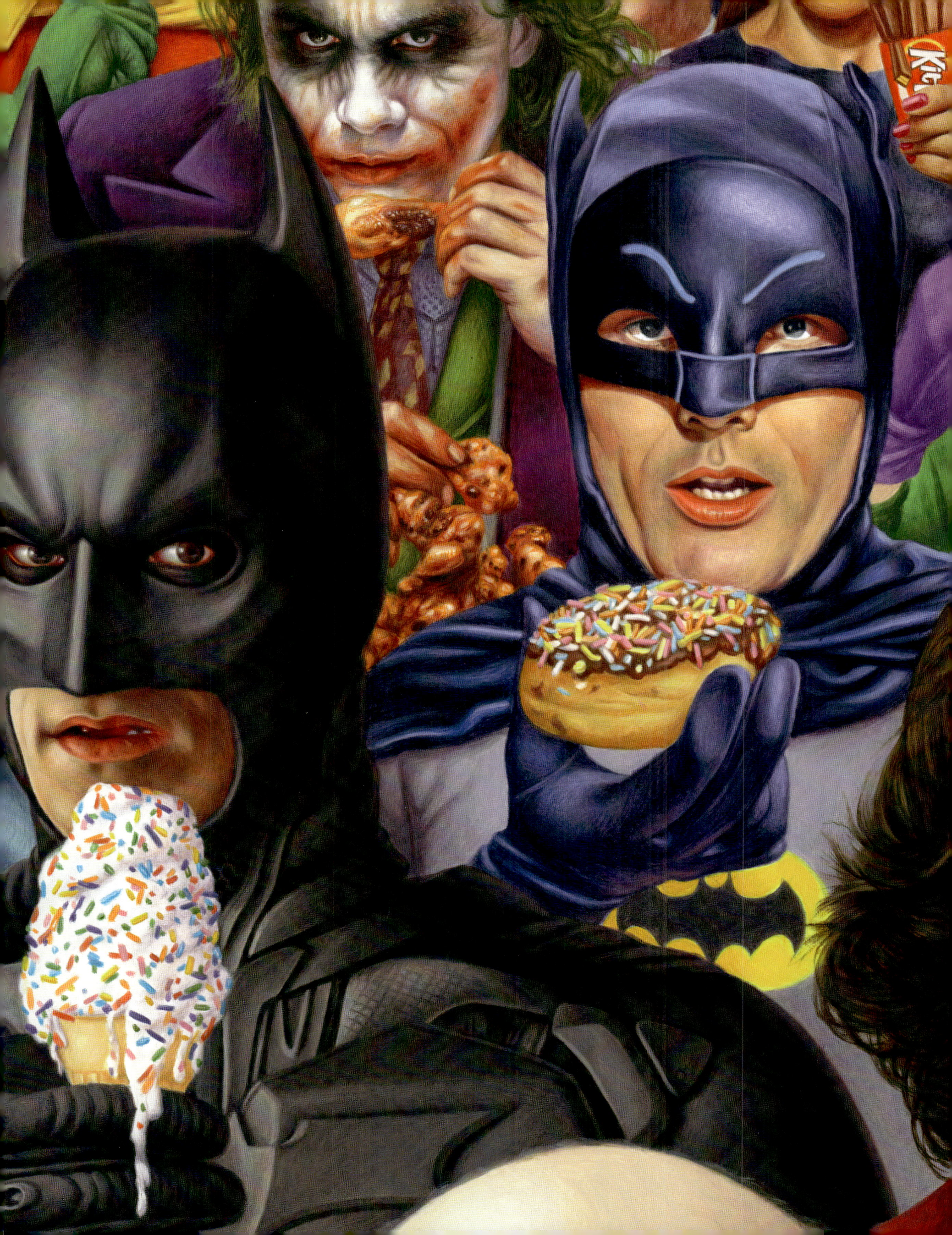

ACKNOWLEDGEMENTS

My family — AKIKO AND RONAN IWASAKI

ROBERTO AGUIRRE-SACASA AND BARCLAY STIFF

MUSTAFA AKTAS

DOMINIK ALEXANDER

AELISA AND FILIPPO CIPRIANI

JOHN DRESSER

ILHAN AND BIRCAN EROGLU

STERLING FOX

BRUCE FRISCH

BENJAMIN FERNANDEZ GALINDO

GREGG GOODMAN

BRUCE HELFORD AND JAN COREY

MERRY KARNOWSKY

SAL KAROTTKI

STANA KATIC

JOHN KEATING

DOV KELEMER

BENJAMIN KRAUSE

ROB LANDREM

DAVID LOPES

ROBERT LUZIO

LAURENT MARTHALER

TRIXIE MATTEL

MARK PARKER

FLOREN PEREMEN

ALEXANDRA SHIPP

MORGAN SLADE

BEN STEVENS

PENG TANG

LINDA TESNER

BARIS AND ILKE TURKER

MARK ULRIKSEN

CINDY VANCE

CEM YILMAZ

EMRE YUSUFI

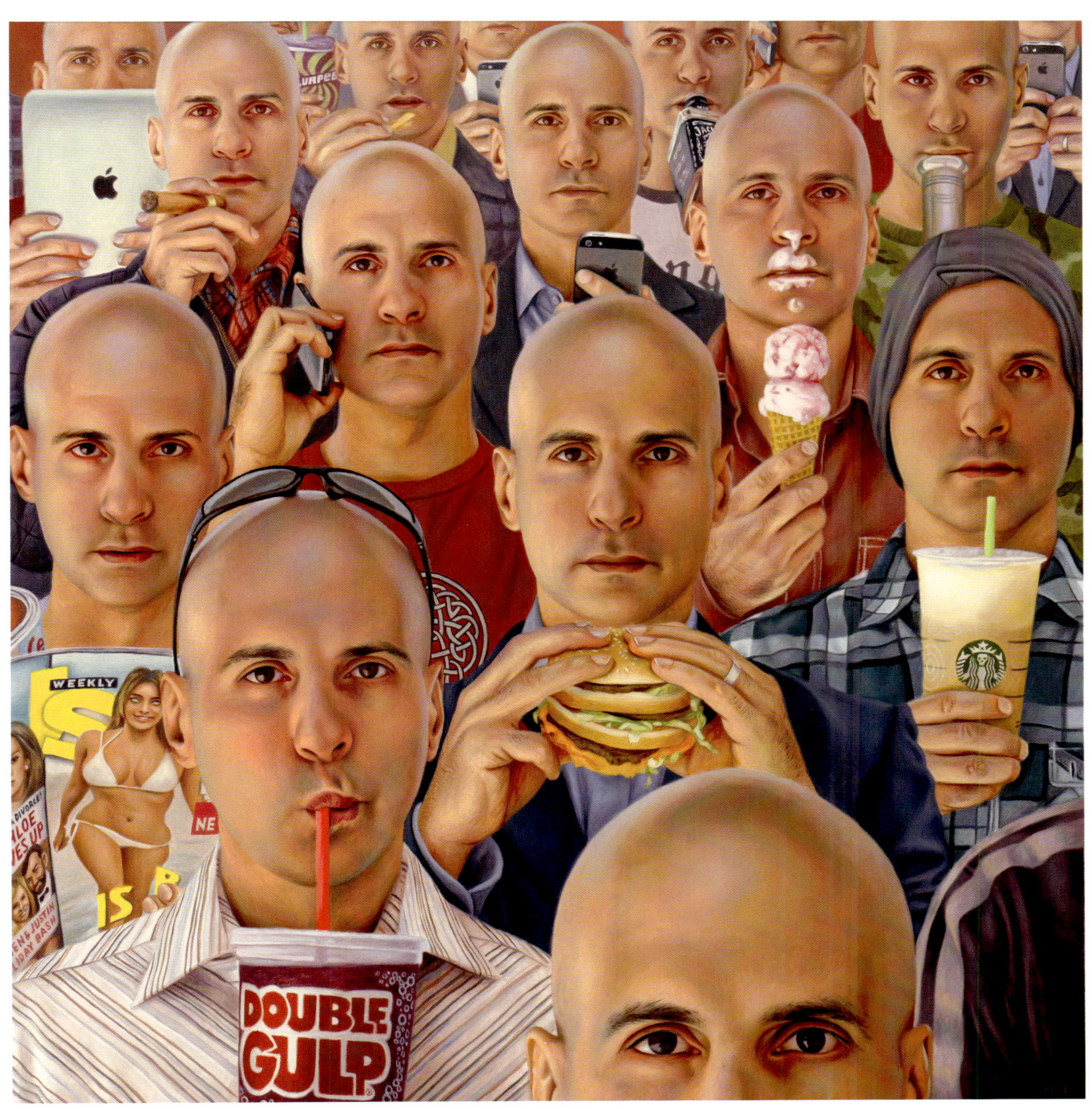

NARCISSISM

Oil on Canvas / 28" x 28" / 2014

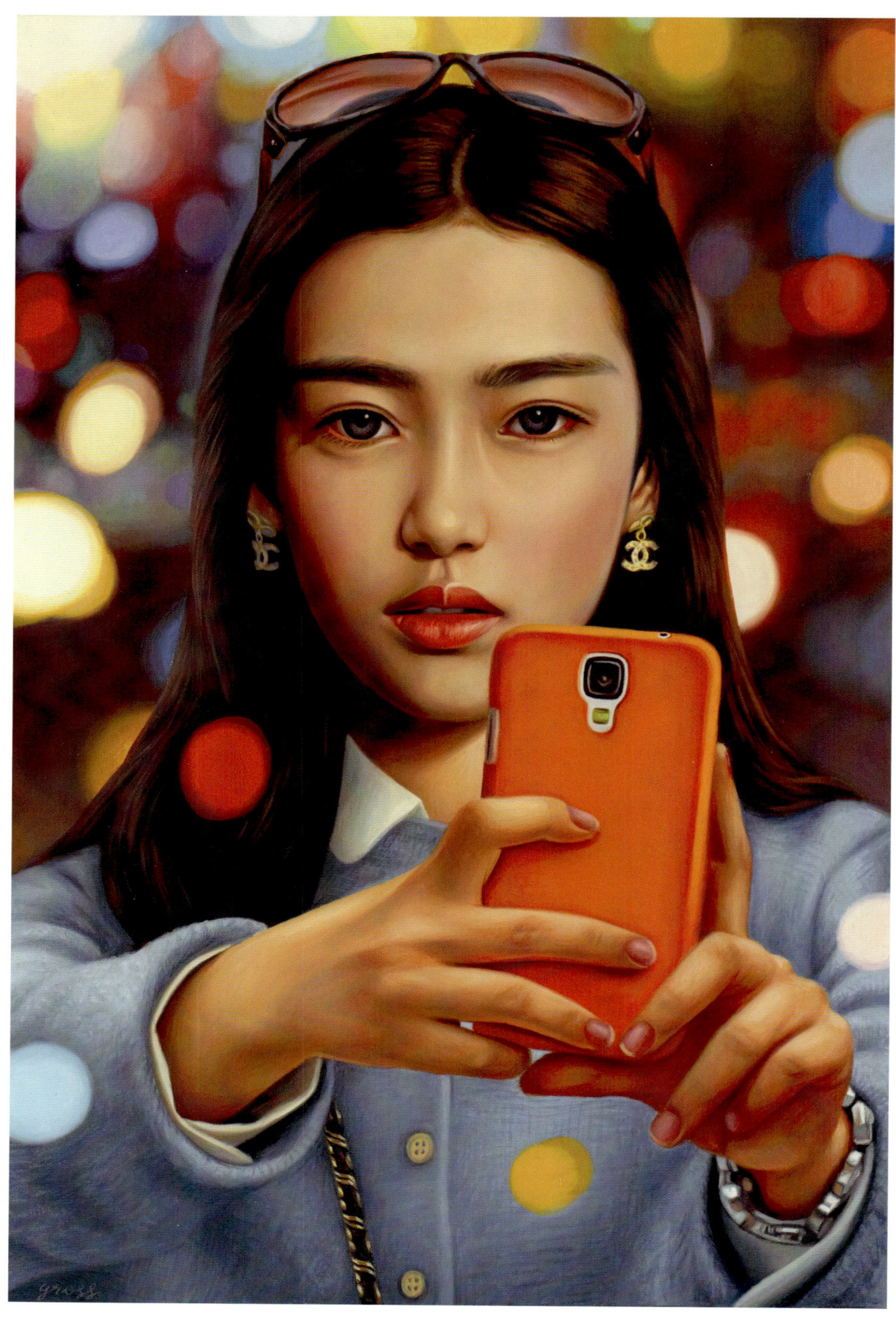

SELFIE
Oil on Canvas / 22" x 15" / 2014

(*following page*): DAYDREAMER
Oil on Canvas / 31.25" x 46" / 2014

www.alexgross.com
www.artofalexgross.com

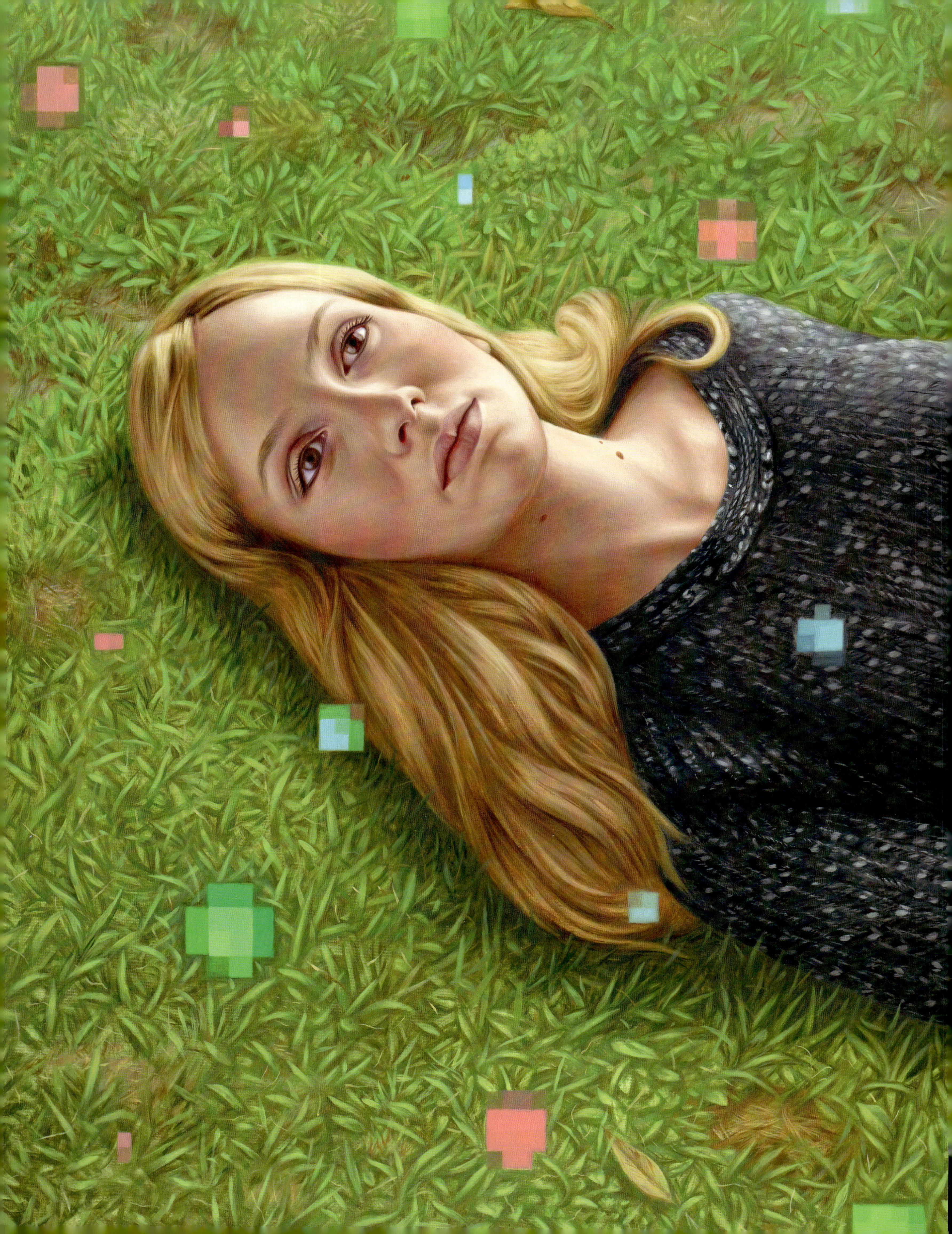

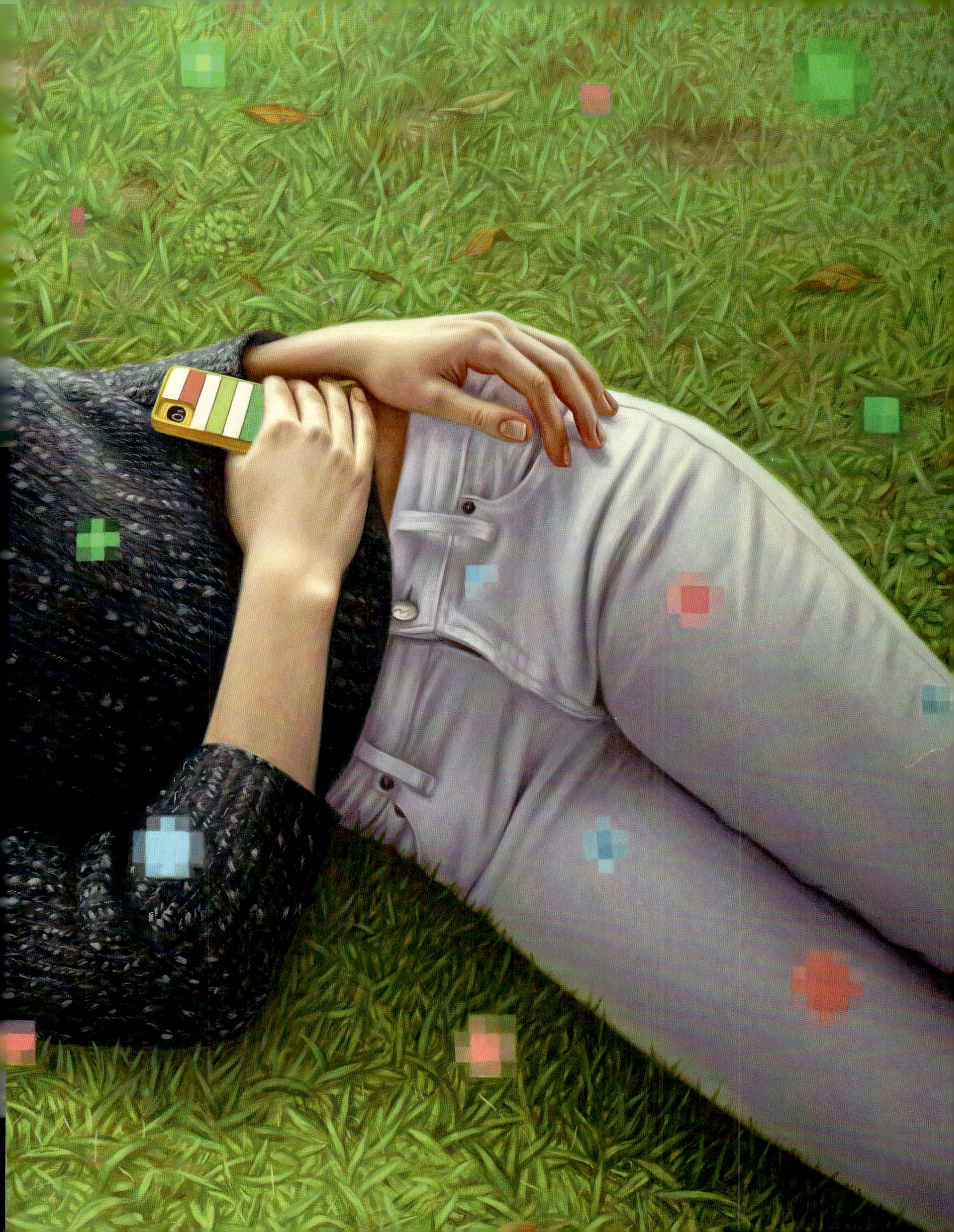

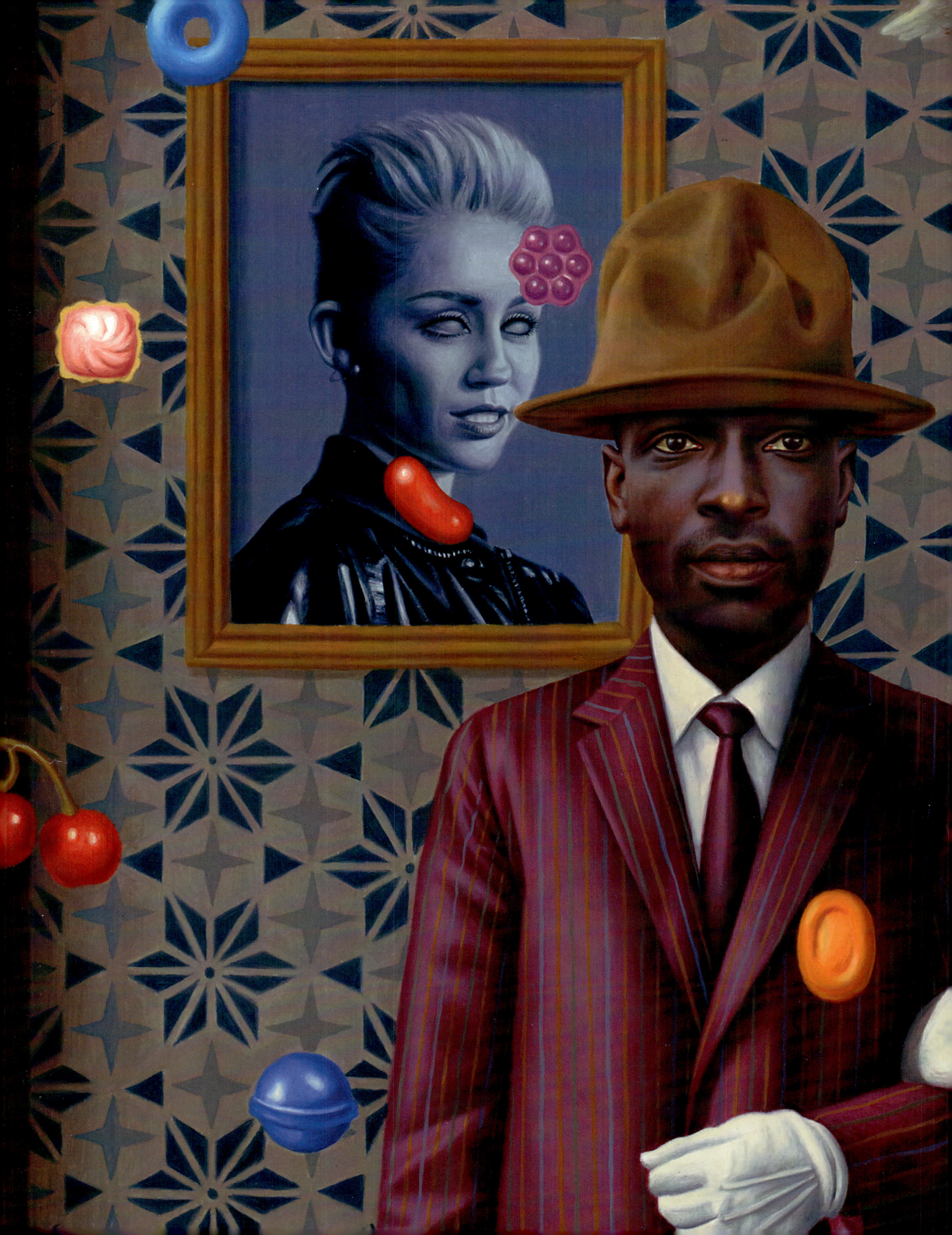

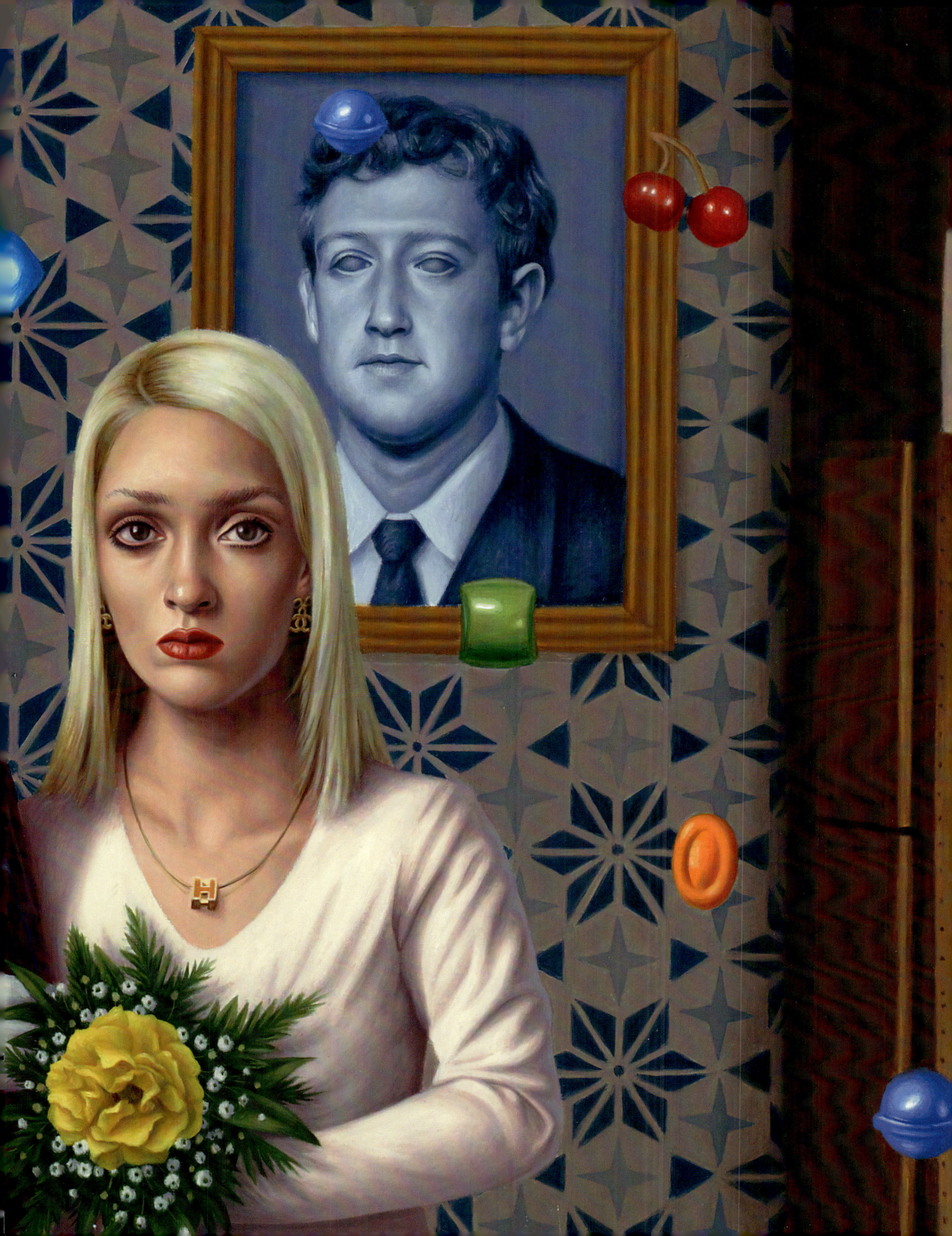

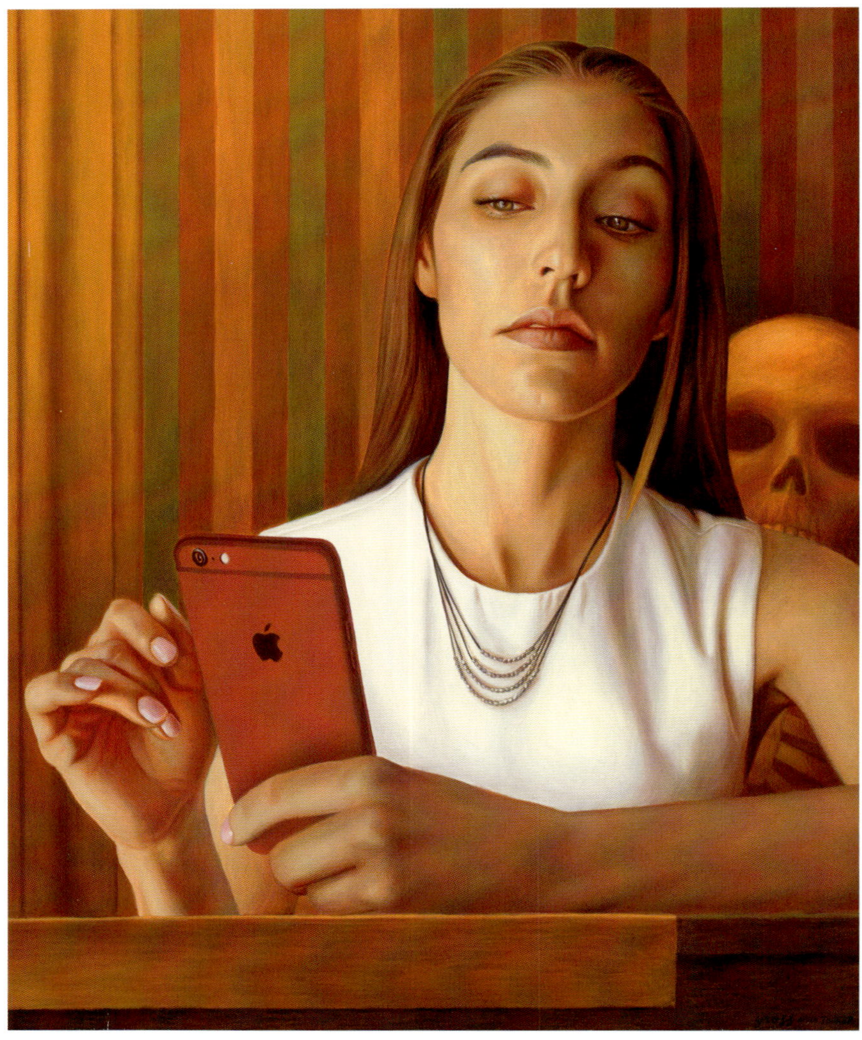

MIRROR (*After Tooker*)
Oil on Canvas / 23.75" x 19.5" / 2017

First Published in the United States of America, June, 2024
First Edition
Gingko Press Inc.
217 W Richmond Ave, Suite B, Richmond, CA 94801

ISBN: 978-1-58423-802-7
Library of Congress Control Number: 2024904523
Printed in China

Designed by Alex Gross and Cindy Vance

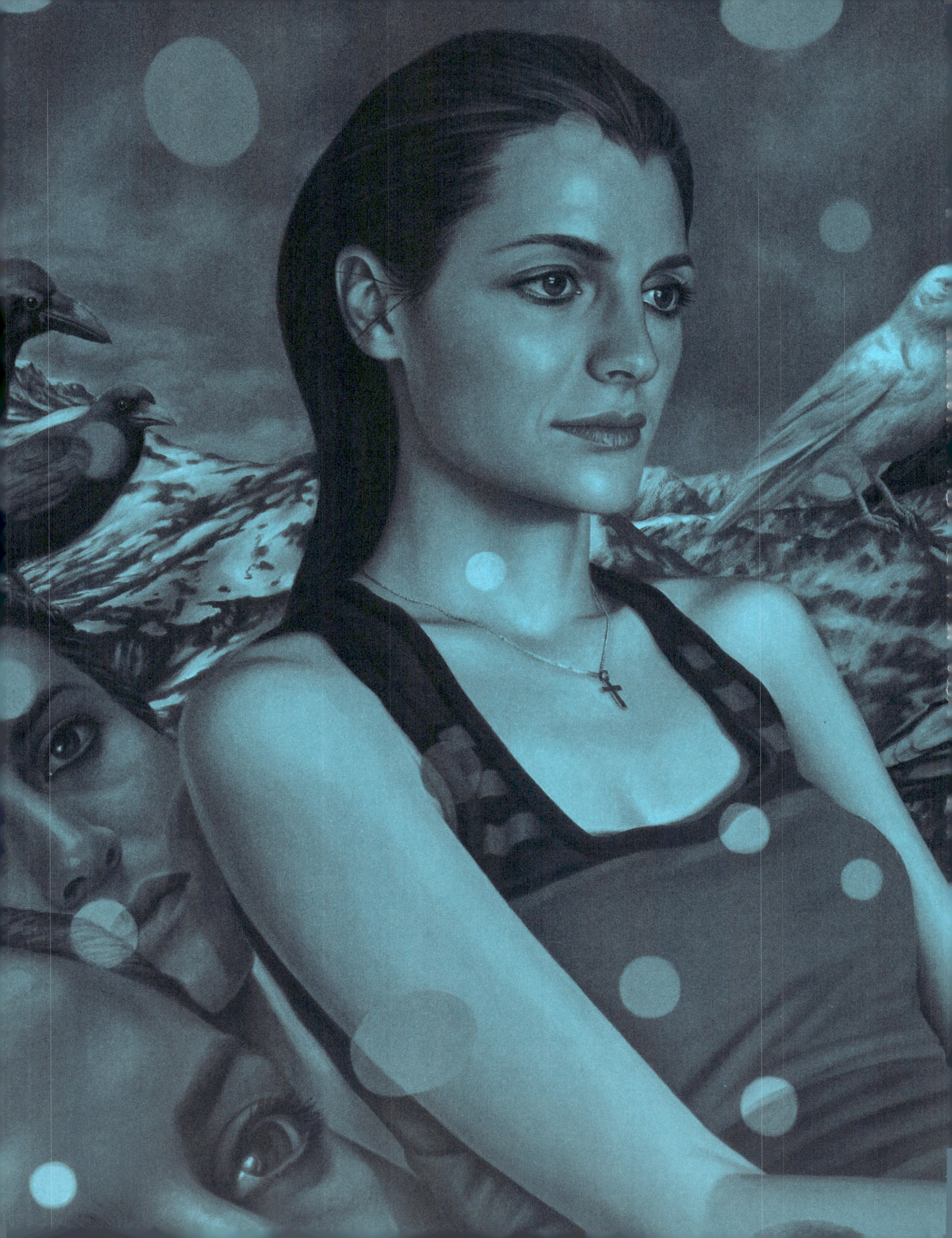